CLIMATE CHANGE:

OUR CHILDREN ARE IN DANGER

THE GOLDILOCKS PLANET IS NO LONGER JUST RIGHT

Mary Guay

DEDICATED TO LILLY

I wanted to name this book For Lilly: A Clueless Great-Granny Goes Green, but that sounded like a children's book. As I write, I refer to the book as For Lilly. It helps me focus. She is the reason I am writing this serious book about saving an Earth capable of supporting her generation.

Earth has provided for man for millions of years. In the last two hundred years, we have taken from the Earth without giving back to such an extent that we have altered the balance of nature, putting our children's futures at risk.

Our generation will be asked, "Why did you destroy the Earth you were given and leave so little for us?" To answer "I didn't know what I was doing" is of no value. I don't want to hear, "You wasted so much, cared so little, and now it's too late."

Lilly, Great-grandma is learning all I can and doing everything possible to protect you from harm.

AND
JANET MALLETT (1946-2011)

Thirty years ago, my sister told me I should write a book. See? I do listen. Today, I have a sense of purpose. Now, I'm ready.

———

Thank you Eckhart Tolle. Your words touch and inspire me.

> **You are here to enable the divine purpose of the universe to unfold. That's how important you are.**

TABLE OF CONTENTS

INTRODUCTION

Why didn't I know our generation is destroying the Earth? Well, I just didn't. I thought I was an environmentally conscious American consumer. In December of 2010, I saw an interview with Prince Charles; he explained his new book, *Harmony* (2010). What he said about the destruction of our planet alarmed me enough to order a copy. Then Wally, my husband of fifty years, and I left for a month-long vacation on the Island of Roatan.

Roatan might be considered third world; however, the people have a joy Americans lost long ago. Living there rekindled childhood memories of peaceful summer vacations spent with my Grandma Meister. That month was the perfect backdrop for arriving home to find *Harmony* waiting to educate me and rattle my world.

Prince Charles has an important message and a sense of purpose I admire. He warns of global devastation. What he said hit home like a bull's eye on my heart. Chapter 1 contains the facts that compelled me to learn more and take action. I thought, "Why didn't I know this was happening, and what can I do to pass a livable planet to our great-granddaughter, Lilly?" There was a wave of guilt when I thought of Lilly and her future, until I remembered the words of Maya Angelou.

> **When we know better, we do better.**

I researched global warming for a year and a half. My unique book is a compilation of the scientific facts and the consequences. All are clearly explained. There are more than one hundred actions I have tested, used, and am passing on to anyone who wants to reduce their carbon footprint.

Wally is a wonder when it comes to dealing with rapid changes as I set out on my mission to do all I could. He lives with me, which is like being at ground zero. We must wake up while there is still time to save our planet. Ignoring this "lump" could be deadly for everyone. Do not wait for someone else to decide there is a problem. People are watching *Survivor;* we need to be survivors.

I hope to peak interest so that others make changes that benefit their lives, our world, and future generations. Some facts seemed unbelievable. The sociologist in me wants you to have accurate scientific information. As you read the disturbing facts, which we do need to know, remain focused on solutions. Do not be incapacitated by fear. If you feel the urge to set the book aside, resist that idea and jump ahead in the book to the solutions you can use to decrease your carbon footprint. Our sense of power or powerlessness determines how we react to bad news. People seldom realize their value until faced with a crisis requiring bold, decisive, and immediate action. Life threatening news about yourself or a loved one changes everything. We want specialists to explain reports, and we do whatever it takes to survive. Do not kid yourself; global warming is life threatening. We need reports explained. We need to take immediate action. We need to do whatever it takes.

I care about you and know you love your family as much as I love mine. I hope to leave you feeling inspired and motivated, rather than discouraged. Maslow's Hierarchy of Needs inspired a tool I, as a social worker, used for years. I call it "Mary Guay's Hierarchy of Happiness."

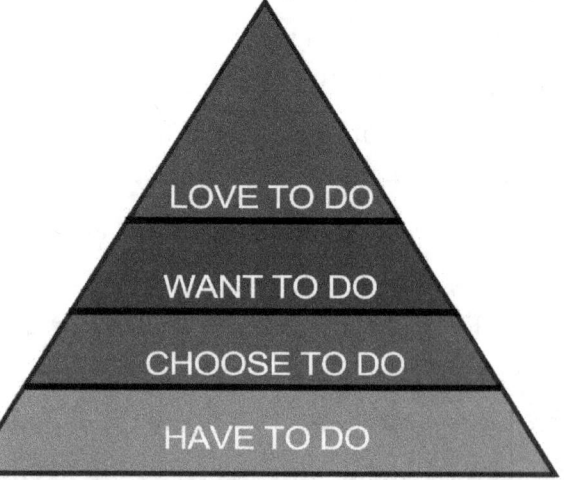

When faced with something that is ours to do, we can "reframe" that task from HAVE TO DO, elevate it to CHOOSE TO DO, WANT TO DO, and reach the top where that same task is something we LOVE TO DO. In facing issues and taking action, we stretch beyond our comfort zones and discover new meaning, purpose, abilities, and greater feelings of self-worth. I hope readers will reach the point where they love to do all they can to live sustainably and help pass a livable planet on to our children. Personal growth gives life new meaning.

Too often we exist at the bottom level; we feel we HAVE TO DO one dreaded thing after another. What if instead of feeling tired, resentful, guilty for putting it off, used, unappreciated, etc., you could feel like a person of value who knows you can do anything that is yours to do? Notice I did not say a person who can do everything for everyone else. At the top level, you know your priorities and you discover abilities, which have been within you all the time.

To "reframe," you take the situation you decided looked awful, study it closely and differently. Then, in your mind, you polish it, buy a nice mat, place it in a gold frame, shine a spotlight on it, and appreciate what is before you. A saying displayed in my home is, "I can hardly wait to see the good that will come of this." There is good in any situation, but sometimes you have to be willing to look really long and hard. Global warming is something none of us can hide from; we must face it, and the sooner the better. Once you start doing your part, you will discover a bright side to this problem.

Read the entire book; ask, "Can this be true?" I questioned what Prince Charles wrote. I dug deeper and learned that scientific investigations prove what he said is true. The facts and changes needed to save our planet are not too big to face; they are too big to ignore.

PREFACE

WHAT WOULD POSSESS A GREAT-GRANNY TO WRITE HER FIRST BOOK?

I never dreamed I would write a book for any reason. Now I believe I was destined to write *For Lilly*. In my heart, this book is *For Lilly: A Clueless Great-Granny Goes Green.* That is what really happened. A long-dormant Mary was waiting to develop into a person who is willing to explore, wants to learn, is determined to understand, and is re-born to take action. At first this unfolding process pulled me along. I didn't realize it was happening, until I became so compelled I could not turn back. I retired from social work with hospice, was asleep in my cozy cocoon, unaware of any threat to Lilly's future, but now there was a reason I needed to fly.

My husband Wally and I have two daughters, seven grandchildren, and a great-granddaughter, named Lilly. She is the first of our fourth generation and symbolizes the hope we have for a positive future for our family and for all children. I was in the delivery room for the births of four of our grandchildren and for Lilly's arrival.

A GREAT-GRANNY'S COMMITMENT

What a wonderful night! Three generations of women gathered to welcome a new generation. We were there *For Lilly* and we always will be. When I first held her, Lilly's tiny hand wrapped around my little finger, and at the same time, around my heart. My daughter had become a grandmother. My granddaughter had become a mother. A new generation, we may expect it, but that does not begin to capture the emotions felt that night. Becoming a great-grandmother was a monumental event. I held Lilly for the first time, and in that instant of pure joy and wonder, I made a commitment deep in my heart. I vowed to always love her and keep her from harm.

Lilly is a happy, healthy, and well-loved little girl. Seven years after that beautiful birth and my vow to keep her from harm, I am writing this book to inspire others to join in a movement to save the Earth. I offer information, insight, many hands-on things you can do, and motivation to inspire action, so that future generations are able to live in a world capable of sustaining our loved ones as they grow.

CLIMATE CHANGE:

OUR CHILDREN ARE IN DANGER

THE GOLDILOCKS PLANET IS NO LONGER JUST RIGHT

CHAPTER 1

THE FACTS FROM *HARMONY* THAT AWAKENED A CLUELESS GREAT-GRANNY

Seven billion people share the same address and landlord–Earth and Mother Nature. The issue, whether we call it global warming or climate change, is like an ominous cloud engulfing all of us. Global warming IS global. I thought it meant summers are hotter in Syracuse, Los Angeles, and Moscow. In general, they are; however, the term global warming refers to the average temperature of the entire Earth, which includes land, sea, and air. There are some colder winters and cooler summers, but the trend is that year after year the entire Earth's average temperature is climbing, with most of the increase in the last thirty years. We throw a cloud of greenhouse gases into our atmosphere that acts like an overcoat, and it will not blow away. Earth cannot re-absorb that cloud fast enough to prevent increased accumulation. The only way to slow this is for man to reduce the release of greenhouse gases and to make corrections where possible.

Americans squander resources at double the rate we did in 1968. Consider the square footage of your home, the number of TVs and cars you own, the size of your closets, the quantity of toys and electronics, the trips to the store or fast-food restaurants, the number and size of the trash cans it takes to haul off what you discard, the amount of food you eat, the size of your waistline, and the processing and transportation used for all the stuff in your life. Americans' consumption and waste has skyrocketed in our lifetimes. The changes were gradual and barely noticed, but the results are deadly.

The disruption to the lives of baby boomers from rising sea levels, disastrous changes in weather patterns, and depletion of natural resources has been minimal. The effects of global warming could make Lilly's life a daily struggle for survival. The information, predictions, and future scenarios available are staggering. What can one person, this great-granny, do to help? Until recently I hardly knew there was a problem. Now that is a problem, a problem many people have in common. We are clueless!

Retirement was going along blissfully, as in "ignorance is bliss." There were some sad events. I had two sisters. My youngest sister died in September of 2011. The middle sister died in 2001. It seemed strange that I, the oldest sister, was the last one left. One wonders why. I had no sense that my life had some new or big post-retirement purpose.

My husband and I were going on a one-month dream vacation on the Honduran Island of Roatan, in the Caribbean. Before we left, I saw Prince Charles's interview, ordered *Harmony*, packed our bags, and we flew off to enjoy the tropics. That is how easy it was for me to go from concerned to forgetting about it. Snorkeling among the beautiful reefs off Roatan, I forgot I even ordered the book.

LESSONS FROM ROATAN

We spent a very relaxing month in a lovely rustic duplex on the beach. It was not a "resort," but it was just what we wanted and could afford. Our unit was under the forest canopy, which did wonders to keep our place cool. Big porches on the front and back of our island home had hammocks where we stretched out, talked, snoozed, read books, and watched a steady stream of humming birds visiting a feeder three feet away. On Roatan, we didn't have to do anything at any special time. We turned the clock to the wall and lived by nature's clock.

We learned that the power goes out often and the minimum time for the restart cycle was one hour and forty minutes. When the air-conditioner quit, we discovered there would be no repair until some part came from somewhere and they found someone who knew how to fix it. That would be about a week after we left. These experiences were valuable lessons for us when we returned home.

The people of Roatan have time for their families. No air-conditioning—electricity out—no problem. The islanders have no need for A/C and take things in stride. Americans can get their knickers in a knot about anything. We must have everything, and everything must be just so.

Our duplex had no glass windows, but it had screens and built-in louvered slats made from local timber. When it rained, we closed the slats. The rest of the time, the Caribbean breezes lulled us into a relaxed state of mind. We saw no thermometers and no one talked about the actual temperature. It is remarkable how much less it bothers you when there is no number to prove it is so hot you must take control. The first two days after the A/C quit were unbearable, and then something changed. We went native, acclimated to the weather, dressed cool, went barefoot, and snorkeled.

Each day we walked to the end of our long dock, climbed down the steps, and relaxed into the beautiful Caribbean. I can close my eyes and feel the soothing warm water, adjust my mask and snorkel, and greet the fish. The French grunts were the first fish I saw. They are eight to twelve inches long and silvery gold with fine shimmering blue stripes. Many fish seem to shimmer, while others look velvety. Schools of fish float like clouds in the sea and are content to let me be a fish with them. Wally and I swim to the reef, while fish effortlessly open a path for us. When we reach the coral heads, we see my favorite, the beautiful rainbow parrotfish. They are up to two feet in length and look like sequined works of art. Their eyes are lined as if ready to go on stage.

The younger parrotfish have similar markings, but in pastel shades. If you are ever where you can snorkel with tropical fish, do not let that opportunity pass you by. The way the fish glide, as if they are one with the gentle current, is hypnotic. After swimming the reef for an hour or more with the parrotfish, blue tangs, sergeant majors, queen angelfish, groupers, an octopus, and many other varieties of fish, we always came out of the water in a peaceful state. Any thought to hurry was erased; our walks along the beach were like drifting strolls. Just remembering our swims relaxes me and brings a smile.

My dream is to take Lilly to the reef and watch her joy as she snorkels with those lovely creatures. Reefs around the world are dying, and I want her and all my children and grandchildren to come to my reef and meet my fish.

Roatan has one hilly-winding main road forty miles long, with little roads and settlements off to the side. Often when we were driving along a peak, we could see the blue, turquoise, and lavender sea to the left and right of the island. There is no fancy tourist district, yet. The souvenir shops all carry about the same thing. Shopping mostly involved taking a taxi to town to buy the food we couldn't get off the produce truck—once the flyswatter crisis passed.

Each week we took a cab to Coxen Hole, the closest town with a supermarket. One week there would be a good supply of something, like breast of chicken, and the next week, none. It depended on what came in on the supply boat. I was already a vegan and had brought cans of black beans, organic brown rice, and my rice cooker from home, so the fruits and vegetables from the truck that pulled into our parking area twice a week was all I needed.

The longer we were on Roatan, the easier life seemed. The constant need to have something done, repaired, located, or bought ASAP drifted away. The happy and leisurely feeling typical of the islanders was contagious. They were very poor by American standards; however, we admired the rich joy they took in their children, how they set aside time to see the beauty in nature, and their gentle acceptance of whatever happened.

Early in our visit, I decided I must get to town to buy a flyswatter. Guess what! They didn't know what a flyswatter was! Then one day in a little dirt-floored shop in West End Village, I spotted a dust-covered flyswatter hanging on a nail. The guy wasn't sure what it was, but agreed to sell it. When I explained its purpose, he wondered why one would bother. That flyswatter is one of my favorite souvenirs from Roatan. It reminds me of a time when, for a month, I learned to relax and not think about what I wanted to buy, had to do, or had to have a certain way.

These were perfect lessons and just the right background for what was about to become my mission, my purpose, maybe even the reason the oldest sister is the one who is still alive. There is something I have to do.

There May Be a Reason the Oldest Sister Is Still Here

I have enjoyed reading Eckhart Tolle for several years, and I am always drawn to a message in the front of *The Power of Now* (Tolle 1997).

> **You are here to enable the divine purpose of the universe to unfold.**
> **That is how important you are!**

The Roatan vacation was over, and in the big box of mail waiting at the post office was *Harmony* (2010) by HRH the Prince of Wales. His message is that we are damaging the Earth so severely by our actions that we could cause Earth to become uninhabitable for future generations. That would be Lilly!

Prince Charles explains the Earth can continue to support man, only if we shift to a sustainable course. The information is from scientific research, published by the United Nations, government agencies, and research groups. It is not hearsay, hype, or unsubstantiated data.

Once we were home, we could control the temperature, and we

started "needing" to adjust the thermostat. We could buy whatever we wanted as soon as we thought of it, and we started "needing" many things. We could have things done ASAP, and we started "needing" prompt responses. Ah, life was back to normal. The leisurely feeling was slipping away and I missed it. Why were we unable to keep a little of that island state of mind in our everyday life now that we were retired?

Later chapters of this book explain in detail the many areas that threaten our world. I will describe changes Wally and I made in our attempt to walk more gently on our planet. Some of our results are rewarding, motivating, surprising, and spectacular successes. I can hardly wait to hear the surprising results readers achieve. Our new life started when we read Harmony. If I had not read the book, I would have remained clueless and my research and discovery of ways we can make a difference in our home would never have begun.

> **It takes a rare person to hear what he does not want to hear.**
> Dick Cavett

PRINCE CHARLES' EYE-OPENING INFORMATION

Dozens of topics grabbed my attention as I read *Harmony*. I was amazed how little I knew about global warming and the many life threatening issues. The following facts from *Harmony* started my journey.

Temperatures 5.4 degrees F higher than at the beginning of the industrial revolution were last seen three million years ago, and the sea level was eighty feet higher than now.

Earth's average temperature is rising. Most of the 1 to 1.5 degree rise since the industrial revolution has been in the last thirty years, and each year the temperature rise is accelerating. That caught my attention.

Ice caps will not melt immediately; however, it won't be long before our house is in trouble if it isn't already. No one says the sea level has risen in southwest Florida. Our daughter's home is supposed to be at the highest elevation in Collier County. Their bank required flood insurance beginning May 1, 2012, because FEMA has "moved and redrawn" the flood zone boundaries. Collier County is Florida's largest county with 2,025.5 square miles and 285,170 residents. What is happening? The housing crisis hit Naples, and no one wants to say anything to discourage the recovery. They just redraw flood lines with no explanation.

Our home is six feet above sea level (the last we knew); with a rise in sea level, our home and much of Florida could be in trouble. How many seaports around the world could need relocation over a brief period? Doing whatever we can to slow global warming may be the most cost effective and humane action we could take.

Wally and I searched to find things we could do to slow global warming. By February of 2011, we turned off our A/C—at the circuit. That may not seem like a revolutionary move, but in south Florida, we often reach 85 degrees or more on February afternoons. In 2013 we turned the circuit off in early October.

We live in a fifty-five and older community of manufactured homes, and the A/C units are outside. Many of the homes belong to "snowbirds," who are here a month or two each year. During bike rides, we can hear our neighbors' A/C units running day and night, twelve months of the year, even when outside temperatures are well below seventy and the homeowners are living in Cape Cod or Ann Arbor. Our neighbors are not thoughtless people; they simply lack knowledge about global warming. If they can afford to pay the electric bill, high-energy use is not a problem to them.

Our utility company brags about low rates but ranks high for dumping large amounts of greenhouses gases into the atmosphere. Despite our abundant sunshine, only a small percentage of our energy is solar. Maybe having the cheapest energy is not the bargain we need.

I propose we conserve energy in the home, pay a higher rate to convert to solar, and still save money. There are reasons to rethink our use and source of electricity.

Fifty-five million years ago, the Earth's temperature was 9 degrees F higher. Earth was ice free, and the sea level was 243 feet higher than today. The Intergovernmental Panel on Climate Change (IPCC) predicts a 9-degree temperature rise and a corresponding 6-foot rise in the sea level, as the ice melts, by the end of this century. "NINE" degree temperature rise is not a typographical error. As I proofread the chapter, I once again could not believe this, so I re-verified the information. "NINE" is correct, and it could be even higher. The rise in sea level would continue to accelerate as more ice melts, and the newly exposed darker oceans and land absorb ever-increasing amounts of heat from the sun.

The IPCC is an affiliate of the United Nations and is a group of two thousand scientists and environmental experts from two hundred countries. They continually review new scientific data about global warming and the risks facing the world because of climate change. It is the IPCC reports, issued every few years, that provide the most accurate information. The IPCC is certain global warming exists, man causes it, and man is destroying the climate that makes it possible for humans to live on Earth.

The thought of nine degrees, and six feet in Lilly's lifetime haunted me. Something stirred in me; I began to understand Lilly is in danger. The struggle to learn more and free myself from my cozy-clueless cocoon steadily increased. Scientists have been telling us of the impending crisis for years. I had heard nothing. Cocoons create a false sense of safety and render us useless, but now I hear the news.

The IPCC's "worst-case scenario" was a temperature increase of 10.8 degrees F by 2100. In 2005, 2006, and 2007, the world's greenhouse gas emissions have been above the amounts that would cause that worst-case scenario.

Scientists believe a 10-degree rise, likely caused by 10,000 years of volcanic activity, ended the Permian period 250 million years ago. We're talking about a similar temperature rise in less than one hundred years caused by man's burning of fossil fuels, deforestation, landfills, factory farming, and a population over seven billion.

I read everything I could find on global warming. There are so many interconnected environmental issues, far more than I could have guessed. We emit ever-increasing amounts of greenhouse gases and exceed the rate of the "worst-case scenario" every year. I cannot stand by and do nothing, while we reach a 5, 7, or 9 degree F rise that will destroy our children's future. Now I know the way we are living has unimaginable consequences for our children.

Harmony taught me many things beyond the fact that the burning of fossil fuels was polluting the atmosphere. The temperature of land, air, and water has risen, glaciers that provide water for billions are disappearing, and permafrost in northern North America, Europe, and Asia is melting, releasing billions of tons of carbon dioxide (CO_2) and methane. Permafrost had been a stable foundation for thousands of years. Buildings, roadways, and pipelines are damaged and collapse as the permafrost melts.

Melting ice had not registered with me as something that could lead to devastation. An event never seen before happened in the summer of 2007. A portion of Arctic sea ice, twice the size of Great Britain, disappeared in a span of two weeks. The same thing happened again in 2008. Some scientists now say the Arctic Ocean could be ice-free by the summer of 2015. Ice reflects 80% of the sun's rays and heat back out of the atmosphere. The dark surface of the ocean and land, once ice is gone, absorbs 90% of the heat from the sun. This creates an ever-increasing, self-perpetuating warming of the oceans and lands, leading to further ice melting. Some scientists are trying to calculate a "tipping point," where the process becomes so rapid that it is too late for man to take effective measures to prevent the "worst-case scenario."

On July 10, 2012, ABC World News anchor Diane Sawyer gave a brief report about the **Greenland ice-sheet melting thirty times faster than it was a decade ago**. That news definitely warranted a follow up; there was none. After researching issues related to global warming for over a year, I have learned some reasons why we are not alarmed when Greenland's ice sheet is melting thirty times faster. Incidentally, ten years ago scientists were alarmed by the rapid increase in the rate of ice melting on Greenland. Are we thirty times more alarmed? No, we don't remember the report or understand there is a threat to our children's future.

It is difficult for cocooned Americans to take needed action when politics and special interests stall, lie, deny, and try to create confusion. Many public servants are so obligated to those who paid to get them elected that they do nothing to save our planet. Attempts to reach an agreement or pass a law die somewhere in a maze of dead ends put there by those who want business as usual. There are laws of nature that oil, coal, and natural gas companies cannot change with their power and influence.

Other details about how we are damaging our atmosphere and world were news to me. Americans bury 222 million tons of household waste a year, and landfills are one of the biggest methane producers in the world. Landfill gases are 50% methane and up to 40% CO_2. Methane is twenty-five times more damaging to the atmosphere than CO_2. Although China has 20% of the world's population and the United States has 4.4%, in 2007 Americans were producing half again as much garbage as China. In 2013, China's booming economy created more waste than the U.S. (but not per capita). Americans have not decreased the amount we send to landfills. We also send electronic waste to China and India to be recycled.

There is an eye-opening account in *Confessions of an Eco-Sinner* (Pearce, 2006). Pearce tracked where his computer was recycled. He writes that the United States sends over 300,000 tons of electronic waste abroad every year. His computer was recycled in a city on the outskirts of Delhi, India. Ten year-old Rajesh's job was to lower circuit boards into a big drum of hot acid to remove the copper from the keyboard. The boy wore rubber gloves but no goggles or breathing mask. Once the acid was of no further use, they poured it into an open sewer running down the side of the narrow dirt street. Rajesh's six-year-old brother works there too. When boys first start working, they have headaches and feel "giddy." After work, someone gives them a strong drink and they feel okay. We feel okay, knowing we have responsibly recycled. The American businesses are handed papers authenticating the items are being reused, refurbished, or recycled. Then Rajesh and thousands of little boys like him do their job.

I now have a small voice that whispers I should check things out for myself. Too often, we dismiss our doubts because it is easier to believe someone else will take care of everything. That goes for people and for the businesses that send the electronics to some far-off land and get their authenticating pieces of paper.

We do not bury or send all our garbage to China and India. There is a man-made plastic vortex in the Pacific five hundred miles west of California. It doubled in size between 2000 and 2010, is nearly six times the size of Great Britain, and contains 100 million tons of all kinds of trash, such as plastic bags, bottles, cans, and chemical sludge. Rotating ocean currents, called the North Pacific Gyre, keep the mess in a somewhat stable position. This plastic vortex is not the debris heading for the west coast of the U.S. from Japan's tsunami.

The first American woman to circumnavigate the globe alone, Tania Aebi, described what she encountered in *Maiden Voyage* (1989). She wallowed in a sea of garbage, where currents converged in the Indian Ocean one hundred miles off the coast of India. She wrote, "Black oil covered the surface" and "I was mired in sludge, bags, plastics, Styrofoam, dishwashing-liquid bottles, flip-flops and wrappers coating the hull of the boat with a thick black film. I lamented how any sea life could survive such appalling pollution. Indeed, here the ocean seemed completely barren of life and the scene was sad enough to make one cry." She encountered that more than twenty-five years ago and before the population rose by nearly 50%.

We cannot keep buying and throwing away single-use items. There is no "away!" Plastic bags made from oil take forever to break down. As they do, the chemicals are eaten by sea creatures and enter our food chain.

I was shocked to learn the slashing and burning of the rainforests of the world contributes 17% of the CO_2 and billions of tons of methane to the greenhouse gasses building up in our atmosphere. The Amazon Rainforest releases 20 billion tons of water into the air daily, providing rain for South America, the North American prairies, southern Europe, and northern Africa. These clouds are like "flying rivers." Forests sequester vast amounts of carbon, naturally and free of charge. Boreal forests, in cooler climates, are also cleared for lumber, industry, and land to grow crops and livestock.

We are farming in ways that devour Earth's resources so fast that Mother Nature cannot keep up. Man destroys the soil, squanders the world's water supply, and strips away what our children will need to raise their food. Agribusiness farming methods use antibiotics, hormones, fertilizers, pesticides, genetically modified seeds, and wasteful irrigation methods. Insecticides kill the bees needed to pollinate and produce one-third of our food supply. We are draining aquifers, our source of water from the ground, and they are collapsing.

Farming today is different from when I was growing up. Large corporations now control most of the food production and distribution around the world, forcing small farms out of business. The majority of the food on America's tables has traveled 1,300 to 2,000 miles.

We raise 60 billion farm animals for food, using one-third of the world's usable land and grain harvest, and those farm animals are responsible for 18% of greenhouse gasses. When the cattle are raised on an animal factory farm, a quarter-pound burger requires more than 2,500 pounds of water to produce.

When I was a kid, we had a cow named Bessie-Lou. She had a long and productive life, taking from and giving back to nature as she grazed in her pasture and drank from the creek. Her manure dried in the pasture and gave the nutrients back to the soil. This is part of the nutrient cycle and does not produce the methane that the animal factories put out when they wash away manure by the ton. I had to learn how farming had changed from life sustaining to Earth destroying.

Farm fertilizers are one of the main reasons many bodies of water have algae blooms, creating imbalances and collapsing entire ecosystems. A United Nations survey states one-third of the world's farmable soil is degraded. That happened in the last fifty years. Prince Charles believes the dependence on petrochemicals by corporate monoculture farming is a major factor in the destruction of land and water.

Prince Charles explained how Edward Bernays applied the propaganda skills he used to persuade Americans to join the WWI war effort to the field of advertising for commercial and political purposes. Bernays realized that to have unlimited economic growth, the desire to consume must never be fulfilled.

Mass-media techniques maintain the only condition that makes it possible to sustain compulsive consumerism at an ever-increasing high-octane level. Should we be concerned about the long-term impact on our children immersed in mass media?

Our Earth is in danger because of the way we live. Plant and animal species are disappearing at a rate one hundred to one thousand times faster than the historic rate of extinction. There are many reasons including loss of habitat, climate change, pollution, and over population. We are a species. This is the first time in Earth's history that one species, man, has dominated. The world's population more than quadrupled, going from 1.6 billion in 1900 to over 7 billion today. The doubling of populations within a habitat can eventually make the habitat unable to support that species. Humans are using up vital resources at such a rate that some scientists believe the planet may be entering the sixth extinction, because we are destroying the means to feed our own species.

> **Let us permit nature to have its way.**
> **She understands her business better than we do.**
> Michel de Montayne, French Renascence writer

Stern Review (2006) stated, "If we do not act very soon, the ongoing pollution of the atmosphere can be expected to cause damage to the economy in the coming few decades that would be equivalent to the cost of both world wars and the great depression combined."

Leading anthropologist Gregory Bateson stated, "The major problems in the world are the result of the difference between the way Nature works and the way man thinks." Prince Charles believes our disconnect from nature makes it possible to ignore the damage we are doing, and that nature also holds many answers that will help man right his course.

The Prince told of indigenous people on remote islands near the epicenter of the 2004 tsunami. Rescuers feared all the people would be dead, but hardly anyone was injured. "Nature had told them." The birds and fish were acting differently and the people knew from their folklore what to do. They, like the wildlife their lives depend on, had moved to higher ground in the shelter of the forest before the tsunami even started. Indigenous peoples everywhere know of an interconnectedness and responsibility to safeguard Mother Earth. If we fail to do this, age-old cultures predict, "There will be discord and the Mother's source of nourishment will dry up."

How disconnected from nature are we? How many of us heard anything about global warming, or forgot about the 2003 heat wave in Europe that killed fifty thousand people? We are not the ones heading for the safe high ground; we bask on the beach until we are eye-to-eye with a fifty-foot tsunami!

The wisdom to connect with nature lives within us, but we don't remember. How do we wake up and use the wisdom that can save us all? Could this awakening result in us discovering a new peace, love, and joy we are not finding in all our possessions?

> **Be the change you want to see in the world.**
> Mahatma Gandhi

For Lilly is a different book. One part has the bad news I uncovered doing research. I am sorry to have to tell you Earth's symptoms, diagnosis, and prognosis, but I thought you should know. The rest of the book tells things Wally and I have done to be "green." Sometimes my years as a social worker take over, and I share information and techniques I used to motivate families, patients, groups, workshops, and myself.

Saving the world does not have to leave you feeling drained and deprived. It can empower you, awaken confidence, and you may become a person you like even more. There is wisdom in us all that we seldom realize until we stretch beyond our comfort zone. That wisdom is not something we have to struggle to learn; we REMEMBER that wisdom when the chatter of life and the constant chewing of the mind stops for a while and we are able to know our true value.

Quotes from *The Wisdom of Native Americans* (Nerburn 1999)

The Earth is the mother of all people, and all people should have rights upon it.
Chief Joseph, Nez Perce

All things are connected. Whatever befalls the Earth, befalls the children of the Earth.
Chief Seattle, Suqwamish

Let us put our minds together and see what kind of life we can make for our children.
Sitting Bull

CHAPTER 2

THE LIBRARY, THE BOOKS, AND MORE EYE-OPENING INFORMATION

Since retiring, I've been a regular at the Collier County Public Library. Once I started reading *Harmony*, my life began to change and I went from reading mysteries to doing research. I have a real mystery on my hands. As I read fifty books, I kept thinking of Lilly. What will her life be like? I hope to live at least another thirty years and perhaps play with a great-great-grandchild. Will Lilly even dare bring a child into the world if the future looks too bleak?

We become different people when we discover a compelling purpose. We choose to do things that have greater meaning, and we start to realize our inner value. After reading, questioning, and searching for ways to make a difference, I am freeing myself and changing into a person who has a divine purpose. I hope you discover similar transformations in your future.

I can no longer ignore global warming. Not knowing robs us of time to slow the disaster speeding toward us. I do not want truth withheld from me to protect me from being upset. Unknown truths are still true. When they are life threatening, the sooner we know the better.

> **A good friend who points out mistakes is to be respected, as if he reveals a secret of hidden treasure.**
> Buddha

LET ME BE TEACHABLE

Book choices fell into two categories: What is global warming, and What can I do about it? I looked for *An Inconvenient Truth* (Gore 2006). All copies were out; I had a copy put on hold and browsed the environmental books in the library. It would be well over a year before the KNOWING that I would write a book popped into my head, never to leave. The cocoon started getting uncomfortable. As I read, layer after layer fell away; I started understanding global warming.

I grew up in the snow belt on the eastern end of Lake Ontario and always wished the brutal winters were milder and shorter. For a while, global warming sounded pretty good. We moved away in the late 1970s, but we still had friends and family there. Shorter and milder winters sounded as if they finally got a break. No! The books educated me. When I graduated from high school, no one had heard of global warming.

Earth and all who live on it can adapt to change to some extent. Species that can migrate adapt more easily. Stationary plants and coral reefs are less able to change and need things just right to survive. So many balances in nature are essential to sustain life as we know it. My earlier thoughts that warmer weather might be nice were the thoughts of someone who was "clueless."

It was as if I'd just found out the rash I'd had for years was melanoma, and in order to survive I needed the best information and treatment available. For answers about global warming, I needed an expert. I found Lester Brown and his books. The news was not pretty, but at last I was ready for straight answers.

FAVORITE AUTHORS

I learned the Earth's problems are as deadly as a long-ignored cancer. Finding Lester R. Brown was like finding the doctor you can trust and who will do all he can to save your life. He has devoted more than forty years to research and writing about global warming. College courses on the environment and the risks our civilization is facing use his publications as textbooks. Many details in the chapters on global warming, land, water, and food are from his *Plan B* series. In case you wonder what Plan A is, that is business as usual and deadly. It is interesting to see the changes between Brown's earlier books and his most recent ones. Things are changing faster than anyone could have imagined!

The Rough Guide to Climate Change (Henson 2011) confirmed what Prince Charles had written. If you read about our planet and see IPCC reports, they are the gold standard for accuracy. Every few years the IPCC releases a current review. Henson said, "The IPCC has compiled the most well organized scientific collaboration in the history of humankind and formed a consensus that all the nations of the Earth must work together to solve the crisis of global warming."

The 2001 IPCC report predicts temperature rises by 2100 ranging from a low of 2.5 degrees F if man acts quickly to reduce greenhouse gas emissions, to a rise as high as 10.4 degrees F if man continues on our present path. In the United States, IPCC reports are not big news, even though it is the most thorough statement ever made by climate scientists about the Earth. Longtime environmental researcher and activist James Lovelock called the IPCC's 2001 report, "The scariest document ever written."

No wonder great-granny was clueless. How could anything be more newsworthy? Who decides we would rather see weeks of news coverage about some celebrity's overdose? Have you ever heard of the IPCC reports? Lester Brown and many other authors, researchers, and scientists wait for the latest IPCC report with more interest than the

Americans who needed to know the verdict in the O. J. Simpson trial.

When I mention O. J. Simpson's trial, does a mental image of O.J. sitting in the courtroom and Marcia Clark speaking to the court come to mind? Nearly twenty years later, people still remember "the glove." That trial had daily live coverage for months. There was no such coverage in America for a report on a life and death crisis for mankind! Some government leaders, corporate powers, and media outlets did such a good job covering up the news that few Americans ever heard the Earth could be uninhabitable for man in less than two hundred years and in utter collapse during our grandchildren's lives.

Who decided what news to broadcast the day they released the last IPCC report? Do not wrap me in a stronger cocoon; I must be free!

Scientific studies in the years since the 2001 IPCC report show steadily rising greenhouse gas emissions exceed the worst-case scenario. The IPCC's report in 2001 carried predictions forward through the 22nd century and wrote, "We could see only a remnant of humanity eking out a diminished existence in the polar-regions and a few remaining oases left of hot arid Earth." A local TV station has a slogan, "All the news you need to know." I take offense at this omission. I am teachable. Why would anyone want me to be clueless?

I do not want to be terrified by earth-shattering news in the near future. However, report enough to let us know we need to be mindful of our energy use and other actions that are destroying the planet. That is news we need to know! The tragedies of Pearl Harbor and 9/11 could pale in comparison to the grim reality facing the entire world! Like many cancer patients who don't learn the facts early enough, we could get horrible news and find it is too late to be saved. Global warming is news everyone in the world should know, but for some reason in the United States, it seems to have been classified "Top Secret." That IPCC report spent years swept under "the RUG!"

"The RUG" is tucked away after the final chapter. I am getting a clearer idea of who bought and paid for George's oval rug and many other rugs scattered in the offices of our Capital. Money from big business gets rugs into congressional offices, offices of high-level appointees, and into the offices of many panels, committees, and agencies. The cost of the rugs was not an issue when it came to controlling the votes to determine policies, enforce regulations, and decide who to tax, who to fine, and who gets billions in subsidies. The possibility of choosing a few Supreme Court justices would be the icing on the cake. Those rugs were worth every penny. Look what big business pulls in. What's a few million dollars per rug? It's just good business. Decisions and policies may lack the "global conscience" about environmental destruction that Canadian Prime Minister Martin felt the United States was lacking, but big business was able to get the bottom line that matters to them. In the end, I suspect the taxpayers paid for every rug.

If information on global warming crept into a news report, some "think tank" would have equal time and point out that not all scientists and reports agree. The names of the think tanks are impressive, but many are employees of big business whose job it is to create doubt. Those cocoon tenders are one reason we need to do our own research; they are not letting the facts be known. Scientific reports about the exact number of feet the sea level rises and the time when such a rise will occur "disagree," but there is no doubt whatsoever about global warming being real. Predictions cannot agree; we have yet to see if man acts quickly before reaching tipping points when we can do nothing to avoid damaging the Earth so severely that man can no longer survive on the planet. There are many tipping points; some are pretty shaky already.

Big Coal (Goodell 2006) was an eye-opening book. I thought coal was on its way out, but while the U.S. population increased 140%, coal use in the U.S. increased 400%. As I read Big Coal, the most frightening thing I learned was the unimaginable depth of the influence exerted on U.S. laws and policies by people appointed to high-level positions. There was a direct connection between financial contributions from coal, railroad, and utility industries and the United States being the only nation to refuse to ratify the Kyoto Protocol calling for signers to agree to a cap on CO_2 emissions. A cap on the United States, the worst CO_2 polluters in the world, is something the coal, railroad, and utility companies in America did not intend to allow. The United States never ratified the Kyoto Protocol. That was a shameful and destructive choice on the part of George W. Bush. I have to wonder, if America had cooperated and aggressively moved toward developing wind, solar, and geothermal technologies, would the world be building pollution-free plants today instead of all the coal plants that are bursting onto the scene in China and other developing countries? America is a world leader. At that pivotal point in time, the U.S. turned and marched pompously in the wrong direction.

The literature still holds out hope Earth can be saved for man, and many authors offer plans to stop catastrophes. I began searching for information to tell me what I could do to help. A favorite book is *No Impact Man: The Adventures of a Guilty Liberal Who Attempts to Save the Planet and the Discoveries He Makes about Himself and Our Way of Life in the Process* (Beavan.2009). I bought a used copy and some to give away. Beavan is a sociologist with a sense of purpose and a sense of humor. He comes across as a naive friend that had no idea what he was in for when he decided his next book would be about something he really cared about– global warming. He decided his research would be to try to leave no carbon footprint for a year. Then he told his wife of his grand plan. They live in a ninth-floor Manhattan apartment with their

18-month-old daughter and their dog. He refers to his family as "ten legs and a tail."

Beavan chronicled his efforts to have no trash, use no toxins, only buy local, use no gas or electricity, etc. This book gave me the willingness to try some pretty outrageous and rewarding things in our home. He learned that rules and laws make sustainable living difficult in the United States, even impossible. We are on a treadmill, living a disposable lifestyle and unaware of the many ways we are marketed and pressured into forced consumption. In addition, we find our lives are not enriched by all the stuff we thought we wanted. We are mindlessly living in a crisis, believing this wastefulness is normal.

An Inconvenient Truth was finally available at the library. It is easy to understand, is a quick read, and has many pictures and graphs to illustrate and emphasize problems. When reading about the Greenland ice-sheet melting, the pictures pop into my mind. I know what a moulin looks like and how dangerous it is when many form. Being a seventy-year-old lady, my first thought about moulins was, "It's as if Greenland has osteoporosis in her ice sheet." When that slips, it could be the end of a number of island nations in the Pacific and Indian Oceans.

Gore points out there is hope and a huge opportunity for economic growth if we respond to the need for alternative energies. He has firsthand insight into reasons why America has been so slow to act. Things people are able to do at home are important, but we also need to work within our communities, at state and national levels, and with large corporations. Gore's book also comes in a children's edition.

One Earth (Brower 1990) has wonderful pictures to look at with children. You can see the destruction had started before 1990, nearly twenty-five years ago. It has only gotten worse. The pictures show what we're doing to our oceans. Seeing what desertification looks like makes it easier to comprehend the scope of that problem. There's an aerial view of a mountain in Washington State showing one side with a virgin forest and the other side clear cut and about bald. The caption told how the ecosystem was destroyed, animals killed or displaced, and the soil carried away because it had lost its protection from the sun and wind and rain erosion. Earth is a beautiful home and must be sustained as nature intended.

Global Warning: The Last Chance for Change (P. Brown 2007) is also a picture book a family could read together, look at pictures, and discuss what is happening to our Earth. There's a two-page spread of the Earth with little flags in many areas telling the problems each area faces.

I always thought of Mother Earth as lovingly providing for me and mine. Humans are lousy tenants. Mother Earth is there for us, but she can only work within the laws of nature. Man stepped so far out of bounds that our future is in jeopardy. Seven billion mouths to feed certainly pushes the limits, but Mother Nature can renew our lease if we abide by a sustainability clause. Most of us don't know the clause exists. We are teachable and there are important things we need to learn about sustainability.

Americans are such a problem. Mother Earth can accommodate China, India, and Japan easier than she can keep up with Americans' spoiled and self-indulgent ways. I had not realized I was living that differently from the rest of the industrialized world. We prospered to the point that we lost all awareness of boundaries. I think of the things I was marketed to buy and worked to accumulate. I felt entitled to spend my money any way I pleased. I had no idea I was robbing my grandchildren of a secure future. My research was giving me a new perspective. Americans are caring people, but without knowledge we have developed some very destructive habits that put every person on Earth in jeopardy.

> **The first day or so we all pointed to our country.**
> **The third or fourth day we were pointing to our continent.**
> **By the fifth day, we were aware of only one Earth.**
> Sultan Bin Salman al Saud–astronaut

Beyond Oil: The view From Hubert's Peak (Deffeyes 2009) has thorough information about the world's oil supply, and how close we are to a drastic decline in oil, worldwide. For hundreds-of- millions of years the Earth stored carbon from decayed plants and animals in the form of oil, coal, and natural gas. Man has used over half the oil in the last one hundred years, and released the carbon sequestered in the oil over millions of years. It is the last half century when our tail pipes and smoke stacks spewed out most of the CO_2 and other greenhouse gases. I had never heard of King Hubbert or his predictions and had no idea we are putting CO_2 from oil into our atmosphere at a rate 4,000,000 times faster than the carbon was stored.

If we continue to rely on oil and trucks for distribution, the oil shortage and skyrocketing cost of transportation will mark the end for the "big box" stores. We would be living local, working local, and getting our food local and seasonal. I am voluntarily trying to do some of those things. However, the changes the books tell about are far more radical and forced on us by desperate circumstances.

Greasy Rider (Melville 2008) convinced me I would never want to drive a car around the block on french fry oil, let alone across the country. Two guys made many stops to check out things that benefit the environment. One big disappointment was Al Gore's huge house in Nashville, lit up like a Christmas tree. The way they referred to it was, "The Friggin' Taj Mahal." In a follow up, they learned Gore retrofitted the big old mansion and purchases green offset credits.

If the term green offsetting credits is unfamiliar to you, think of it as a voluntary fine one chooses to pay to an environmental project to make amends for damages one does to the environment. There are websites that calculate the damages for you. I have thought about offset credits and decided not to go that route. Wally and I are investing in going green at home. We turn off our lights, turn down or shut off our hot water heater, and do whatever else we can think of, thank you. We plan to keep the carbon safely sequestered in the ground in the first place. It's against my principles to waste energy, release excess greenhouse gases into the atmosphere, and then think I can buy my way out of it. Turn off the darn lights, Al!

That gets me on my soapbox. I bike ride at sunset. I used to think it was pretty when ground lighting in our community flashes on at dusk to light up the palm trees lining our streets. Now it frustrates me. Those palm trees do not have to be shown off all night; we see them all day. Then I considered the "safety-issue" and I wonder how many billions of hours of needless lighting are on in the name of safety in every city, every year. I think I can remember how to hold a flashlight. Lights are left on in the name of love: "I'll leave the light on for you, honey."

Dark is not bad. Dark is not dangerous. Dark is peaceful and very hard to find. For thirty years I've looked for a place where there is no light pollution at night so I can really see the stars. Try it sometime. Homes far out in the country have "security lights." Secure from what, it certainly is not going to keep us safe from global warming.

For the life of me, I cannot figure out how Americans habitually use seven times more energy than the rest of the world. After two years of studying about the environment, I think it is ludicrous to leave lights on to be safe. They sold us a bill of goods and we paid dearly for those lights. Dare to see if you can be safe in the dark all night long. How many lights could you turn off? What other crazy ideas have crept into our thinking that contributes to that tally of seven times above the average Earthling? All that was over Al leaving the lights on, and by the way, no one was home!

Twelve by Twelve (Powers 2010) is a special book that reminded us we have a solar shower bag on our sailboat that would work very well for the house. When you read about someone else using one, it seems more logical to at least give it a try. I would love to live in that little twelve by twelve house off the grid for a month. It's owned by a doctor who has everything she needs, and she enjoys the peacefulness, simplicity, and free time allowed by an unencumbered lifestyle. It sounded wonderful.

That peace is a treasure within each of us that many seldom recognize. For people who always have to be entertained, it could be a challenge to find the value of solitude. The words, "I wouldn't know what to do with myself" are all too common. We don't have to DO anything. To just BE is refreshing and inspiring. That is what we forfeited in the name of progress, getting ahead, and having it all. Peace and serenity are not for sale; they are just there, waiting, if you can spare the time. I love to hear trees whisper, brooks babble, and birds sing, so Twelve by Twelve was a pleasure to read. It gave me hope that many people who need to make adjustments in their lifestyle can end up with more contentment and joy than they have ever known. There are quiet places where you can just BE and have your spirit lifted. That is priceless.

I hope everyone watches the documentary Gasland (Fox 2010) to understand why cheap and clean natural gas has a deadly dark side. Gasland is about natural gas wells being drilled, lies, water-air-land contamination, brain lesions, disabilities, deaths, drinking water that lights on fire, dumping toxins in streams that kill fish for thirty-five miles downstream because their gills were eaten by the toxins dumped, and the clincher is the "The Halliburton Loophole" that makes this legal. It's all in the natural gas chapter.

I learned the way we eat in America is not only killing us, but increasing starvation for millions each year, destroying our planet, and polluting the atmosphere. The Ultimate Weight Solution (McGraw 2003) reminded me,

> **It is not possible for me to be overweight unless I generate and adopt a lifestyle that sustains the extra pounds.**
> Dr.Phil

I hope to be leaving a little more food for the children in Africa by not loading my plate. I don't go to Dr. Phil for the scientific aspects of a proper diet. I needed an attitudinal adjustment to be willing to eat the healthiest foods for the planet and myself.

Michael Pollan's book, *Food Rules* (2009), is brief, informative, and comical, but the rules are lifesavers and planet savers. I'll give you a few.

> **Eat food, mostly plants and not too much.**
> **Don't eat anything your grandmother wouldn't recognize as food.**
> **Avoid food products containing ingredients third-graders cannot pronounce.**
> **If it came from a plant, eat it. If it was made in a plant, don't.**
> **The whiter the bread, the sooner you're dead.**
> **Eat when you are hungry, not when you're bored.**

There is much more to this little book, including information about how Americans are turned into corporate profit makers addicted to and buying "food-like" factory products.

Eat More Weigh Less (Ornish 1993) tells about medical miracles doctors did not think were possible. Since 1977, Dr. Ornish has been treating patients with advanced heart disease. I saw him on Oprah, accompanied by one of his longtime patients who twenty-five years ago had been waiting for a heart transplant. Under Dr. Ornish's care, the man went off his meds, had no surgery, and was restored to good health. Now there is a diet with reward points. The advice I got from his book was, "Total change is easier than gradual change; it allows your taste to change." That is the most reliable way to convert to being a vegan if you wish.

The China Study (Campbell and Campbell 2006) is a lifesaver for Americans. Dr. Campbell compares how the people of China and America eat. He states that Americans are encouraged to eat health-destroying food-facsimiles, enabling the food industry to make huge profits at our expense. The greatest profit is in factory-made, monoculture, agribusiness fast food with Monsanto-type formulas. Dr. Dean Ornish said of Campbell and *The China Study*, "Everyone in the field of nutrition science stands on the shoulders of Dr. Campbell, who is one of the giants in the field. This is one of the most important books about nutrition ever written—reading it may save your life." Read the book. You won't be watching your children die prematurely from complications of diabetes, heart disease, or many types of cancer if you heed his words.

The recommended foods are plant based from the lower part of the food chain. If Americans ate a healthy diet, we could feed all of Africa. I have no scientific data to back that claim; it's just a gut feeling. Wouldn't it be great to have a healthy country and know our choices made it possible for millions of starving people around the world to have enough food to grow and develop physically and mentally? Starvation affects the development of a child's brain.

Eat to Live (Fuhrman 2011) is the book I find most useful for restoring this great-granny's health, and it is certainly environmentally friendly. It motivates people who want to become vegan, lose weight, and improve their health. He explains we are addicted to the sugar, salt, and fat in the Standard American Diet (SAD) and our palate now craves the foods that are killing us. He encourages us to allow our palates to learn to enjoy healthy foods. We need to realize our palate is "unfamiliar" with foods like kale, and rather than saying, "I can't stand kale," be willing to retrain your palate by eating unfamiliar foods until they become familiar and delicious. Craving suicidal foods was one of my downfalls. When I heard on TV that the average American couple needs $250,000 in retirement savings for medical expenses alone, I thought *my new palate saves me a fortune*. America's eating habits are a major contributor to global warming and world hunger, and we are killing ourselves. Here is a correction we can all live with.

I look for every way I can find to decrease global warming. I give and receive fruit and shade trees as gifts. There is another thing I do that saves as much CO_2 from going into the atmosphere as switching from an SUV to a Prius. If someone shows an interest in becoming a vegan, I give them used copies of *The China Study* and *Eat to Live*. These two books change the way a person thinks and eats. Every vegan prevents twenty thousand pounds of CO_2 from entering our atmosphere and is rewarded with good health. If I can help fifty readers convert to being vegan, I will be instrumental in saving one million pounds of CO_2 per year from going into the atmosphere.

Confessions of an Eco-Sinner: Tracking Down the Sources of My Stuff (Pearce 2006) taught me where our stuff comes from, what harm we are unintentionally doing to other people and other lands, how to choose items that leave a smaller carbon-footprint, and how naive I was about so many of my seemingly insignificant purchases. Many items we bring into our homes have had their passports stamped many times. He writes about, "My T-Shirt, Slave Labor, and the Death of the Aral Sea." That is one topic; it's all connected to cotton.

Rising Powers Shrinking Planet: The New Geopolitics of Energy (Klare 2008) tells how everything we thought we knew about being the strongest power on Earth has changed. Klare claims we're living in the past and military strength no longer insures security. I thought about that. Oil is declining. America is dependent on huge oil imports. China is building a huge cash reserve. China wants more and more oil. China is not our enemy. We depend on China to buy our bonds to cover our overspending. You may wonder where this is going. Just let me ramble a bit and see how the pieces start to fit.

We are not doing nearly enough to get America free of our oil, coal, and natural gas addiction. We spend billions to have a strong army, but our weakness is no longer the threat of invasion. Spending billions to control oil by military action leads to conflict and increases the money we borrow from China. Oil dependence threatens our national security. We need to rectify this "Achilles Heel," emphasizing conservation and switching to wind and solar power. Klare would make a good five-star general for the energy war we are facing.

There is a new reality. Oil is declining everywhere and prices will soon explode through the roof. China needs more and more oil to grow her economy and take care of her people; "Houston we may have a problem." Whatever country can pay for the oil gets the goods. "My money trumps your army." We might not have as much luck going to our banker, China, when the bank wants to buy the oil. China has enough financial power to apply pressure when needed in the future.

One-example Klare sites of our vulnerability was the "UNOCAL Affair." Do you remember that? It was in 2005, around the time Anna Nicole Smith died. When I mention Anna Nicole, murky facts start surfacing; she had a baby and a couple men claimed they were the father. People let her live in and out of drugged stupors. What a mess, remember?

Do you remember as many murky facts about Union Oil Company of California (UNOCAL)? It was in the news because the government and Chevron wanted public support to stop the sale of an American energy company to a Chinese company. Chevron announced to its executives, "It was no longer possible to assume that global hydrocarbon reserves would keep growing indefinitely and that Chevron's aging fields would be adequately replaced with newfound deposits." Chevron's $16.5 billion bid to buy UNOCAL was expected to fly through Congress. Then an unsolicited cash offer from the Chinese National Offshore Oil Corporation (CNOOC) for $18.5 billion was announced. *The New York Times* said, "Capital Nearly Speechless over Big China Bid" and "None of them had remotely considered that a Chinese firm would seek ownership of U.S. energy assets considered vital to the economy." China withdrew the offer, but that will not always be the case. According to the "Fair Trade Agreement," the offer was not out of line. In 1990, Citi Service was sold to a state-owned company in Venezuela. Fifteen years later, the world has changed. Oil companies and governments know oil supplies are dropping and production cannot meet the demand. This is not a brief situation. That is the way it is and will be until oil is gone or civilization topples because a tipping point is crossed.

> **A new chapter in the history of international politics has begun, one in which the pursuit and control of energy resources would be the central dynamic of world affairs, and governments.**
> Michael T. Klare

The headlines were about China endangering our oil supply and security. Not once did it mention a need to decrease America's dependence on oil. We heard what Chevron and the government wanted us to hear; I hardly remember it. Reasons for not remembering could be, I didn't want to know, and the government wanted it forgotten once China withdrew their offer. There was no need to start a push for alternative energies or conservation. There was money to be made from the status quo. Gas-guzzling Hummer vehicles would be a future hit, spelling profit, gas sales, and bigger and better things to come.

Global warming is the "elephant in the middle of the room" that no one wants to look at or talk about. It is time to look. It is time to talk. It is time to protect our children. Study the symptoms, understand the diagnosis, and act before the prognosis is terminal.

WARNING

DO NOT STOP READING THIS BOOK!

THERE'S NO TIME TO ROLL OVER AND PLAY DEAD!

I Wish It Weren't So

The following pages contain the most disturbing news you will ever face. It brings back feelings I had as the hospice social worker at the hospitals in Naples. I met with the patient and family after the doctor made the referral to hospice. I could not change the facts, and just like the families, I wished it weren't so. Some patients or families frantically denied the patient was terminal and life expectancy was measured in months, weeks, or days rather than years. Others were angry, believing if some doctor, test, or treatment had done what he/it was supposed to do, the patient would not be dying. Patients felt guilt for not visiting the doctor sooner or for leaving their families. Everyone was doing the best he could and all were in pain.

I felt I had a "divine purpose," then as now, to offer help, answer questions, provide information, and to give hope and strength to get through this natural part of life. I loved my job. I didn't want patients struggling more than necessary, fighting a reality that marched on despite denial. No matter what warnings I got from the doctor, nurses, or social worker about the chaos behind the patient's door, I wanted to knock, reach for the handle, and enter their world. For seven years, with more than two thousand patients and their families, before I knocked and entered, I lifted the lid on my clipboard and read a quote from *A Course in Miracles* (Schucman and Thetford 1975).

> **I am here only to be truly helpful.**
> **I am here to represent Him who sent me.**
> **I do not have to worry about what to say or what to do, because**
> **He who sent me will direct me.**
> **I am content to be wherever He wishes, knowing He goes there with me.**
> **I will be healed as I let Him teach me to heal.**

That's how I feel now. These are difficult realities, but we need to know the truth. I want to bring hope, provide tools to do what needs to be done, and help you discover your value and power. I want to help you find peace in this situation. And yes, I wish it weren't so.

I am an author, only in the sense that I'm putting this in a book. I would rather enter your room and be by your side. On March 26, 2012, as I was walking to the market. I received a clear message. After studying and making changes in our home, my journey to help others understand the problems facing Lilly's world was about to begin. My mind was searching for ways to help others understand and take action for their families. Out of nowhere, as my feet hit the pavement with five steps, five words came out of my mouth, "I will write a book." I was shocked, but the knowing came with each word. My answer was, "And so it is." When I returned home, I immediately started writing. Eckhart Toole's remark about having a divine purpose now made sense.

I don't know how to be an author, but "I do not have to worry about what to say or do, He who sent me will direct me." He has directed me before. I have to remember that over and over. I try to write properly and to give you accurate facts. I may make some mistakes. Do not let my errors stop you from finishing the book and doing research for yourself. My intention is only to be truly helpful.

I feel an urgent need to write and publish *For Lilly*. Her world is under attack, and it seems as if everyone is as clueless as I was. Global warming is not news any of us would want to believe. I have tried to give you every dastardly fact. Someone has to talk about the hard stuff. There are examples of what we have done in our home to live more sustainably. You will also find tools and techniques to empower you and help you discover your own value and power.

For Lilly goes from telling you man is destroying our Earth, to a book about how to experience a peace and joy you have never known. When I consider the subject matter I feel compelled to give you, I may not worry about how to do this, but I am curious.

I had those same feelings during my work with hospice, bringing the difficult facts to new patients. I was willing to be directed. Often, I entered into chaos and left with both others and myself feeling hopeful and with an understanding of what to do.

CHAPTER 3

THE GOLDILOCKS PLANET

We do not like to hear bad news and are not often confronted with in-depth news about global warming, so we think it must not be a problem. We're waiting until it is front-page news day after day: **"Global Warming Threatens Our Children's Futures**." The fact that it is true does not put it on the front page. Few politicians dare make it an issue. Lobbyists spring into action to counter any attempt to shed light on problems requiring corrective changes by the industries they represent. The media also fails to do in-depth reporting on the most life threatening event man has ever faced. Journalism gets more mileage from reporting about celebrity scandals than a world in crisis.

For years, no one understood the Earth's temperature was warming in a threatening way, instead of from a natural cycle. A huge problem today is that we do not want to change our behavior. The U.S. economy is based on cheap fossil fuel, and Americans have been convinced we are irreversibly dependent on oil. We elect officials, but the power elite wield more influence over many politicians than do the people at home. Global warming was not started intentionally, but the continued burning of fossil fuels is a train that is hard to stop. Only when enough people learn the facts and demand action will millions of voters carry the weight to force our government to wage an all-out war against global warming.

Two years ago, I thought I was being a good Earthling. We gave up one vehicle when I retired and did less driving in our gas-guzzling van. Using canvas bags for all my shopping, changing to energy-efficient light bulbs, and swearing off all paper products except toilet paper was enough to appease my environmental concerns. Everything has changed. Wally and I kept studying and making more changes as our thinking shifted. Some changes cost money; many save money. Money and convenience are no longer the main issue. Our children's lives, Lilly's life, will play out on the Earth we leave them as their stage. Choices I make today take into account how they affect that stage I think of as "Lillyland." That concept helps me put my heart into my efforts to be a green granny. Global warming is not too big to tackle; it is too big to ignore.

First, I wanted to understand what is warming and why it is a problem. About ten thousand years ago, the Earth had warmed, many North American glaciers had melted, and there was water covering much of the land. An enormous wall of ice prevented that water from flowing into the North Atlantic. One day that ice dam broke and the water rushed into the North Atlantic, leaving North America with our five Great Lakes; however, Western Europe was in for trouble.

The world's ocean and the wind currents circulate heat and cold so the climate stays livable in many areas. Ocean currents are regulated, in part, by the level of salt concentration in the ocean water. Higher salt content makes the water heavier and it sinks. The fresh water from North America suddenly flooded into the North Atlantic, reaching the area of the Thermalhaline Pump just south of Greenland where the driving force for ocean currents originates. The fresh water diluted the ocean water's salinity and the sinking-pumping motion slowed when the water was no longer heavy with salt. Then the pump stopped. The Gulf Stream was no longer pulled to the North Atlantic by the sinking-pumping motion. The steamy air that evaporated from the Gulf Stream when the warm waters met frigid Arctic air was gone and Western Europe went into a mini ice age that lasted nine hundred to one thousand years. The salinity gradually returned and the Thermalhaline Pump slowly regained its movement. Western Europe's weather during that ice age was similar to what the Arctic has today. Eventually, Europe thawed and the planet became a great place for man to thrive.

The first time I came across the information about the wind and ocean currents, I was amazed. Nature does a lot of balancing I never read about when I was in school. Check the Internet for Thermalhaline Current, Thermalhaline Pump, or Global Ocean Conveyer Belt. There are reasons it could be something to be aware of for our future. The Greenland ice sheet is like a finger pointing straight to "the pump."

What has happened since the Earth's climate became so suitable for humans? If we are in trouble now, what is causing such a sudden change? There are complex reasons why the Earth is warming, after having a stable temperature for nearly ten thousand years. Great-granny decided to try to explain it as a fairy tale. The idea came when I read that Earth has a nickname: "The Goldilocks Planet."

EARTH BECAME THE GOLDILOCKS PLANET

Once upon a time, there was this beautiful little blue planet called Earth. It had been through many changes in 4.5 billion years. Different creatures had come and then disappeared. It had been hot part of the time and covered with lots of ice at other times.

10,000 years ago, one million people lived on Earth. With all the changes the planet had been through, the climate was finally "just right" for humans to thrive. Earth became man's Goldilocks Planet. The climate was controlled by a delicate and thin atmosphere, which let in enough of the sun's rays to warm the planet. The atmosphere also allowed excess heat to reflect off the ice and radiate back out through the atmosphere so the Earth did not get too hot. Earth was not too hot or too cold; Earth was "just right."

Nature had rivers of wind in the sky that carried the heat from the equator and warmed the land and sea to the north and to the south. These winds were like rivers because they also carried moisture and rained down on the land so that man had water to drink and to raise his food. The oceans also had great currents that helped warm and cool more places so that man had more places to live. Fish swam in the waters of the world and fed many people. Goldilocks now had a home and nature had laws to keep Earth just right. Man used what he needed to live, gave back to the Earth, and man thrived.

There were scraps, feuds, and even wars at times, but that didn't alter the delicate balance of the atmosphere. That never failed. For thousands of years the water, wind, air, and land temperatures stayed just right. The Earth provided for man, and man, with his marvelous brain, found ways to make life easier and better.

In 1 AD there were 200 million people. They had tools, fire for heat and cooking, animals to help with the work, and some people lived in cities. Even with 200 times as many people as there were 8,000 years earlier, the Earth and its atmosphere remained just right. The Earth was so big there would always be enough.

By 1830 there were 1 billion, or 1,000 times as many people. They lived in nations; people had big cities, or worked the land in the country to provide food for themselves and others. When the soil was overworked and depleted, or when people felt too crowded, they cleared land and settled in new areas. Most of the farming fit into nature's balance. The sun shown, the sun's energy was stored in the plants, animals ate the plants, then other animals ate some of them, but in each step of this process nature gave and received back what was needed for the just right cycle to go on forever, it seemed.

By 1930 the Earth had 2 billion people, or 2,000 times as many. It took 10,000 years to reach 1 billion and only one hundred years to add another billion. People were living longer because of better nutrition, medicines, and improved sanitation. By now, man was burning a lot of oil and coal. Both were cheap and many things were made from oil. Some parts of the world had electricity and roads that trucks used to transport food and manufactured products great distances. All seemed well, and the Earth and her atmosphere were still just right. After all, the Earth is so big there did not seem to be a limit to what she could provide for man. The great rainforests still filtered and put billions of tons of moisture into the air every day. There were billions and billions of other trees to absorb the extra carbon man produced by burning fossil fuels and wood. The world was in a great depression, but the people never had to worry about the atmosphere.

In 1960 the population passed 3 billion, or 3,000 times as many people. It took 10,000 years to reach a living population of 1 billion, another one hundred years to reach the 2nd billion people alive and eating on Earth, and a mere 30 years to have the 3rd billion showing up at Mother Nature's table for their meals. Nations were "industrialized" and "developing." Advertising stimulated the economy. Television, magazines, and newspapers let people know what was new and better. It hadn't reached the point that many things were single use. People were not ready to pay a thousand times more for a glass of water from a "safe and convenient bottle," when the water from the tap was perfectly fine. Who could imagine such a crazy thing?

Mother Nature was starting to struggle, but for the most part, man was not taking things like water and trees from the Earth faster than she could replenish them. There were a lot more mouths to feed, and some of the people had made great progress in using Nature's capital.

Fossil fuels were another issue. Mother Nature, for 400 million years, had safely sequestered the carbon from decayed plants and animals in the ground in the form of fossil fuels. This was how Mother Nature kept the climate just right. Now man was digging, drilling, and burning the stored carbon. Nature cannot re-sequester carbon stored away over millions of years if it is released into the atmosphere within a few years. The atmosphere has no way to let that much CO_2 out into space, so it built up in our thin, fragile, and just right atmosphere. It started feeling as if people were putting an overcoat around the Earth.

By 1960 some scientists noticed CO_2 levels in the atmosphere were rising. Ice core samples from the Antarctic and improved technology revealed that historically, when CO_2 levels rise, the Earth's temperature also rises. The ramifications of that rise were only starting to be considered. This "climate change" was new to man. There had been brief changes in the past caused by naturally occurring events, but now they were looking at something that was not only remaining in the atmosphere, but also accumulating faster each year. Few scientists recognized this was the first signs of a threat to the human species.

The Earth's CO_2 level has been meticulously measured and recorded daily since 1958 and has gone from 315 parts per million (ppm) in 1958 to over 400 ppm by the summer of 2012. We know that as the CO_2 concentration rises, so does the Earth's temperature.

By 1975 the world population reached 4 billion, 4,000 times as many people. Holy cow, each billion is arriving a lot faster! What is going on? It took 10,000 years, then one hundred years, then 30 years, and now just 15 years to add another billion. No matter how hard Mother Nature tried to keep the balance just right, she found the needed corrections were outside the laws of nature she had to work with. It was not just that awful carbon problem from oil; man found more ways to take carbon from the ground and forests and dump it into the air.

People were using plastic money so advertisers could cue them to go buy the newest, the improved, or the latest color. All those "in" turquoise and pink refrigerators would have to go. Avocado green and harvest gold was the way to go for an updated kitchen, and they needed a matching trash compactor to make the stuff hauled out of their homes manageable. More women worked outside the home so the family could afford new necessities and modern conveniences. The economy and profits grew. That is how the industrialized world measures a country's success. The GNP and the GDP must always climb. If it lags, people are urged to buy-buy-buy to stimulate the economy. Economists watched for any sign of a recession, so they could take quick action. However, no one saw news about rising CO_2 levels.

Corporations were big and powerful, spread into many countries, and had great influence on world leaders. The owners and major investors in these corporations became very wealthy. They knew they could never have too much money, and they hired advertisers and created "think tanks" to peddle their wares and protect their image. The government provided subsidies and protected the corporate interests, sold on the idea that the economy must endlessly keep growing.

With 4 billion mouths to feed, the world's water tables were dropping, and global warming was changing the climate that Mother Nature had previously been able to keep just right. Man was using resources faster than nature could replace them; that fact was ignored. The rich were getting richer; the industrialized world was buying a lot of stuff, and sorry to say, Mother Nature started running low on resources. She can only work within the laws of nature. Man was over-riding limits. Laws of nature do apply to man, but for a while, man can keep the economy growing by spending their children's future. That was the 1970s, a mere shadow of what was to come.

By 1990 the population had reached 5 billion, or 5,000 times as many people, but now the Earth was not able to keep the balance. The rich seek power and money and our children will pay the price when this big Ponzi scheme collapses. America is the world leader for mindless consumerism. We dine from the top of the food chain, enjoy our love affair with beef, and use up to seven times the land and water resources needed to supply our nutrition.

It is not just food we splurge on; we buy everything we can pay for with cash or credit. Business as usual continued to grow and grow the economy. Over time, Americans have become accustomed to spending, depleting, and polluting at a rate seven times the rate of the average Earthling. In our minds, only the amount of money we do or do not have will cap our spending, depleting, and polluting lifestyles. Once we had the convenience of one car, TV, telephone, and bathroom. Now, if we can afford it, the sky is the limit. Get a car for every kid old enough to drive, put a TV in every room, get the eight-year-olds their own phones, and be sure each child has his own bedroom. Sharing is so inconvenient. Buy a boat, get jet skis for the kids, buy a ski lodge, get a cabin on the lake, and take time to enjoy life by flying to Europe. What will they sell us next?

How did we get so out of touch with how destructive our way of life has become? In a later chapter, you'll meet a woman who was raised in India and has been in the United States nine years. When asked how she would describe Americans, she was thoughtful and finally said, "Americans are very frivolous." I do not want to be frivolous, but I am a product of our culture. It's not easy to find where all the little changes took place that made me believe I wanted so much stuff. At some point I interchanged the word "need" for "want." I think I need all this stuff, while at the same time I'm taking from what Lilly will REALLY need.

> **There must be more to life than increasing its speed.**
> ## Gandhi

By 2000 the world population reached 6 billion, or 6,000 times as many people. In ten years, the world's population increased by 1 billion people; so much for stabilizing the rate of increase. It took 10,000 years to get from 1 million to the first billion; now we add one billion people in 10 years. All of the maladies mentioned from 1960 on are getting worse. New terms are creeping into our vocabulary.

Carrying Capacity is one of the laws of nature that could present a danger in the near future. The carrying capacity numbers for man differs, depending on the lifestyle of the population and how much stress each person puts on the environment. The rule of carrying capacity states, "Any population that increases indefinitely will eventually outgrow its natural support systems."

Another term is <u>Environmental Refugee</u>. Where can a million starving, ill, and homeless people go when there is no food? They walk in hope of finding anything to eat. They are unwelcome in bordering countries and often endanger the food supply of their already hungry neighbors.

<u>Failing State</u> is the term used to describe a country when it breaks down to such a degree that the government is unable to function, provide healthcare, education, or security for its people. Leadership is gone and often civil war breaks out. There are now sixty countries identified as failing or at risk. Somalia is #1 and only exists on maps. There is no way the United Nations or the International Red Cross can safely provide aid in Somalia. It is too dangerous; trucks are hijacked and people are killed or taken hostage. Industrialized nations spend $8.5 billion dollars a year to protect their shipping interests from Somali pirates. In the past, we feared leaders who had too much control over their citizens; today we are at risk because countries' leaders have no control.

Global warming is a big player in the failing states. Environmental refugees and exceeding carrying capacity limits are problems the government can't handle. The world's population is more than **7,000** times what it was 10,000 years ago. Some scientists are contemplating whether the Earth is nearing the sixth extinction. Laws of nature have been violated, and we may be nearing some tipping point of no return. Lester Brown explains, "Nature is the time keeper and we cannot see the clock."

I believe in happy endings. To have a happy ending we hypnotized-over-consumers need to "snap out of it!" We do not have the luxury to drift slowly from our hyper-consumer mentality. We have a distorted view of what Earth has to offer and consider it normal to spend and consume in ways we would have considered crazy in 1960. When I say snap out of it, I mean at warp speed

Ted Turner felt an early *Plan B* book by Lester Brown had so much information essential for government leaders to know that he gave a copy to every member of Congress, leaders in the White House, and to many other officials and people in industry. Unfortunately, the leaders at the time had such an allegiance to oil, coal, natural gas, railroads, agribusiness, and the power elite, that the message was ignored. I believe Americans wasted or were robbed of valuable time. We are all influenced by and have alliances with friends, but leaders have a duty to lead.

George W. Bush claimed to be interested in protecting the environment when he ran for president, but after taking office, he announced he didn't believe global warming was a problem. We squandered eight years when there was so much to do.

Bill McKibben, author and environmentalist, wrote about how politicians and corporate leaders wanted gentler names for global warming. They chose "climate change" because it is less alarming and less detrimental to businesses and the economy. For years they hid behind those words, pointing out that climate and weather always change in cycles. Well, this is not an average change. McKibben suggested we skip the debate about climate change or global warming and see if "Hell on Earth" might get someone's attention. Earth is no longer the Goldilocks Planet.

> **Our generation has inherited an incredibly beautiful world from our parents. We must not be the generation responsible for irreversibly damaging the environment.**
> Richard Branson at 2006 Global Initiative Summit in New York

CHAPTER 4

GLOBAL WARMING

GREENHOUSE GASES 101 (THE OVERCOAT)

There are three naturally occurring greenhouse gases, plus water vapor, and three other gases that are not naturally occurring in the atmosphere. These seven gases plus other pollutants we cast off make up "the overcoat" that is overheating the Earth. Mother Nature may be getting a new tenant; she is having trouble keeping up with man's destructive ways. She can only do so much to keep the atmosphere balanced. Earth has had five known evictions (extinctions). Reasons for extinctions are not clear, but no other tenant ruined his own home. Earth will go on; she always has. Man could stay longer if he was not covering Earth with a sweltering overcoat. We had better help the lady off with her coat.

Earth's thin and delicate atmosphere is comparable in thickness to a sheet of paper around a soccer ball. CO_2, methane, nitrous oxide, and water vapor, were in the correct balance to allow man to enjoy a livable climate. This precise balance allows heat to enter the atmosphere so that Earth is not a frozen planet. It is also mandatory that the correct amount of heat escape from the atmosphere, or Earth will be too hot for the human species. That fragile atmospheric shield is what man is destroying by releasing excessive greenhouse gases.

CO$_2$ should make up 63% of the atmosphere and takes one hundred years to break down. Nature provides the proper amount, but man is adding extra CO$_2$. The Keeling curve is a graph that shows the increase in carbon dioxide levels in the atmosphere since 1958, when the CO$_2$ concentration had already reached 315 ppm.

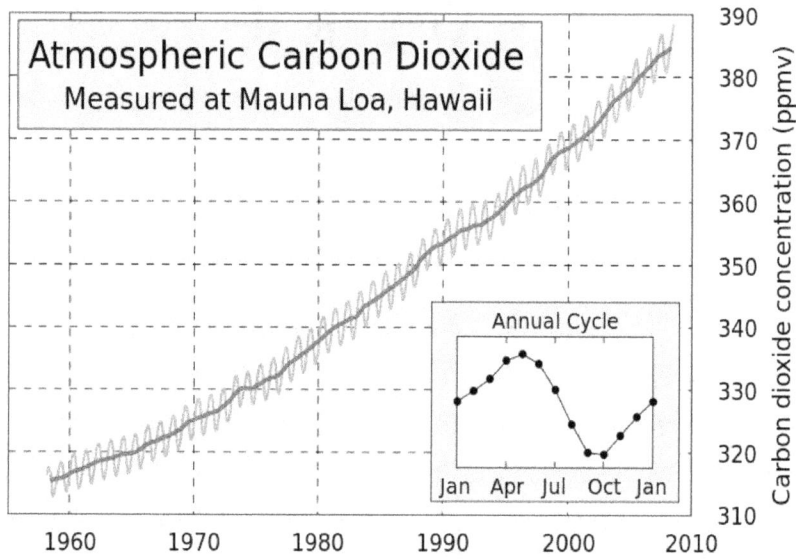

Al Gore explained, "If you think the up and down zigzag of the Keeling Curve indicated the CO$_2$ concentrations go up and down, it's true. Most of the land and vegetation on Earth is in the Northern Hemisphere. Each spring and summer, leaves and other vegetation put on new growth and absorb more CO$_2$. During the fall and winter, vegetation dies back releasing CO$_2$. It is the overall direction of the CO$_2$ accumulation that is the concern. Go back and look at the Keeling Curve and all the zigzags are there, but draw a line and the direction is undeniable." Measure and you'll see the rate of acceleration increasing dramatically, with an ever-steeper climb predicted.

It is crazy for us to play games with our children's future... We have a heavy obligation because we now know what is happening to our climate and what will be a highly predictable set of

outcomes if we continue to pour greenhouse gases into the atmosphere.

We also know we have an alternative of even greater prosperity if we apply the new technologies that are now available to us.

Former president Bill Clinton, Montreal Climate Talks, 2005

Scientists study past CO_2 levels and past temperatures using ice cores from Antarctica. There have been regular change cycles about one hundred thousand years apart, but Earth had never in the previous 650,000 years reached a CO_2 level of 300 ppm. CO_2 and temperature increase in unison. Man skyrocketed CO_2 levels past 400 ppm in July 2012.

We dig, drill, pump, and dump millions of years of stored carbon from the ground to make and run every imaginable contrivance from crayons to rocket ships. Enterprising humans have released half of the carbon from dead animals and vegetation stored in the ground as oil for 400 million years into the atmosphere in the last 150 years, most of it in the last sixty.

Tropical rainforests hold half the carbon present in live vegetation around the world. That helped Mother Nature. However, man has been destroying the rainforests at a rate that, instead of storing carbon, releases enough carbon to contribute 10% to the additional manmade CO_2 in the atmosphere. Slashing and burning releases CO_2 the fastest, but every tree cut is a step in the wrong direction. Any cutting of the forests that is not sustainable needs to be examined. We do many things in a frivolous manner when there are better options. The fast buck isn't necessarily a bargain.

Fred Pearse, in *Confessions of an Eco-sinner*, tracked the origin of his belongings. For his socks, cotton grown in Cameroon was trucked to the west coast of Africa, shipped around the Cape of Good Hope to India, trucked sixteen hours to a village to be spun, trucked back to Mumbai, and loaded on a ship to Istanbul. After a long drive to be dyed, it was returned to Istanbul for knitting. Fred's socks cross Europe to England. Socks for Americans cross the Atlantic, are trucked to warehouses and stores, and finally driven to our homes. I gave little thought to energy used and CO_2 produced to make something new for me. Getting the resources, making, and transporting each item in so many steps and in so many places is a big part of how Americans use so much more than the other people of the world. We buy far more than we need.

When you look at your clothing and consider that a pair of socks traveled ten thousand miles to be stuffed in your drawer with ten to twenty-five other pairs, might we consider slowing down our clothes shopping? Make this your mantra: "Get enough, but not more than you need." After reading Fred's book, my strategy for helping the lady off with her coat includes no longer buying more than I need. Realizing my concept of what I need is distorted, I first say, "I'm not buying anything; I have a lifetime supply." Then I ask, "Is this something I can buy at the thrift store?" *The No Impact Man* inspired me to try thrift stores before buying new. What a find! I got a beautiful bathing suit for $1, cut off the original $75 price tag, and washed my brand-new, never-before-worn bathing suit. What a sacrifice for the planet!

Methane in the atmosphere has increased by 60% because of the activities of man. This gas is twenty-five times as potent as CO_2 for holding the heat in the atmosphere and takes eight years to disappear. Methane sources are belching cows, tanks of liquid manure from the factory farming of livestock for our meat, landfills, rice paddies, peat bogs, our cars, homes, and industry.

Cattle grazing in pastures leave manure to dry in the field; it decomposes and fertilizes the land without giving off methane. If you eat beef, can you eat less and find a source from cattle raised in pastures? You won't ingest the antibiotics and hormones found in factory-farm meat.

Nitrous oxide is 310 times as strong as CO_2 and lasts one hundred years. The amount in the atmosphere increased 17% due to man's use of fertilizers, burning of fossil fuels, and burning rainforests. When the soil in the rainforests is disturbed, the bacteria produce nitrous oxide for two years.

Water vapor is a greenhouse gas because it holds in heat and has increased due to global warming. As temperatures rise, water expands in volume. This expansion also raises sea level.

Sulphur-hexaflouride (SF6) and PFC are not natural greenhouse gases; they are by-products of industry, aluminum smelting, semi-conductors, and the electric grid used to deliver our energy.

HFC is the substitute for the banned refrigerant CFC, which damages the ozone layer. The bad news is that HFC accumulates as a greenhouse gas in the atmosphere.

> **The identification of humans as the main driver of global warming helps us understand how and why our climate is changing, and it clearly defines the problem as one that is within our power to address.**
> Union of Concerned Scientists, 2006

IF MOTHER EARTH WERE TO HAVE A HEAT STROKE, WHAT WOULD IT LOOK LIKE?

I compare horrible heat waves to Mother Nature having a heat stroke. Tens-of-thousands of people die in prolonged record high temperatures. Just like human victims, who cannot adjust to such heat, Mother Nature cannot cool down to a healthy temperature. Moreover, each year it gets worse. The years from 2000 to 2010 were the hottest decade on record. Look at some of the decade's events.

2001- President George W. Bush takes office and announces, "Global warming isn't a problem at all." I guess we believed him. What a relief; Detroit could get going on those Hummers.

After 9-11, it was clear sailing for Bush-Cheney. In the name of national security and independence from oil from unfriendly countries, environmental laws were gutted and overturned. The Halliburton loophole allows oil and gas companies to avert inspections by the Environmental Protection Agency (EPA). In 2005, Vice President Cheney pushed the Energy Bill through Congress. I did not know what the bill did until watching the documentary *Gasland*. The Energy bill was supposed to be good for America—but not my America. It exempted oil and gas from the 1970 Clean Air Act, the 1972 Clean Water Act, the Safe Drinking Water Act, the Super Fund Law, and provided many more perks for oil and gas companies.

Canada's oil from tar sand is very expensive to extract. Boreal forests are scraped from the landscape and then the oil company drills deep into the earth. Steam and many chemicals are forced in to liquefy the oil enough to extract it. If the oil company could use benzene instead of steam as an emulsifier, the oil would be much less expensive to produce. However, benzene is a carcinogen; therefore, in Canada benzene is not an option. Canada doesn't have the Halliburton loophole. In the United States, the 2005 Energy Bill exempted oil and gas companies from having to disclose what chemicals they pump into the ground to extract natural gas or oil. Benzene is one of many known carcinogens put into the ground that ends up in people's drinking water, streams, our water tables, and in our blood streams. What an injustice; what an abuse of power! Some fields near natural gas wells vent undetected methane into the atmosphere. A landowner placed an eighteen-inch cone over bubbling ground water in his field. He lit a match and had a methane torch. No one knows how much land, extending out from fracked gas wells, has undetected methane escaping into the atmosphere. There are apparently no regulations governing gas companies, no matter the damage or danger they cause. Cheney-Bush turned out to be the oil and natural gas industries' dream team.

The news in August 2012 was that there is a "drilling frenzy" as the new Halliburton technology makes it possible to extract natural gas from shale. It was reported as great news because the United States' CO_2 emissions are now as low as they were in 1992, thanks to power plants turning from coal to natural gas. This was a public relations stunt to encourage landowners to think leasing their land was a good idea. This "new" technology has been used fifteen years. There may be more harm done by fracking in relation to global warming, but Americans are led to believe we have done our part to reduce CO_2 from energy production. China and India are the bad guys; they're building coal plants. Whatever they do, America is still responsible for our actions. Methane is under the radar and perfectly legal, like benzene in the drinking water.

We were hoodwinked in the name of national security. If the U.S. wants freedom from foreign oil, I ask, "Who owns the sun and the wind?" In the interest of national security and freedom from foreign oil, we should explore sustainable energy. Eight crucial years were lost and the American public is left with a legacy of laws that cripple our ability to regulate, inspect, or clean-up. We are also saddled with oil and gas lobbyists more powerful than the officials they control. No bill gets past them.

Many in Congress vote with oil and gas, and if one cooperated with the other side, it's time for him to go. Senators and Representatives, take notice. Indiana (R) Senator Dick Lugar served thirty-six years, and he was regarded as one of the most knowledgeable senators on foreign affairs. His main fault, according to the Tea Party, was being bipartisan. He tried to come to agreements in an effort to solve problems. The Tea Party had enough of his uncontrollable actions, so they ran another candidate in the primary and spent millions of dollars to toss out Lugar. Indiana now has a new senator who will faithfully vote as told; there will be no working together problem with him.

2003—Fifty thousand people died in Europe as a result of the July and August heat wave.

2004—Florida had four big hurricanes in a row. Brazil had its first hurricane ever. Hurricane Katarina formed in the South Atlantic, and they named her after the area she hit. Hurricanes cannot form in the South Atlantic. Something's been messing with Mother Nature's temperature and ocean and air currents. Hurricanes, typhoons, and cyclones are the same weather phenomenon, just originating in different oceans (Atlantic, Pacific, and Indian Oceans). Hence, the Brazilian Katarina was a hurricane and a very big surprise.

2005—The hottest year on record (at the time). It seems like we heard that in 1998 and again in 2011 and 2012. In 2012 every month was the hottest ever recorded in the United States.

2005—In July, Hurricane Dennis damaged the oilrigs in the Gulf of Mexico, and Katrina hit them in September. When Al Gore's book went to press in April 2006, one-third of the oil production facilities in the Gulf of Mexico remained crippled, including the largest oil platform in the world.

2005 had some other significant hurricane milestones and an opportunity to learn the Greek alphabet. We used up our alphabet and continued with Alpha, Beta, Delta, Epsilon, Gamma, and Zeta. That addresses increased frequency and number.

Severity also flourished. The intensity of a hurricane is determined by barometric pressure. When you live in an area subject to hurricanes, you watch the barometric pressure. If it falls, the hurricane strengthens. In 2005, three of the six hurricanes with the lowest recorded pressure arrived. Wilma had the lowest, hit Naples, gained strength as she crossed the state, and caused more damage on Florida's east coast than we had from the direct hit. The assumption was that hurricanes weaken as they pass over land. That is not true with the lowest barometric pressure readings. Inland Americans take notice. In the past, tremendous rainfall caused destruction after landfall. Now you can add hurricane force winds farther inland.

Hurricane Rita was the fourth lowest pressure reading. I was visiting my sister Jan and my mother and attended a benefit in Branson, Missouri, for the victims of Hurricane Katrina. We returned to Jan's after the benefit and waited for relatives evacuating for Hurricane Rita. They left Houston early and still had traffic jams for the three hundred miles to the Arkansas border.

Hurricane evacuation routes in Florida changed after Katrina and Wilma. Floridians are advised to hunker down at home or as close to home as possible. Crossing to the opposite coast does not help much if the hurricane has a very low pressure and keeps building. We are in a mandatory evacuation zone. It takes time to batten down the hatches, so we have half our windows covered with clear hurricane shutters all summer long. It is an exhausting job to prepare for a hurricane and then face traffic jams. Many elderly people in our area need local shelters. We would probably go to Tampa early and be with our oldest daughter, her family, and Lilly.

Hurricane Katrina ranked the sixth lowest on record, another example of the drive behind a hurricane with a low-pressure reading. Did you know Katrina made landfall in Miami? It did not fall apart crossing Florida and reached the hottest Gulf of Mexico waters on record (at the time). When Katrina made a second landfall in Mississippi, it nearly filled the Gulf of Mexico, and we were still getting torrential rain in Naples. New Orleans' levees were in disrepair and the city had many extremely poor people who could not evacuate. The city was a disaster waiting to happen. The death toll from Katrina was 1800. The expense of preparing for and recovery after the bigger hurricanes in our future could drain the government coffers and our bank accounts.

Global warming did not create hurricanes anew, but we may be seeing "a new" breed of hurricane in our future. In 2011, Vermont had terrible damage from Hurricane Irene. In 2012, Hurricane Sandy slammed New York and New Jersey. The hurricane zone may extend farther north as the Atlantic waters heat up. Systems we counted on can fail when Mother Nature has a heat stroke.

Gulf waters can reach 90 degree readings in the summer. What a hurricane could do with that! The oilrigs look like bowling pins when a hurricane fills the Gulf. Some hurricanes could bowl quite a few strikes; I pray there is never a "300 game." When there is no gas to be had, our car stays put; fifty-two miles per no gallons of gas equals nowhere. It seems as if something is always going wrong with our oilrigs in the Gulf of Mexico and the price of gas takes another leap. *I hope there is never an oil spill in the Gulf.* That was a pre-BP thought. Wouldn't it be great to have wind and solar power?

When someone dies of a heat stroke, systems fail, and little can be done to rectify the damage. Mother Earth has many systems that play a part in keeping our Earth in a healthy balance for man's survival. David Viner, a Russian scientist, said about the melting permafrost in the Siberian tundra in 2006, "When you start messing around with these natural systems, you can end up in situations where it is unstoppable. There are no brakes to apply. This is a big deal because you cannot put permafrost back once it's gone."

Scientists consider the atmosphere the most vulnerable part of the Earth. It is thin enough that man's behavior can unbalance it to the point the Earth becomes uninhabitable for man. That sounds like a heat stroke. Things look okay, until one day, Earth is so overheated that systems start failing and a series of catastrophic events cause a domino effect. Multi-systems failure claimed my sister Jan's life, but the chemo tipped the dominos into play. That chemo-blend in our atmosphere could be a ticking time bomb.

2005—The Amazon rainforest, the lungs of the world, was dying due to the overheated Gulf of Mexico. This assault was over and above deforestation for timber and farming. Global warming wreaked havoc on larger trees, which could not adapt quickly to excessive heat caused by the warmer Gulf waters to their north. Additionally, 2005 brought a terrible drought to the Amazon, drying up some of the tributaries of this great river. These tributaries are like major rivers. Steamships were stranded; the only means of transportation came to a halt. There are no roads. To add to the devastation for the innocent indigenous people, fish in the tributaries died. When the rains returned, the rivers filled, but the fish that provided the people's food and livelihood were gone.

2006–President George W. Bush eloquently states in March "I told the world I thought Kyoto was a lousy deal for America." The world was impressed, lousily.

2006–When temperatures rise, we advise people to find some way, some place, to stay cool. Ignoring the warnings can be deadly. Yet we ignore information about global warming. We do not listen, do not remember, and do not get it. Americans seem conditioned to ignore, to assume global warming is all a part of a natural cycle, and to do nothing to take corrective action individually or especially, to demand our government act responsibly. Dr. Michael Oppenheimer, of Princeton, said on *Oprah*, "The last 50 years sticks out like a sore thumb. The temperature has gone up and up and up. It bears the imprint of human activity." Somehow this did not equate to wake up, do something, this could be deadly!

Two more of Earth's systems being decimated are ocean currents and wind currents. They form an incredible circulatory system that moves heat and moisture from the equator and rainforests. This moderates the climate and provides rain to grow food for billions of people. Both the ocean and air currents need many variables to be just right. These currents were stable for nearly ten thousand years, but now they are having difficulty keeping that balance that makes man's life on Earth, in our present numbers, possible.

About one-third of the CO_2 emissions sink into the oceans. The oceans absorb the increasing amounts of carbon to their own detriment. The excess CO_2 is responsible for an increase in carbonic acid, which makes the oceans more acidic. Increased acidity prevents the formation of coral and the shells for shellfish. In 1880 the Earth had an abundance of coral reefs in the Atlantic, Pacific, and Indian Ocean. Man's use of fossil fuel has another victim. The optimal areas for the oceans' coral have been reduced by over 50% since the pre-industrial era. If we remain on the current path, by 2050 the oceans will no longer support living coral.

I never again want to see a dead reef. Wally and I took a snorkeling excursion booked on a Caribbean cruise; it was awful. The dead coral was ghostly gray and there was not a fish in sight. Coral is a sensitive living organism and suffers when ocean waters are too hot. The summer of 1998 started our long run of the hottest summers on record. That summer, overheated waters killed 16% of the oceans' coral. Pollution from shore and dynamite fishing does the same.

If you do go snorkeling, never touch the coral with anything (hands, feet, or fins). Do not wear sunscreen in the water; it is deadly to some of the creatures. Wear a wet suit or an old pair of pajamas (for sunburn protection). Anchor at a distance and swim to the reef, instead of anchoring on the reef. The reefs may die soon, but I don't want to be the cause of some dying sooner.

An Inconvenient Truth has a world map showing the shrinking areas where coral can survive. Reefs are essential for the world's fishing stock. I don't know what other ramifications the loss of the coral will produce. For the islands that count on the reefs to attract tourists, their economy will suffer. It would be too depressing to return to Grand Cayman, Roatan, or the British Virgin Islands if the coral died.

2010–Russia baked in a heat wave during July and August. Moscow had eleven thousand more deaths than the previous year for the same two months. Morgues and funeral homes were backed up, and crematories running 24/7 overheated. The air was suffocating from the heat and smoke. Siberia was burning with two to three new forest fires daily. Russian presidents had historically been reluctant to acknowledge the reality of global warming.

> **An increase of two or three degrees won't be so bad for a northern country like Russia. We could spend less on fur coats and the grain harvest would go up.**
> Vladimir Putin, Russian President, October 2003.

After the 2010 summer from hell, Putin said, "Man has caused global warming and the entire world needs to act as quickly as possible to save the planet."

In December 2007, Australia's newly elected Prime Minister Rudd signed the Kyoto Agreement his first day in office. Sadly, the United States Congress never did and it's a dead issue. All the influence-peddling in Washington kept Congress hog-tied. Vice-president Gore signed the agreement years ago, but the United States Congress was too beholding to outside interests to allow ratification by the country causing the most damage.

If thousands of people died in Washington D.C., as in Moscow, due to a heat wave, and the forests of our country were going up in flame, would our elected officials take action, or would the lobbyists spin it as, quite the weather we are having—some cycles are worse than others.

If you think thousands could not die in a major American city, don't be too sure. Our electrical grid is subject to failure and automatic shut down when it detects a major problem. If Bos-Wash (a term that describes the heavily populated megalopolis from Boston, through New York City, Baltimore, and Washington, D.C.) and its millions of people crank up air-conditioners day and night for weeks because temperatures are above 100 degrees, we cannot be sure the grid would meet the demand. Once the 100-plus degree temperatures heat up the concrete and asphalt of the cities, there is a heat-island effect, and cities remain hot day and night. A rolling blackout could be a rolling death trap. Would the puppeteers leave town, go where they could have air-conditioning, and fiddle while the country burned?

The reason the very young and the very old die quickly in heat waves is their metabolism cannot adjust to extreme temperatures as well as the general population. This decade is looking like another hot one.

2011–Hottest year ever recorded. We are used to hearing this. "What do we do?" Ignore it, of course. Air-conditioners still run when we aren't home; lights are on in rooms someone left hours ago, and empty office buildings are lit up like Christmas trees all night. There are so many streetlights on you would think the city got a two-for-one special. Families watch four TV sets, there are three cars parked in the yard, and the A/C is set so low half the family wears hoodies. Everyone enjoys one or two long hot showers a day, clean clothes are laundered instead of being hung up after being worn once, and there are a dozen "runs" to get something that could have waited until you needed to go to the store,… yada yada yada. Color us mindless, clueless, at risk, dangerous–color us red, white, and blue for being typical Americans.

2011-2012 was the year of no winter in the northeastern United States. Strange weather we're having.

In 2011 and 2012, Houston area headlines read, "Hell or High Water." In 2011, the forest fire just north of Houston went on for weeks if not months. Bastrop and Magnolia, Texas lost many homes to the fires. Firefighters came from many states and filled the hotels north of Houston for August and September 2011.

My sister Jan worked long hours to help her hotel manager keep up with all the extra work from being at full capacity with super hungry and super dirty firefighters day after day. Jan's breast cancer came back after seven years and she started chemo. Within three weeks, the chemo killed her. Her doctor said Jan had one of the worst reactions to that drug she had ever seen. Jan worked thirteen hours on Wednesday and went in at 3a.m. on Thursday. She came home at 9a.m. feeling "bad." By noon, she went by ambulance to the emergency room, and at 3p.m. the next day, she was dead. The chemo had destroyed her white blood cells. Sometimes I wonder if that foul, smoke-filled air, with whatever it carried, contributed to Jan's death. She certainly was not getting sleep or taking the time her body needed to fight its own raging fire. In my mind, her death is tied to the time of those terrible fires. I had talked to Jan on the phone Wednesday night and we were joking about something. The next evening, Wally and I were in our van, driving straight to Texas after being told Jan was in the hospital. We made it into the state, but were not yet to the hospital when she died.

Our poor ninety-one-year-old mother, who had lived with Jan for seven years, didn't know. Jan had gone to the ER Thursday afternoon, and Friday afternoon the family returned to Jan's house. Mom had been getting updates, but it was only in the last few hours of Jan's life that the realization of no hope hit us. Wally and I drove straight to the house. We could not tell Mom over the phone. She was alone. Mom's first words as we entered were, "How's Jan?" All we could say was, "She died."

The chemo had destroyed her white blood cells and system after system failed in rapid order, once the process started. Jan had a "tipping point." Scientist say Mother Earth has "tipping points," too. We ignore symptoms and try to keep doing everything as long as we can. Are we in the Emergency Room, telling ourselves nothing is wrong when we're on the brink of disaster? Frustrated scientists, warning that further global warming will cause our world to suffer a string of catastrophes, have made similar analogies. And I think of Jan.

About the Houston headline, "Hell or High Water," in 2012, Houston flooded. Global warming brings drastic and unpredictable weather.

STRANGE WEATHER WE'RE HAVING

The IPCC reports that even if we reduce greenhouse gases, the weather extremes will continue through 2050, will be more frequent, last longer, and be more extreme. The overcoat does not come off quickly, and some self-perpetuating problems are in play.

July 10, 2012, *ABC World News* with Diane Sawyer reported, "The United States government's *State of Climate Report* says the planet is heating up. The last 12 months have been the hottest twelve months we've ever lived through. The Greenland ice sheet is melting thirty times faster than it was a decade ago." Sawyer never mentioned tipping points or greenhouse gases caused by man. The report took less than thirty seconds, had no interview, no pictures, not even a comment about this being significant; it must not mean much.

Then she said, "The mayor of New York wants smaller apartments built in the city." Would this be a back-door message that if Americans buy into that weather thing, we would have to sacrifice-sacrifice-sacrifice? Suddenly, there's news footage and an interview of a person in a four hundred square foot apartment, with a cat, no less. That deserved a comment and a chuckle. Then they show a smaller apartment, the size the mayor was recommending; it was the size of two parking spaces. The interviewer is shown around this cozy two hundred square foot abode. Yet another apartment is shown; I believe it was 105 square feet. The final shot was of the occupant's frying pan propped on the shower soap holder. She does her dishes in the shower.

In the past, I would have thought nothing of this coverage. Since learning how media of all types are influenced by big business or the power elite and always has to have some sort of rebuttal, I think that world news coverage was bizarre. Nothing whatsoever made the staggering facts about global warming sound alarming. I looked for a follow-up report for days. There was none. Simply by saying nothing more, they treated the report as insignificant. Oh, I can still see that frying pan propped in the shower as I recall the broadcast. A 105 square foot apartment got more attention than the Greenland ice sheet melting thirty times faster than it was ten years ago. By the way, ten years ago, the scientists were amazed at how much faster the ice sheet was melting than they had expected. Now it is melting thirty times faster. Ouch! If a major portion of the Greenland ice sheet were to slide into the sea, no one knows how long it would take to melt. There are too many unknowns, but the water is warmer every year. If the entire ice sheet melted, the sea level would be twenty-three feet higher.

Some enterprising people are considering hauling ice to lands with little water. How fast would ice melt in the Middle East? When the ten thousand-year-old Larson B ice shelf broke off the Western Peninsula of Antarctica in 2002, it took thirty days to melt. It was small, only the size of Delaware. That removed support holding the ice sheet on the land. The sheet's movement toward the sea is eight times faster since losing the Larson B shelf. If the Western Peninsula ice sheet collapses, it has a lot in common with Greenland's ice sheet. Once they melt, each would raise the sea level twenty-three feet.

There is a quote in *Global Warning* (2007) by the National Resources Defense Council: "Over the past three decades, more than one million square miles of sea ice—an area the size of Norway, Denmark, and Sweden combined—has disappeared." That quote was six years ago and covered a thirty-year period. Last summer (2012) in the Arctic Ocean alone, one million square miles of sea ice disappeared. Everything is accelerating, yet the United States remains unaware.

The newscast that came closest to alerting the clueless was on July 24, 2012, when NASA reported about the Greenland ice sheet. In a four-day period, the thawed ice area of the ice sheet jumped from 40% to 97%. The surprised scientists said, "This was extraordinary and went all the way across the ice sheet, including to the 3,200 meters above sea level summit. In the past the highest area to show melting on the surface was at 2,000 meters. To have the surface area of melting jump from 40% to 97% was unheard of." There was no mention of global warming or a promise to viewers that there would be more news on the significance of this latest development. This was not sensational news.

Americans want sensationalism, as long as it requires little or nothing from them. In the mid-90s, reporters were running all over trying to find out what size gloves O. J. wore, the size of the gloves in the courtroom, where the gloves were bought, if O. J. had arthritis with swollen fingers from the disease, old football injuries, or medication. It is not as if we are not interested in the news, yet the melting on the ice sheet to the tip of the 3,200-meter summit sort of slipped by most of us.

July 14, 2012, news included these facts: "60% of the U.S. is suffering from drought; one thousand counties in twenty-six states have been declared in a state of emergency, and 75% of the food production could be affected by a corn shortage."

An August 29, 2012, news report stated that, "While Hurricane Isaac was hitting the Gulf Coast, this summer's drought is turning out to be good news for the farmers in the Dakotas not affected by the drought. The corn and grain prices are up 39%." When I heard this I wondered, *How many thousands more children will starve to death each day because food prices are so high the United Nations and other charities cannot afford to buy as much food?* This is called reducing population by increasing mortality rates.

The Weather Channel's Dr. Forbes showed pictures so that people could understand what was causing the drought. Drought cycles grow worse as the time of extreme heat continues. Heat pulls more moisture from the soil, but the moisture pulled out is not enough to cause rain. Drier ground holds more heat; the loss of moisture goes deeper into the ground and crops fail. In the background, a huge cloud of dust engulfed a tractor, showing how they are now losing their top soil. The drought was expanding and there was no relief in sight.

FYI: Many crops do not pollinate if the temperatures are too high, even if it does rain.

Forbes shifted the topic slightly to what was of most concern to Americans. "Watch for higher prices in the grocery store, except meat prices should remain steady. Ranchers lacking grassland or grain to feed livestock will be reducing their herds. This should keep meat prices steady this year at about four dollars a pound. Next year, beef could go to five or six dollars, or more a pound." There was no utterance of the forbidden global warming. After such news, Americans are asking, "Should we fill the freezer with beef now or wait a month?"

July 17, 2012, headlines included, "Worst drought in half a century. With corn affected, Americans will pay the price." We use corn in everything from food, feed, ethanol, tires, and shampoo. The things you learn when you're trying to understand global warming–shampoo? The drought is a multi-billion dollar loss. One farmer interviewed said, "In my thirty-three years of farming, this is the first time I've never had a crop."

The news continued, "Washington D.C. hit 101 degrees today." Then they listed a slew of northern cities that continue to register record highs. Americans think, *I bet beef prices will really drop soon; let's clear some space in the freezer, or, maybe there's a sale on freezers at Sears.* Yah, let's plug in another appliance and burn more energy 24/7. Lilly, how do we get out of this mess?

The rapid melting of Greenland's ice sheet has one other unique twist. The Thermalhaline Pump I mentioned earlier is a vital piece of our climate control. If the Greenland ice sheet suddenly collapsed into the North Atlantic, it is possible the Thermalhaline Pump could again slow or stop, affecting the entire planet.

THE THERMALHALINE PUMP

The land, water, and air are warmest at the equator, where the sun's rays are most direct. Earth's air and water temperatures are moderated by great streams of air currents and ocean currents. The mechanism that keeps the ocean currents moving is a precise balance of changing water temperatures and changing levels of salt (salinity). The current takes the super-warm surface water from the equatorial region of the Atlantic Ocean by way of the Gulf Stream northward around Florida, out to sea off the coast of the Eastern United States, and toward Greenland.

Gulf Stream waters converge with the frigid air from the Arctic and Greenland, and gigantic amounts of the stream evaporate into the atmosphere. Air currents and the Earth's westward rotation bring the heat and moisture to Western Europe. London and Paris are farther north than Montreal, Canada, but enjoy a much milder climate due to this effect.

When the water evaporates so quickly in the North Atlantic, the salt remains, salinity increases, and the water becomes much heavier. The heavy water sinks to the bottom of the ocean at the rate of 5 billion gallons of water per second. The cold water, deep in the ocean is pumped southward along the eastern coast of South America, then flows east near Antarctica and into the Pacific. This long world-circuit eventually brings the water back to the equator and the Gulf Stream.

Some scientists are concerned the Thermalhaline Pump could slow or stop again, as it did a little over ten thousand years ago. As the Greenland fresh water ice-sheet melts, it becomes more porous and less stable. It's possible a great portion of the Greenland ice sheet could collapse into the sea, like the Larson B did on Antarctica's Western Peninsula. Moulins are like rivers down through an ice sheet. They melt the ice faster, but also create a flowing river of water between the base if the ice sheet and the land under the ice. No one knows what the consequences would be if a major portion of the Greenland ice sheet plummeted into the sea. How fast would it melt, what would it do to the sea level, and how would it affect the ocean currents and the Thermalhaline Pump? A rapid rise in sea level would displace hundreds of millions of people and the croplands that feed nearly a billion people would be under water in Southeast Asia.

Humor creeps into my thoughts to ease my mind when something stressful is staying on my radar. My mind strays in odd directions. Mary's Musings is what my husband calls it when my warped mind goes wandering.

MUSING ABOUT THE THERMALHALINE PUMP

If the Greenland ice sheet cracks, hits the skids, and thousands of salt-free ice chunks the size of Rhode Island, Connecticut, and Delaware are dumped into the North Atlantic just above the pump, could it melt slowly enough that it doesn't lower the salt concentration enough to stop the Thermalhaline Pump? Where is Bill Nye the Science Guy when you need him?

If all green grannies donate the salt we're not supposed to eat, could we keep the pump running? Or, are the chunks flushed causing a "pump attack?" It's like trying to prevent a heart attack: the specialist's reports are a concern; you feel okay, but with those reports, if there's a problem, it could be "THE BIG ONE."

Now, imagine it scares you enough to change; 300 million Americans have to follow the doctors' orders, too. What about Congress? There could be a breakdown getting anything passed to help slow global warming.

People in China and India are dreaming of living the American lifestyle, buying every luxury that hits the shelves. If they follow the leader, will they make the right turn with us? Shucks! I just remembered the sea level would rise either way. I don't think my home can be converted to a house boat.

The weather news the day I am preparing this book to go to press is: **Typhoon Halyan Hits the Philippines and Is Deadliest Natural Disaster on Record**. Severity of weather increases as the Earth keeps warming.

ONE MORE PROBLEM WE CANNOT IGNORE

Discussing population, from the standpoint of doing something to control it, always seemed as if it was none of my business. My thoughts changed when the choice became, address the fertility rate, or face a soaring infant mortality rate. Seven billion and gaining eighty million more people every year may be nearing the breaking point for man on Earth. The eighteen thousand children who die of starvation and related diseases every day reached the carrying capacity limit in the regions where they lived. Those figures were from 2007, before the price of grain tripled and the World Food Bank had to severely cut the quantity of food purchased because of the higher cost.

One of the marks of an environment reaching and passing its carrying capacity is a rapid population growth so stressing the environment that the population cannot be maintained. Food supplies dwindle and resources are stripped, leading to an even faster demise. That is how a species becomes extinct. Man is causing the extinction of one-third of the existing plant and animal species by destroying habitat, over-harvesting, or poisoning. Disappearing animals and plants makes it more difficult for the poorest people to survive.

World food shortages cause death by starvation for 7 million children a year. That number may be doubled by now, as recent reports from relief agencies suggest. You may think the rise in grain prices is due to flooding, draught, and heat waves; you are right to a small degree. We have added two continuous trends to the equation of food supply and demand. From the food to feed everyone, deduct four to seven times as much grain to provide meat, dairy, and eggs for the affluent who can afford to pay for them. The supply is the same, so just take it from the poorest; they have no power to stop you.

Soybeans are a great cattle food and gives rapid growth to provide us with our hamburgers and steaks. Three billion more people are aspiring to climb their way up the food chain. More people will lose their grip and die from the bottom of the chain. Soybean production is fifteen times greater than it was in 1950, but the cattle get most of the soybeans.

The other item that you can deduct from the limited food supply is the corn and other crops that no longer become food to eat, but are sent to the distilleries to make ethanol and bio-diesel for our cars and trucks. Starving people in sub-Saharan Africa cannot compete with someone filling the tank of an Escalade. There is ethanol in every drop of our gasoline.

The United States is the largest corn producing country in the world. In 2009, the United States grew 416 million tons of corn; however, 119 million tons of that corn was distilled into ethanol for our cars. Are we reducing oil consumption by having a blend with ethanol in our tanks? Probably not. Ethanol reduces miles-per-gallon and uses a lot of energy to grow and produce. No one mentions the jump in the number of children dying of starvation each day; that is relevant to me.

Farmers are paid more for corn to make ethanol, and more distilleries are being built. Car corn has replaced people corn, tripling grain prices. Aid organizations cannot afford as much grain for the starving people. We are upset by the jump in our food prices; those starving die.

What a difference between a person born in the United States and one of the 900 million born in sub-Saharan Africa. Food prices go up; we grumble—they die. We don't have much in common with our nameless brothers and sisters. Our worlds are polar opposites. They have more in common with the polar bears. Both love their young, they search for food, and they are both dying because of the way other people live and destroy the Earth. The ties are even greater. The polar bear in search of food can't reach the ice that had always been there, they swim and swim and swim, and eventually she and her cub drown. The mother in Somalia finds no food, aid no longer comes, she carries her baby and leads her little ones, and they walk and walk and walk. They may make it to Kenya or Ethiopia, or they just die. Nearly all babies reaching refugee camps die.

> **Those least able to cope and least responsible for greenhouse gases that cause global warning are most affected.**
> **Herein lies an enormous global ethical challenge.**
> Professor Jonathan Patz, World Health Organization

What does this have to do with the fertility rate or birth control? Population is controlled by the fertility rate or mortality rate when the environment can't support the population. Sadly, it seems easier to increase the mortality rate than to deprive Americans of their meat and the big pickup truck for dad, the SUV for mom, and cars for the kids.

Addressing the fertility rate costs money. The most effective solution may surprise you. Starving families will send their children to school if meals are provided, especially when a ration is sent home. Girls in the poorest countries are kept home to work, but if there is a food program, they are sent to school. Girls who attend through middle school marry later, have children later, have fewer children, can better take care of their smaller family, and the family has a better chance of climbing out of the starvation level of poverty. If food distribution expands to include pregnant women, nursing mothers, and preschool children, the infant mortality rate drops further. Children no longer have permanent physical and cognitive damage from malnutrition. Educated girls learn about abstinence and other contraception choices, family planning, and caring for their young. In the poorest countries, as much as 25% of the children are so malnourished they are too weak to walk to school.

The anthropologists who live in the villages among the people say, "Many women live in fear of their next pregnancy; they just don't want to get pregnant." What must it be like for that mother, worrying she will die and leave her child without a mother, that the new baby will die, or that the older child will be at even greater risk of death with less food available? One of the reasons the fertility rate is so high in the poorest countries is that adults hope one or two children will live to provide for the parent if the parent lives that long. That is their social security system.

When people are starving, dying, and migrating from place to place in search of food, the government often has broken down and cannot safely distribute aid. The countries with soaring birth rates and no jobs are subject to crisis when uneducated, unemployed boys and men become angry and start warring amongst themselves. They are prime recruiting candidates for terrorist groups. The unrest that grows within a country is a part of a country's slide into the desperate condition of being one of the world's sixty failed or failing states.

Population control by education, family planning, and basic medical care is far more humane than the alternative. It's estimated that reproductive care and voluntary family planning for the 215 million women in extreme poverty could prevent 53 million unwanted pregnancies, 24 million induced abortions, 1.6 million infant deaths a year, and if condoms were distributed, the prevention of AIDS would be more effective. As conditions improve, there is a greater chance to deliver aid.

The fertility rate will not be low in these countries, but it may be lowered enough to help them out of the deadliest poverty range. A 3% growth rate in a country per year multiplies the population by twenty in a century. What a disaster that increase would be. The United Nations has a range of three population projections. The mid-range, 9.3 billion by 2050, is the most realistic. The high end is 10.5 billion by 2050. The best-case scenario is a population of 8 billion in the year 2042. All projections show the population leveling off or slowly declining beyond

2050. I hope the decline is related to decreasing fertility rates, rather than increasing infant mortality rates.

Abraham Maslow's Hierarchy of Needs

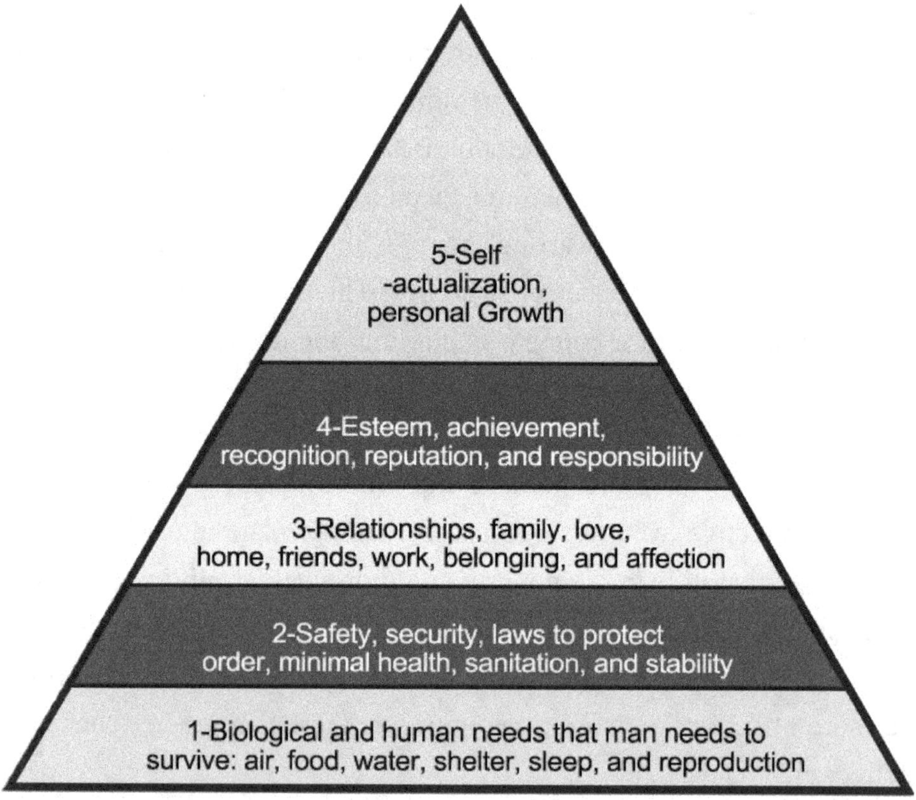

5-Self
-actualization,
personal Growth

4-Esteem, achievement,
recognition, reputation, and responsibility

3-Relationships, family, love,
home, friends, work, belonging, and affection

2-Safety, security, laws to protect
order, minimal health, sanitation, and stability

1-Biological and human needs that man needs to
survive: air, food, water, shelter, sleep, and reproduction

We're all motivated by human needs. Maslow studied monkeys and then people for many years. He noticed that the most basic needs must always be satisfied before one moves to the next level. A billion people struggle for the most basic needs of survival. Some don't even have the food and water necessary to live; they die.

The Bill and Melinda Gates Foundation donated $10 billion for research and vaccinations to prevent childhood diseases and deaths in the poorest of the world's children. It saddens me that the greed of so few causes so much destruction to so many. Then I read about Bill and Melinda Gates and feel there may be some hope for the precious little ones.

A line from the *Course in Miracles* says, "I am my brother's savior," or "We are our brothers' savior." Where do I go from here to make a difference? I keep asking questions, writing, studying, and trying to open my mind to thinking and seeing in a different way. I'm amazed I didn't wonder, realize, see, or hear things more clearly years ago.

I'll leave you with a visual aid as a reminder there are other ways of looking at things. Do you see a young lady or an old woman? We may not see the whole picture at first glance. Many things deserve a second look. To assume you have the whole picture of global warming and the state of the world can leave you blind-sighted. One day you may go from being blind to having it blindingly clear. When we see better, we do better. Now go change a light bulb and let's get started.

CHAPTER 5

ENERGY

ALL ENERGY IS FROM THE SUN

All energy comes from the sun. There are two kinds of energy, current and ancient. We use current energy upon or soon after it's arrival from the sun to grow plants (which feed animals), provide solar heat, and generate movement of air and water to make wind and water currents. The food we eat contains our energy source; we are eating recent energy calories from the sun. We release CO_2 (carbon and oxygen) and water back into the air with every breath.

Ancient energy is stored carbon from as long ago as 400 million years. Mother Nature safely stored the excess carbon from dead animals and vegetation that used the sun's energy while they were alive. Our atmosphere had an ideal balance with the correct percentage of CO_2 remaining in the atmosphere until man started releasing it from the fossil fuels and peat bogs, and melting permafrost in massive amounts.

Humans are a unique species. We tamper with nature's atmospheric balance, take energy for granted, form habits that release ancient carbon in excess, and do not understand the consequences. There seems no reason for concern. Is there a problem? Should we be concerned? Yes! Sorry to break this news to you, but this is something you really ought to know. Global warming is caused by burning ancient energy and releasing hundreds of millions of years of stored carbon into the atmosphere at a rate greater than Mother Nature can handle. It takes a very specific atmosphere to provide the climate man needs to thrive and we are destroying it!

Dinosaurs resided on Earth for a long time, something changed, and they became part of Earth's history. The cause of the dinosaur's extinction may have been an asteroid hitting the Earth or thousands of years of volcanic activity, which would have reduced their current energy source. Species came, stayed, and when the environment could no longer support that species, it became extinct. Mother Earth supported new inhabitants and has had many tenants.

MAN'S TIME ON EARTH—LET'S NOT RUSH IT

It seems to us that man has been around forever, but only in the last ten thousand years has the fragile and unique balance in the thin wrap of atmosphere around the Earth been perfect for man to thrive. This ten thousand years man is enjoying is about 1/40,000th of Earth's history. I never thought of it that way, going through periods, supporting different forms of life, and having very different climates. If we shrunk Earth's history to fit on a twenty-four-hour clock, the ideal climate for humans has existed for one fifth of one second.

Robert Ornstein and Paul Ehrlich, in *New World New Mind* (Walsch 2011), placed Earth's history on a one-year calendar. January 1 at 12a.m. is the beginning of Earth and midnight December 31 is present day. Each day equals 12 million years. The first life form, simple bacterium, appeared in February; the first fish arrived November 20; and dinosaurs roamed from December 10 until Christmas. The earliest Homo sapiens entered the picture at 11:45p.m. on December 31 and recorded history is within the last minute. Using this time frame, man is destroying his own habitat in a split second.

Time marches on and the climate changes; new residents appear. No other species changed the climate enough to make the planet unlivable for its own kind. I don't want Lilly struggling to live on a planet where our time is running out.

WELL, SPECIES, WHAT SHOULD WE DO ABOUT THIS PREDICAMENT?

Maybe most of that carbon should have been left in the ground. The price of oil, coal, and natural gas may be deadly prohibitive, and we're only realizing this in the last split-second of Earth's History. There has always been infinite current energy available from the sun. We may have made a fatal mistake when we turned from current energy as our source and started unearthing carbon to use as fuel.

When I say the last 200, 150, or 100 years, I understand the majority of the damaging carbon release has been in the last fifty years. Releasing of carbon started slowly. The population was only 3 billion in 1960, compared to over 7 billion today, and the average consumption of fossil fuels per person has also sky-rocketed. Man is ravaging the atmosphere as surely as a stage-four cancer destroys its body-home.

Again, I ask, "What should we do about this predicament?" If you said, "Nothing," that's the wrong answer. We can't waste more time. Stop waiting for the next guy to do something; he's waiting for you to do something or waiting for our leaders to act (waiting-waiting-waiting). And, it's time to stop clinging to the false belief engrained in us that we must use fossil fuels to get our energy. **We can produce energy in ways that do not destroy the temperate climate we need to live.** So why aren't we doing that?

My fact-finding mission took a twist I never anticipated. There are forces whose mission is to maintain the status-quo. They know the deadly facts, and they know what is at stake. We are addicted to oil; they are addicted to money and power. That roadblock is what I did not expect to find, not to this extent. The powers in charge do whatever it takes to keep fossil-fuel money flowing, and they'll pay any amount to keep a lid on information about CO_2, global warming, and rising sea levels.

I am not an authority and only recently learned a few things. Please get concerned enough about what I told you and do your homework. Don't count on our leaders for the facts. After being elected, President George W. Bush told us he didn't believe there was such a thing as global warming. While campaigning for president he insisted the U.S. needed mandatory CO_2 reductions in order to slow global warming. He wanted the environmental vote and his backer wanted to keep environmentalist Gore from winning. Oklahoma Senator James Inhofe claimed, "Global warming is the biggest hoax perpetrated on mankind." Bush and Inhofe's reasons for making those statements have nothing to do with protecting our future. Do your homework; get this lump checked out, before we all check out. The question is what direction to take? There is no map; we've never been down this road before.

Over 7 billion people using varying amounts of energy is part of the problem. The way we're living cannot be sustained. When people understand the dilemma, we may re-think family size and re-consider how to live and care for the family we already have. One way that makes sense for me is to look at what I can do to stop releasing so much carbon into our atmosphere. I intend to live differently and smarter.

KEEP THE NUMBER ONE ISSUE NUMBER ONE

Global warming, caused by man's altering the atmosphere by releasing billions of tons of greenhouse gases, is the NUMBER ONE issue. The CO_2 in our atmosphere in 2011 was 760 billion tons. I don't know the correct amount to maintain a livable climate, so I can only provide the number for future reference. CO_2 in the atmosphere was at 315 ppm in 1958, already above the ideal atmospheric blend, and in the summer of 2012, we passed 400 ppm. Scientist are certain the Earth's temperature rises as the amount of CO_2 in our atmosphere rises.

The effects of global warming could have billions of people warring for food, water, land, and other resources. Maslow taught us man is a survivalist. When the most basic needs cannot be met, we do whatever it takes to meet those needs, endangering millions, possibly billions of people as life becomes a fight for survival. Living and prospering in America, that kind of warring world does not seem even remotely possible. I never considered a world at war for food, water, and a space to live as a threat at any time, let alone within Lilly's lifetime, perhaps even mine. I fear some facts were missing from the blissful reality I was living before 2011. Lilly's reality may be anything but blissful as she lives her life.

Man had been burning wood for thousands of years. A few people, a few trees, no problem. That is ancient history. It is today's way of life that violates Mother Nature's laws, while she stands by and watches helplessly. Man has to notice the problem and make the changes on his own behalf.

I Know How I Live; I'm an Energy-Burning American

I know how I live and I know the following figures have something to do with me. The generating of electricity in the United States is our largest CO_2 emitter. These figures are from 2007 so they will be slightly off, but we have not had an epiphany and done an about face. In 2007, 38% of man-made CO_2 emissions were from generating electricity. The percentage is actually down in the United States for 2012, because we are burning more natural gas instead of coal. No one measures the methane increase from the natural gas obtained from fracked wells. We are still burning a fossil fuel, and the parts per million of CO_2 in the atmosphere passed 400 ppm, an extremely dangerous level, and is climbing faster than ever. The unmeasured but still deadly methane level is also rising.

Using fossil fuels to generate electricity means we burn the fuel to heat the water, make the steam, and turn the turbines that produce the electric energy. All methods that burn fossil fuels, wood, solid waste, garbage, or biomass release CO_2 into the atmosphere.

The zero CO_2 emissions are from wind, solar, apparently nuclear, tidal wave, geothermal, hydroelectric and others that may surface in the future. Hydroelectric may be clean, but dams create other problems an overcrowded world can no longer accommodate.

Nuclear plants bring problems with them that in an ideal world should be avoided. Critics say our children will be dealing with the radioactive waste from nuclear power plants for ten thousand years. That has a promising sound to it; I worry the children could be extinct in two hundred years.

Making sense of the numbers that measure electrical use can be confusing. Appliances use watts measured "per hour." Electric bills charge by KWH, which are 1,000 watts. Our home is total electric, and in 2009 we used 13,030 KWH, averaging 1,085 KWHs a month. We have always been conservative, so our bills were lower than most of our neighbors. Since learning about global warming, we searched for ways to reduce our electrical use AND WE DID! In 2012 we used a total of 2,372 KWH, for an average of 181 KWH a month. We made enough changes to use less than one fifth the electricity in our home for an entire year. Chapter 17 will explain our efforts and successes. Our highest month's usage was 1,831 KWH in August 2009.

My dream goal is to be at least one KWH below that for an entire year. It may seem trivial to try shaving off another 45 KWH per month, but in today's world, it's our business to learn what we can do to protect our children's future. Each KWH is a big deal when you multiply it by every American's monthly electric bill. Many of you will have lower KWH usage because you measure some of your energy in gallons of fuel oil or cubic feet of natural gas. It's still burned and contributes to the climbing CO_2 in the atmosphere. Conserve on your oil and gas as much as you can. The most important KWH any of us has control over is the KWH we conserve by never using it. If you're lucky enough to get your power from wind, solar, or geothermal, do what you can to conserve so that you can add clean energy to the grid for others to use instead of burning to get their power. The world needs to *learn never to burn*. That doesn't solve all our problems, but it's the direction we need to go, so we'll be around to solve other problems.

Another way to reduce CO_2 is to buy less stuff. Everything we buy comes from resources, is processed, manufactured, transported, over-packaged, "needed," bought by us, and eventually a lot of it rides to the landfill. Every step requires the use of energy, and we get our energy primarily by burning a fossil fuel. It gives a new meaning to the phrase, "That's a *smokin'* outfit you're wearing."

An Ace-in-the-Hole to Save the Planet

YOU are my ace-in-the-hole. By educating you, or rather you educating yourself, to the problems we face, you become a problem solver. Our way of thinking changes when a life and death factor appears. I look at many things in an entirely new way. I'll give you one example of a new thought. Americans have been convinced to buy obese refrigerators to store convenient factory-produced food-facsimiles. The giant food corporations make more money with more processing. We burn more energy to cool our huge refrigerator-freezers. We "try" the new food-facsimile advertised, or that the kids begged us to purchase. Then, depending on the family, either the food spoils, gets freezer burn, or you have to eat it before it goes bad. In the latter case, the family now has more in common with their obese refrigerator. No matter, the food business made a sale, the appliance company got you to buy a bigger fridge, and the power company increased its profits. That's good for business, but you now have an huge refrigerator that's burning more energy; you spend more money to buy and power it; you work more to pay for over processed food, some of which will spoil; and you overeat nutrient-depleted processed food. For the grand finale, you and your family are heading down the road to obesity, diabetes, heart disease, and cancer. Look at the people walking down the street or in the mall and tell me that thought does not ring true.

When it comes to home energy use, you may not duplicate our savings, but you will be amazed at the changes you can make. We bought a "leaner" refrigerator. We sold our big one to a typical American couple who are retired and needed a big refrigerator-freezer for their utility room. That used to make perfect sense to me.

Not many of the changes you make in your home will cost money. The new energy-efficient light bulbs cost more at first, but every bulb soon pays for itself and starts saving money. We have the compact-fluorescent lights (CFL) that use 25% of the energy used by the old incandescent bulbs. The newer LEDs use only 15% of the energy. If it is feasible, we'll replace the bulbs we use most and give those CFLs to family or someone on a low fixed income who has not been able to afford to make the switch. We have some widows in our neighborhood who struggle to make ends meet between social security checks. They don't waste a lot of energy. At night, they have one light on. That's the bulb to replace first.

We're told to purchase "off-set" and "energy" credits to make up for the energy we waste. First of all, if you know you're wasting energy, can you cut the amount of waste? Then, instead of sending your money off to someone who claims he will use it for the environment, use that money to reduce your own energy use. Save it, so that when you need a new washer, you can afford the high efficiency model. Or, help people on low incomes by replacing their most frequently used incandescent light bulbs. That's a gift that keeps on giving to the planet, to the people you gifted, and to Lilly. Another benefit is that it just plain feels good.

THE BRICK WALL

An aggravating problem keeps popping up: Americans are addicted to fossil fuels. The supplying of those fuels and electricity is handled by monopoly-like industries that do not want things to change. I picture them as a "brick wall."

Fortunes were made in oil, coal, and natural gas. Business owners and corporations believe it's a good business-practice to invest money and exercise their influence to maintain the status-quo. The new element in this equation is, we're up against a life and death situation if we stick to status-quo and energy business as usual. This should mean something, but nothing persuades the profiteers to consider the good of the planet over the profits going into their wallets. The power they wield has been there for many decades; their influence has invaded our country at the highest levels of national, state, and local governments.

A "clueless" population makes ideal consumers marching along with the status-quo. There used to be a slogan, "keep her barefoot and pregnant." That was one way suggested to control your wife. The powerful want to keep American consumers "clueless and scared." We're told that to protect our country, we need to aggressively go after our own coal, oil, and natural gas. Every one of those fuels only provides energy by burning and releasing carbon. When are we urged to buy less electricity or merchandise? Never. Profits must continue. We keep doing what they tell us in the name of national security and a healthy economy. Just be scared, don't try to find other solutions to the problems we face. When Romney said during his presidential campaign that he was not willing to spend "trillions and trillions" to "TRY" to lower CO_2, that was a deceptive scare tactic! Trillions and trillions is what we spent on a war to try to keep control of foreign oil.

Tens of billions subsidize the "brick wall." Some of those billions could set us on the clean-energy track. Romney's statement was carefully crafted and was aimed at making the American public unwilling and afraid to look for clean-energy alternatives. That sounds to me like a "tank thought" put together by some "think tank." How many of you think that no longer using oil, coal, and gas would be impossible and would ruin our economy? Where did that message come from and how true is it? Is there something wrong about spending billions of dollars to silence or discredit the information we all need to know to protect our children's futures? Are these messengers the ones we want to follow blindly a minute longer? I don't trust the profiteers to tell me anything but what they want me to hear; they want us "clueless."

There may be a few corporate leaders and politicians able to hang on to the belief (with a death grip) that there is no such thing as global warming. George Bush knew it was real in campaign speeches, but then decided it was not a problem on January 20. Bush didn't pick many of the worst appointees; he let Exxon Mobile, Peabody Coal, Halliburton, and the Burlington Northern Santa Fe Railroad (BNSF) just send in their men. Then, they told George what to do. Bush is a symbol for avoiding, delaying, preventing, and deceiving his country, so eight years created even greater problems and a terrible Oil War. Our country is left with loopholes in our laws that Cheney skillfully gutted, allowing fossil fuel companies to destroy our air, land, and water. Wells are being drilled and more power plants are being built that lock us into going in the wrong direction even longer. Money that could be used to encourage the expansion of solar and wind power goes to subsidize the richest companies in the world. Using our tax dollars to subsidize the energies that burn is another method of delaying solar and wind development.

ARE AMERICANS ASLEEP AT THE WHEEL?

Global warming leads to more frequent, more severe, and more unpredictable weather. Jeff Goodell, author of *Big Coal*, told of a conversation with an energy industry consultant in the early stage of researching his book. The consultant was aware of the crisis and the energy industry's efforts to hide the truth. The consultant joked, "A ferocious hurricane would have to wipe out New Orleans before America would wake up to the dangers of global warming." Goodell went on to say, "By the time I finished the book that hurricane had arrived, although the awakening had not." He was referring to Hurricane Katrina.

You may think Katrina had nothing to do with global warming or the burning of fossil fuels. The facts were not presented in a way that global warming would be connected to the disaster. I remind you, Katrina hit Miami first and remained strong enough to emerge in the Gulf and rebuild. Hurricane Katrina had the sixth lowest barometric pressure ever recorded for a hurricane and the hottest Gulf of Mexico water temperatures ever recorded to fuel Katrina's building. Hurricane Katrina was so large that when it hit the Mississippi coast, we were still getting torrential rains from the same storm here in Naples, Florida. I don't recall hearing or thinking about global warming at the time. Today I realize everything about Hurricane Katrina and the 2005 hurricane season screams, "Climate change," including the frequency. The energy industry consultant, who joked to Goodell about New Orleans being wiped out, understood what global warming could do and thought that might awaken the American public. We are sound sleepers, and perhaps the cocoon tenders of the energy industry were slipping us something. The media also failed to address the global warming connection.

I often wondered how the German people could blindly follow Hitler. Maybe humans are more easily and unknowingly lead in the wrong direction than we ever realized. Just have the powerful control the media; tell us what they want to tell us and what we want to hear, and tell us we are the greatest. We want to believe it. The rest of the world knows about global warming, and they know America is the biggest culprit. We, like the wife of a cheating husband, are the last to know.

Today, energy is political and politics prevent us from protecting our children's futures. We can't trust our leaders to provide us with the truth we need; we've got to do this ourselves. For Americans asleep at the wheel, it is time to Wake Up!

CHAPTER 6

OIL

FUEL + BURN = CO_2 = GLOBAL WARMING

You have probably guessed I am not an advocate of oil and want solar and wind power everywhere it can be used. One problem is that the energy industries have no way to own the sunshine and the wind. They can make money from selling the power they generate and distribute; however, the potential is there for individuals or small groups to produce their own power. The energy companies feel they own the vast American market and must protect that ownership.

THE BRICK WALL—AGAIN

For the eight years the George W. Bush administration misled and misinformed America from our president on down. The chair of the U.S. Senate Committee on Environment and Public Works was Senator James Inhofe, but he protected oil, gas, and coal, not our environment. His stand on global warming remains the same today, and he is still on, but not chairing, that committee. Why, considering his stand on global warming?

> **I have long believed that claims of a consensus that man is causing global warming is the greatest hoax ever perpetrated on the American people.**
> Senator James Inhofe, (2006).

I believe the "hoax" that was perpetrated on the American people was that global warming is not real. Here are some of the views the president and Senator Inhofe ignored.

The position of the United States is hard to accept given the danger the planet is facing.
Nelly Olin, the French Environment Minister, speaking in Montreal in 2005

This is a rogue administration, out of step with the rest of the world and much of America, representing just a small number of powerful industrial interests.
Jonathon Porritt, chairman of the UK Sustainable Development Commission, (2005)

Politicians from other countries pretend that with enough patience and understanding, they will bring the world's largest emitter of carbon along with them to address this unprecedented global threat. They will not.
In the U.S., the White House has become the East Coast branch of Exxon Mobil and Peabody Coal, and climate change has become the preeminent case study of contamination of our politics by money.
Ross Gelbspan, American Pulitzer prizewinner at the Montreal Climate Talks (2005)

President Obama agrees there is global warming and he's making some progress, but it seems as if it is still classified information. Our grandchildren are stepping into a world that is being destroyed by the very people who love them. We want to give our children a world that is safe. Will someone please tell us the truth so we can help?

> **Our generation faces the greatest moral and political crisis in human history.**
> **Will we take the steps necessary to avert catastrophic global warming or will we doom our children to a new Dark Ages in a world that is biologically economically impoverished and defined by ever diminishing quality of life?**
> Robert F. Kennedy, Jr.

Paul Brown, in *Global Warning: The Last Chance to Change* (2007), wrote a frightening view of the powers he perceived as dictating America's actions during the Bush administration. Much of that power remains in place today. He was questioning the powerful lobbyists when he asked, "When thousands of lives are being lost because of climate change, which may soon be in the millions, should more be expected from lobbyists?" He believes there should be a point when greed steps aside to save lives and the planet. Where do the powerful manipulators think their grandchildren will live? The way of life in sub-Saharan Africa could be what we pass to future generations. To understand what that looks like, you can visit websites of humanitarian relief organizations such as World Vision, Compassion International, and Grace Center Foundation (in Ethiopia), which have information and videos. A picture is worth a thousand words.

Could a few powerful groups actually jeopardize our entire planet to fatten their wallets? Paul Brown wrote about actions just prior to the release of the 2007 IPCC report.

> **The fossil fuel industry has been party to misinformation, obstruction and corruption. Warning from the UK's Royal Society was that this was still happening…and the battle to discredit the 2007 IPCC report to be released on April 6, 2007 continued. Even in the hours before the IPCC report on impacts across the world was released, government representatives from the United States,**

> **China, Saudi Arabia, and Russia succeeded in watering down the final report to make the science to appear less certain than it is. For example, a graph showing that billions of people would be at risk of coastal flooding by 2080 was changed to read millions. Some of the scientists walked out in protest. It is hard to understand a motive, except greed, for all this time and money spent to discredit science and damage the political process.**
> **The main motive for those that sponsor, promote and employ them, the corporations and oil rich countries, is to protect their interests.**
> **In other words it is about protecting profits at the expense of many lives.**
> Paul Brown, Global Warning

Russia's Putin had an epiphany during Russia's 2010 heat wave. I want to believe our leaders would put whatever hindrances they have to working to slow global warming aside and say, like Putin did, "Global warming is real and we need to do all we can to save our planet for our children." Our leaders have children they love dearly. I hope they will put their families' safety first–soon.

During the 2012 presidential campaign, I was disheartened to read Romney's response to a voter's question about global warming. I thought, "Oh no, this can't be happening again." The campaign war chests seemed to be limitless in the 2012 election for the Republicans. The people footing the bill, the same ones who had to make sure Bush was in the White House, expected to get their money back many times over.

Right now, I'm seeing the world through the glasses of Lilly's great-granny, whose purpose is to keep her from harm. I see a polarized Congress that votes in blocks. The block that wants fossil fuels discovered, drilled, burned, and dumping greenhouse gases into the atmosphere are the ones threatening Lilly. Not much was said about global warming during the 2012 election campaigns. Someone in the audience had to ask the question. A voter asked Romney, "What is your position on man-made global warming and would you reject legislation, such as cap and trade, which is based on the idea of man-made global warming?" Romney answered, "My view is that we don't know what's causing climate change on this planet. And the idea of spending trillions and trillions of dollars to try to reduce CO_2 emissions is not the right course for us. My view with regards to energy policy is pretty straightforward. I want us to become energy secure and independent of the oil cartels. And that means let's aggressively develop our oil, our gas, our coal, our nuclear power."

NO, NO, NO! Not "aggressively develop our oil, our gas, our coal, our nuclear power." We need an all-out effort to be independent of the oil cartels, and independent of the polluting fossil fuels and radioactive nuclear waste. If we "aggressively develop oil, coal, natural gas and nuclear," we subsidize the richest companies in the world and ignore the energies that can save us. Mitt, you are an intelligent man; you don't know what causes global warming, or as you quickly rephrased it, climate change? Then you throw in the scare tactic of saying, "invest TRILLIONS and TRILLIONS of dollars to TRY to reduce CO_2 emissions." What a carefully crafted and deceptive statement.

The 2012 election is over. The lessons are to question the candidates, see who is backing whom, and check their records before you cast your votes. We do not know who the next candidates will be, but if names start popping up often, see if you can discover their stance on global warming. The fuel industry is more eager than ever to get people it controls into office and appointed to agencies, committees, and leadership positions.

This chapter is headed "Oil," and so far most of what I've written about is politics. That's because that's the way it is. I'll provide information about oil, but if our political leaders and the people who influence them keep funneling our tax dollars to the fossil fuel companies, progress in all other areas is left for individuals to develop on their own. Government and big business are blocking even those efforts. America's addiction to oil is further perpetuated with messages about destroying our economy, returning to living in the dark ages, or becoming a mediocre country.

The consequences of continued global warming are the destruction of the world's economy with the quality of life becoming so deteriorated that we find ourselves in a new version of our own dark age, and yes, our country and all other countries breaking down to mediocrity or total collapse. A country that can no longer provide for its population's basic needs starts collapsing. When water is toxic and drained, land is degraded, the weather is one violent disaster after another, what will our country look like? The threats powerful leaders use to scare us are the very things they are creating. Global warming cannot be paid off and will not bow to lobbyists. Continuing to dump greenhouse gases into the atmosphere will result in unavoidable consequences. That is not political—that is cold, hard fact.

Now, about the substance that man has the misfortune to abuse and be addicted to: oil.

OUR OIL ADDICTION STARTS

U.S. oil was discovered in Titusville, Pennsylvania in 1865, but it wasn't until the discovery of oil from gushers like Spindletop in Texas in 1901 that oil became big business. Spindletop produced one hundred thousand barrels a day and was the largest known oil field in the world at the time. Gulf Oil and Texaco became huge companies supplying oil to the waiting American public. Oil was cheap, plentiful, and one might think, endless.

With oil so easy to obtain, industries and products that might have developed other means of power or production from current energy switched to ancient energy, oil. Huge profits and powerful companies developed. Did anyone ever think the oil might be gone someday, or wonder what would happen if the country were dependent on oil and the oil ran out? When did anyone suspect the CO_2 from burning oil could change the Earth's atmosphere in ways that could make Earth uninhabitable for man?

> **I'd put my money on the sun and solar energy. What a source of power! I hope we don't have to wait until oil and coal run out before we tackle that.**
> Thomas Edison

Did Edison realize man would alter the atmospheric balance by burning oil and coal? He apparently thought oil would run out. Edison fired up his first coal plant on Pearl Street in New York City in 1882. Soot in the neighborhood was a great source of complaints. That soot was carbon; the great release of sequestered carbon was underway. Soon the coal-fired plants were moved out of sight of the well-to-do, and the smoke stacks were made taller to help disperse the carbon away from the people. The slogan for this fix was, "The solution to pollution is dilution." I wish old Tom had "put his money on the sun and solar" in 1882 as he later recommended.

Edison's quote was a surprise to me. It was from a discussion with Henry Ford and Harvey Firestone. Other fuel sources were abandoned by the 1920s. Oil could be refined to gasoline, it was cheap and plentiful, and distribution to where the public could buy it was easy. This meant the range for the automobile was unlimited.

Automakers, oil companies, and tire companies found ways to promote their products. Many cities once had public transportation. Some cities agreed to sell or lease the transit system to an automaker with the understanding that the new owner would maintain, repair, upgrade, continue the service, and at the same time save the city money. That sounded good, but soon after getting control, the new owners stopped the service. Now, folks needed cars, tires, and gas.

THE AMERICAN CAR-LOVING COUNTRY

The United States painfully lacks good public transit. The order of the best methods of transportation for the planet are walking, biking, trains, mass-transit, bus, carpool, car, and the last resort, plane. One author said he lost 3,500 pounds. He sold his car, bought a 22-pound bike, and gets seven miles per potato!

> **One person flying in an airplane for one hour is responsible for the same greenhouse gas emissions as a typical Bangladeshi in a whole year.**
> Beatrice Schell, European Federation for Transportation and Environment, 2001.

America built a highway system and urged people (the developing market of hyper-consumers) to move to the suburbs. Highways carried people comfortably to larger homes, and to and from work in the privacy of their own automobiles. The programming of Americans to prosper and consume geared up. In the 1950s and 1960s most families had one car. Now we have three cars for every four Americans. In 2011 there were 965 million cars in use in the world. Americans own 248 million of those cars; we drive more miles, get poorer mileage, and burn more gas than the next twenty countries combined. That's changing; 1.3 billion Chinese are chasing the American dream.

The Chinese will not buy American cars; China's mileage requirements are far above what Detroit produces. The European Union standard was 52 MPG for 2012. Japan's lowest mileage was 48 MPG in 2010, and in 2008, China required at least 37 MPG. It is too bad we cannot meet those standards when other countries can.

We were going to increase our MPG when the oil embargo hit us in the 1970s. Congress got busy with the Electric and Hybrid Vehicle Research, Development and Demonstration Act. That evaporated into thin air once the gas companies had their oil supply back.

In 2011, Wally and I made the decision to buy a car that gets at least 50 MPG. It had to be a hybrid because we cut back to one car, and no electric car has a long enough range for us to visit family up north.

We try to support the American economy, but the American economy did not support us. Our priority is to slow global warming. We are now the happy owners of a Toyota Prius, named "Emmy Sue." Her full name is "Emerald" because she is the crowning jewel of our efforts to live green. We couldn't wait for American automakers to produce such a car. The Prius has been on the market for many years and has a wonderful track record. People warned us about the terrible expense to replace the battery, six thousand dollars, someone said. The dealer said replacement batteries are two thousand if we ever need one. We haven't met an owner who had to replace the battery. A few people traded their old Prius in after 250,000 miles for a new model with the improved "eco" and "EV" modes. By trading in, they never found out how long the battery lasts. One lady's 2004 Prius hasn't even stalled in 250,000 miles. You would think Detroit could offer us something. We put a man on the moon, but we cannot produce a car comparable to something Japan has been selling to Americans for more than twelve years.

Detroit advertises with a sexy movie star driving a Cadillac that goes 0 to 60 mph is a few seconds. We watch a rugged outdoor man charge his hulk of a truck up a steep rocky slope and teeter on the edge of the Grand Canyon. The wonderful soccer mom totes the joyful team about while they watch TV in the back seats in the lap of luxury. When Detroit put out a high mileage car, consider the advertisement. For a brief time, there was an advertisement for the Chevy Volt. The shy owner stops at a gas station, but not for gas, and is embarrassed when questioned about why he would stop at a gas station. At last, American automakers offered a high mileage car for shy people with weak bladders.

Americans want a dependable energy-efficient car. Most Prius owners wanted an American- made car that got great mileage, but there were none. Detroit wants to make the cash cows, the SUVs and jazzy trucks.

California is a car-loving state and a state that tried to do something to clean their air. At the citizens' request, the California Air Resources

Board (CARB) passed the "Zero-Emissions Vehicle Mandate," requiring that 2% of the vehicles in California have zero emissions by 1998 and 10% of the vehicles have zero emissions by 2003. People wanted to buy the vehicles. That was the reason for the mandate. In 2002, Chrysler, General Motors, and the Bush administration sued CARB to repeal the mandate. By 2003 the CARB mandate was so watered down that automakers got zero emission credits for non-zero emission vehicles. Automakers started development of electric vehicles to meet the requirements but wanted to pull back and remain with the higher profit gas-guzzlers. We tell Detroit what we want and they say, "You can't have it. You're getting big, powerful, and fast."

Is the government trying to reduce our dependence on foreign oil? We import oil. Gas is refined from oil. It takes much less fuel to make the electricity to run an electric car; however, the profit is less for big business.

Hubbert's Peak May Not Have a Military Solution

In the late 1950s, King Hubbert's theory of the world's oil "peaking" and then declining was greeted with skepticism. However, the forecast of U.S. oil reaching its maximum output in the early 1970s proved correct. The United States pays other countries for half the oil we devour. Some countries may use our oil money to harm the United States. We are the world leader for oil consumption, followed by China, Japan, India, and Russia. The argument that moving to solar and wind could ruin our economy seems lame when you consider that the United States imports 50% of the oil we use.

Saudi Arabia's largest oil field, Ghawar, is far beyond peak; they now get as much water as oil from the wells. Mexico's Cantarelle Super Oil Field is nearly drained. Of the world's sixty-five largest oil producing countries, fifty-nine of them have production that has leveled off or is in decline as of 2008. At the same time, the demand for oil is expected to climb by 40%. Many countries are scraping the bottom of their oil fields. We buy oil from countries we might have problems with in the future. The prospect of funding more oil wars seems like an expense we need to avoid.

We have a staggering national debt. Brown University's *Cost of War Project* states the overall cost of the wars in Iraq, Pakistan, and Afghanistan is between $3.4 and $4 trillion. In addition, there is an estimated expense of $1 trillion in benefits for injury and death to the soldiers and their families between now and the year 2050.

When Romney claimed, it could cost trillions to try to address reducing CO_2 emissions, that was not true. However, we have spent trillions on wars in an attempt to retain control of foreign oil. In the process we lost many soldiers, more are permanently disabled, and our country's image around the world is badly damaged. When demand for oil far exceeds supply, will oil-producing nations refuse to sell oil to the U.S. as a way to harm our nation? Is that possible?

Michael Klare, in *Rising Power, Shrinking Planet*, points out that military strength no longer insures national security. Putting financial resources into building the military creates constant wars for oil access. Our demand is ever increasing for the dwindling oil supply. Allocation of financial resources needs to include wind and solar energy development and conservation of energy. The United States responds only when there is an oil crisis and it has to be a big one. We have been in an oil crisis in at least two ways for many years. We are running out of oil, but the worst part is the destruction of the atmosphere. That one is a stopper.

Do you remember the gas crisis in 1979? An oil embargo cut our supply of oil and prices skyrocketed. We filled our tank on even days, and gas lines were long. In 1979 we were unable to produce enough of our own oil to meet our demand. The government urged people to conserve, and the auto companies started researching ways to improve mileage and develop electric cars. We were on the right track.

When the embargo ended, what happened? Gas stations started giving me sets of drinking glasses and steak knives for every fill-up, and cars got bigger. There were few vans and no SUVs. Automakers knew Americans could be persuaded to go for bigger, fancier gas-guzzlers.

I first learned oil was running out when I read about Hubbert's Peak. After reading Edison's comment, I wonder how many people knew this and when they thought it would be gone. No one clued in the public that the oil would dwindle to nothing by the end of this century.

In the early 1900s, when oil became so cheap and easy to use for cars and provided an unlimited travel range, they stopped making electric cars. Jay Leno has a 1909 Baker electric car. Imagine, we could have gone in that direction and developed from there instead of waiting a century.

The news is showing Mars rover, Curiosity, driving around on Mars. I have not seen it pull into a Mobil or Shell station. I do not believe for one minute it's impossible for American automakers to make an electric car that's affordable and meets our needs.

World oil production may have peaked around 2005. Countries guard such secrets. One reason many are certain oil peaked is that when prices rose from $44 a barrel in 2005 to $147 a barrel in 2008, output only rose .2% higher than in 2005. The price more than tripled, but supply could not be increased.

Deffeyes, who wrote *Beyond Oil* and worked with Hubbert, wrote that Hubbert's estimate of the total of the world's oil, including the very hard to reach, was 2.013 trillion barrels. As of 2005, the world has used 1.000748 trillion barrels of oil.

We cannot continue to have 88% of American workers drive to work. The supply and demand rule of economics is getting very uncomfortable. Part of me welcomes running out of oil. It will cause hard times, but that seems to be the only way to reduce pollution from burning oil; we have to run out. Klare explains once half the world's supply is used, "Each new barrel of oil is harder and more costly to extract than the one before. Oil will be deeper, farther off shore, more hazardous to reach, more environmentally damaging, and more conflict-prone from hostile regions. In time, this will also be true for coal, natural gas, uranium, and copper."

Tar sand and oil shale is the bottom of the barrel when it comes to getting oil and natural gas. It is expensive to obtain and it can require nearly as much or more energy than it produces. Recovery from tar sand or shale destroys the habitat of many species, disrupts people's lives, contaminates the water supply, and there is the risk of spills with little ability for inspection or clean up. Brune's book, *Coming Clean* (2008), tells the amount of excavation required to use Canada's tar sand. More earth would be excavated than it took to build the Great Wall of China, the Suez Canal, the Great Pyramids, and ten of the world's largest dams. It may take more energy for scraping, extracting, refining, and distributing than the energy the oil or gas produced will provide.

Klare points out that not one big nation is working hard enough to have alternatives fill the energy gap soon enough, and our world is becoming a danger zone with climate change, energy shortages, and competition for resources. He acknowledges the devastation of global warming, but also brings up the likelihood of having a world in constant conflict for oil. He believes our resources need to be directed toward a cooperative effort to solve our problems. How long can America use our financial resources to perpetuate our dependence on oil when the money is most needed to develop lasting and non-polluting energies?

LET'S USE NEGAWATTS

Most of our electricity is generated by burning oil, coal, or natural gas. A professor gave a list of reasons not to drill, fracture, mine, burn, destroy the environment, and pollute for our power. He said the real solution was "negawatts." That's what he calls the amount of electricity not used when we conserve. Wally and I are using more than ten thousand negawatts a year in our home. I love that term. Hold off on the nasty fracking for oil on Alaska's North Slope or in the northeast for natural gas. America can turn to negawatts. Caribou returning from the

United States and Canada every spring for the calving season and the forty thousand whales that migrate to the North Slope coast wouldn't be endangered by oil spills. There aren't many clean-up crews on the North Slope of Alaska. The companies could let things happen without any annoying inspectors around.

That's the answer; I can use negawatts for Lilly!

CHAPTER 7

COAL

FUEL + BURN = CO_2 = GLOBAL WARMING

> **If you are a young man looking at the future of this planet and looking at what is being done right now and not being done, I believe we have reached the stage where it is time for civil disobedience to prevent the construction of new coal plants that do not have carbon capture and sequestration.**
>
> Al Gore, at the Clinton Global Initiative Annual Meeting

Coal is the world's most abundant energy source and accounts for one-third of the carbon emissions. Many of China and India's 2.5 billion citizens are without power. China has a lot of coal and adds two gigawatts (two billion watts) of electricity from coal a week. At the same time, China is adding power from sun, wind, and the world's largest dam for hydroelectric power. Imagine trying to build power plants and infrastructure to provide electricity for a population two to three times larger than the United States, and the order is stamped ASAP. India is adding four coal fired-fired plants that each generate four thousand megawatts. One megawatt equals a million watts. This coal plant boom is terrible news for the planet; it could push us beyond a tipping point. The United Kingdom and California no longer allow coal plants to be built.

When the Earth's temperature crosses the line of 3.5 degrees F above the pre-industrial revolution level, the devastation will be swift and likely at the point of no return. I knew we had added one to one and a half of those degrees already, but I didn't realize the oceans are storing another degree of added temperature that is in the process of radiating out into the atmosphere. That means we have over 2 of the 3.5 degrees now. The added CO_2 from new coal-fired power plants is moving us toward the 3.5 degree rise at a faster pace than anyone saw coming. Scientists are seeing changes in the ice caps, ice sheets, and glaciers they didn't expect for a hundred years. Soot on ice also cuts down on ice's ability to reflect heat back out of our atmosphere. The ice caps and glaciers were stable for ten thousand years . Now they're disappearing. In my lifetime, man changed our atmosphere from "just right" to "very wrong."

A coal plant emits one hundred times more radiation than a nuclear power plant with the same electrical output. Radioactive toxins are in the fly ash from burning coal. The new Integrated Gasification Combined Cycle technology (IGCC) is supposed to burn clean coal, but it is far from clean. We are too close to the tipping point to just modify. IGCC is 10% more efficient, uses 40% less water, the radio-active fly ash and solid waste is cut in half, and it's nearly as clean burning as natural gas. This new technology is a step closer to the controversial capturing and sequestration of CO_2. No one wants CO_2 sequestered in his or her back yard. Options being considered are storage in salt domes or under the sea.

America—The Saudi Arabia of Coal

America is said to be the Saudi Arabia of coal with 25% of the world's coal. However, like the other fossil fuels, the cheapest, cleanest, and easiest to mine coal is gone. In 2005 an estimated 250-year supply of recoverable coal remained in the U.S. These numbers were partially based on very optimistic figures made half a century earlier and from

1909 when the technology to accurately calculate the coal supply had not been invented and coal was mined with a pick, shovel, pail, and pushcart.

Today we haul coal out in huge trucks and fill train cars so fast the train maintains a speed of two miles an hour as cars are loaded. The Burlington Northern Santa Fe Railroad (BNSF) coal trains haul coal from Wyoming to the Plant Sherer coal-fired power plant in Georgia. Plant Sherer receives ten to fifteen coal trains a day, with up to 124 cars in each train. It's little wonder that the coal companies and the railroads have such a shared interest in coal use increasing. BNSF receives up to 80% of the money paid for each ton of coal delivered to Plant Sherer. Twenty percent of BNSF's annual profit is from the delivery of coal. Goodell mentioned that Plant Scherer burns more than 34,000 tons of coal a day. When using the 1909 predictions of how long the coal would last, I doubt they figured one customer would be using 68,000,000 pounds of coal a day. That could alter numbers a bit over time. No more picking and filling the pail or push cart. Now tops of mountain are scraped off. Mountain top removal is very unpopular with the people who live on the mountains.

Another mining method is to fluff up the earth so the coal is easier to reach. Goodell was invited to watch a "small" blast in Wyoming. Many holes were drilled into an already huge crater, and 55,000 pounds of ammonium nitrate fuel oil (ANFO) went into the holes. When it was detonated, the ground rumbled and heaved. The earth was now "fluffed." Timothy McVeigh used 3,800 pounds of ANFO to blow up the Murrah Federal Building in Oklahoma City. Coal mining uses 70% of the 2.5 million tons of industrial explosives used in the United States each year.

The Scoop on Coal

The Earth may be 4.5 billion years old, but the vegetation needed to start forming coal wasn't present until 400 million years ago. The

United States' oldest coal is in eastern regions. Coal found in Wyoming and other western areas is only 55 million years old and has lower sulfur content than the coal found in the east. The 1970 Clean Air Act restricts sulfur emissions, because they cause acid rain that killed trees. The lower sulfur content of Wyoming's coal put western coal in demand. That coal is sub-bituminous and lignite and has a lower heat value and higher CO_2 emission. Apparently, the Clean Air Act doesn't have CO_2 limits.

Anthracite coal found in the Appalachian area has the highest heat value and the highest sulfur content. The next highest heat value coal is bituminous, then sub-bituminous, and the lowest quality coal is lignite, which produces the most CO_2. Coal is found in zigzag seams sloping downward into the earth. The seams of coal in the east are eight to ten feet wide. The coal seams in the western states are ten or more times wider and much easier to mine. Wyoming's production rate is thirty-nine tons of coal per employee hour, compared to West Virginia's rate of four tons per employee hour.

West Virginia is now a poor, exploited state. The state's income from taxes paid by coal companies has declined, jobs are disappearing, and benefits eliminated to cut costs. Miners who gave the best years of their lives are without jobs, without health benefits, are sick or dying, and live in a state where there's not enough money for decent state services for health or education. This fate is shared by other eastern coal producing states. Between 1997 and 2004, Wyoming's coal production increased 40%, while West Virginia's declined 18%. Coal companies tell eastern miners the loss of jobs is due to environmentalists and regulations. Wyoming coal is cheaper and contains less sulfur; that's what determines how coal sells.

THIS RESOURCE WAS NOT A BLESSING

Appalachian coal companies use "mountain top removal." By 2008, coal mining had destroyed 450 mountains, buried seven hundred miles of streams, and drinking water was toxic. Coal companies blackmail states into allowing mountaintop-mining saying, "If you don't allow us to mine that mountain, we'll leave and your state will be in poverty without the taxes from coal."

> Nearly 150 years and 13 billion tons of coal later, the great wealth of natural resources in West Virginia has been anything but a blessing. Rather than bringing riches, it has brought poverty, sickness, environmental devastation, and despair.
> Jeff Goodell

It would be wonderful if a wind power industry were built in West Virginia and residents received the profits. A documentary aired in March 2013 interviewed Appalachians who want exactly that… to replace mountain top mining with wind farms.

COAL'S HAY DAY
In 1900, coal heated homes, powered locomotives, and produced electricity. Home heating started switching from coal by 1930, coal-fired locomotives were replaced in the 1940s, and by 1950, the push was on for nuclear power plants. After the 1979 near meltdown of Three-mile Island Nuclear Power Plant, gas fueled power plants came into use. In case you think the United States no longer uses much coal, you are wrong. In 2006 the average American used twenty pounds of coal a day, exceeding a billion tons of coal per year.

BIG COAL = BIG BULLY AND THERE IS NO SHERIFF IN TOWN
Coal companies have exploited our land and people for 150 years. Regulations are ignored; mines that are death traps have long lists of uncorrected safety violations. The only time the violations are noted is when coal miners are trapped in a collapsed, flooded, or burning mine. Fines levied against coal companies are so minimal they're a joke and only point out how much power the coal industry has. CO_2 emissions,

no problem, just like all other harmful practices; no one tells big coal what to do. They have friends in high places.

There are some investigations since the Bush era ended, but America is still saddled with agencies, committees, and regulations that have been stripped of their power. One coal company is miffed that the Environmental Protection Agency (EPA) is investigating them and is threatening to sue the EPA for discrimination.

Dr. Diane Shafer attempted to discover the reason many people in the area outside of Williamson, West Virginia were having early-onset dementia, rising rates of cancer, birth defects, and kidney, thyroid, and gastrointestinal problems. She was concerned the drinking water outside the municipal water supply might be involved. Shafer, the only doctor on the county board of health, could not persuade officials to check the water. In frustration, she had a group of citizens get their water tested. Biology professor Ben Stout at Wheeling Jesuit University, a well-known expert on the impact of coal mining on Appalachian streams, tested fifteens wells. Five met federal standards. The rest were contaminated with heavy metals (including lead, arsenic, beryllium, and selenium) found in the slurry ponds of the mining company. Some wells had contamination 500% above federal safety standards. The mining practice of filling old mines with the slurry provides an easy route into the water supply. The report made little difference.

> **The coal companies control everything down here. It's like the wild-west, except there is no sheriff in town. They just do whatever they want and pretty much get away with it. We are taking one of the great fresh-water supplies in the world, and we are screwing it up. You can't fill in a thousand miles of streams, then inject millions of pounds of toxic slurry into the aquifers,**

> **without it having an impact. It's not the mountains of West**
> **Virginia I worry about, it's the people.**
> **Sometimes I think what is going on here is damn near genocide.**
> Ben Stout, Professor of biology, Wheeling Jesuit University

If a coal company allows its workers and neighbors to die from their unethical behavior, would they change their profitable practices for the good of the planet? I wish I could boycott coal. It's not much, but I'm going off the grid for the next five hours.

Oh No! My Power Comes from Coal

At first I thought Florida Power and Light (FPL) had very little electricity from coal, but Georgia's Plant Scherer, the fifth largest coal-fired power plant in the world, is partially owned by FPL. Scherer ranked twentieth in the world's worst CO_2 emitting coal-fired power plants in 2007. As of August 2012, Georgia's Environmental Protection Department is investigating Plant Scherer for coal ash pond leaching resulting in drinking water contamination and air pollution. Coal ash is the source of the radioactivity associated with coal. *Natural History Magazine* reported in 2006 that the Scherer Plant was the largest single-point-source of CO_2 emissions in the United States. In 2012, Halliburton and other contractors are constructing another smoke stack. My antennae go up whenever I hear Halliburton, and that happens often.

FPL is one of the twenty-five companies in the United States that pay the lowest tax rate. *Business Week* (April 2009) reported FPL paid taxes at the rate of 1.3% rather than the normal 35%. FPL claimed they took advantage of alternative energy incentives. That's interesting considering Florida is among the worst CO_2 emissions state for power plants. A fact that could have some bearing on the phenomenal tax rate is that FPL paid five major Washington lobbying firms more than five hundred thousand dollars. So much of what coal, railroads, and utility companies do is swept under the rug. Check out what was swept under the rug after the last chapter. You'll have a better idea why hearing BNSF was tied to my power company made me cringe.

When is Good News Not Good News?

An August 2012 report that U.S. emissions of CO_2 from January 2012 to April 2012 had dropped below the amount emitted for the same period in 1992 sounded like great news. I was relieved, but as I read on, a sour feeling came over me. Natural gas is now cheaper than coal because of the new technology developed by Halliburton called "hydraulic fracturing," or "fracking." It's estimated there's a ninety year supply of natural gas because of the oceans of gas in shale.

CO_2 going into the atmosphere is not decreasing. We remain ahead of the worst-case scenario by a mile. The U.S. is down from 6 billion tons of CO_2 emitted in 2007 to 5.2 billion tons or 16% of the world's emissions. China's dash to chase the American dream is launched and she now emits 29% of the global CO_2 totaling 9 billion tons a year. China has added far more CO_2 than we have cut, and the U.S. may have raised our methane emissions from fracking for natural gas enough to exceed the CO_2 reductions. Methane is twenty-five times more damaging to the atmosphere than CO_2. Leaving that information out of the good news report is an example of how Americans are misled so that fracking for natural gas sounds like a wonderful solution. IT IS NOT!

We have the technology and unlimited wind and solar resources. If we don't use them, the world will continue adding fossil fuel plants to feed man's insatiable appetite for electricity.

CHAPTER 8

NATURAL GAS

FUEL + BURN = CO_2 = GLOBAL WARMING

I'd been studying global warming over a year and started writing this book before the words "hydraulic fracturing" (or "fracking") entered my world in June of 2012. Until then, I hoped cheap, clean-burning natural gas would be the energy to help fill the gap, while we converted to solar and wind energy. Instead, I learned we could have a country spotted with carcinogenic water wells and aquifers, and no way to "unfracture" what has been "freed up" by fracking over half a million wells in thirty-eight states, in people's yards, next to schools, and anywhere gas companies could buy or lease land.

RECIPE FOR DISASTER

Film maker Josh Fox lives in Pennsylvania, and wanted to check out what fracking was after he received a lucrative offer to lease his nineteen acres. It sounded tempting, so he decided to call the gas company to ask some questions. He couldn't even get anyone to take his calls. This concerned him. He began his own investigation and put his findings in a documentary, *Gasland*.

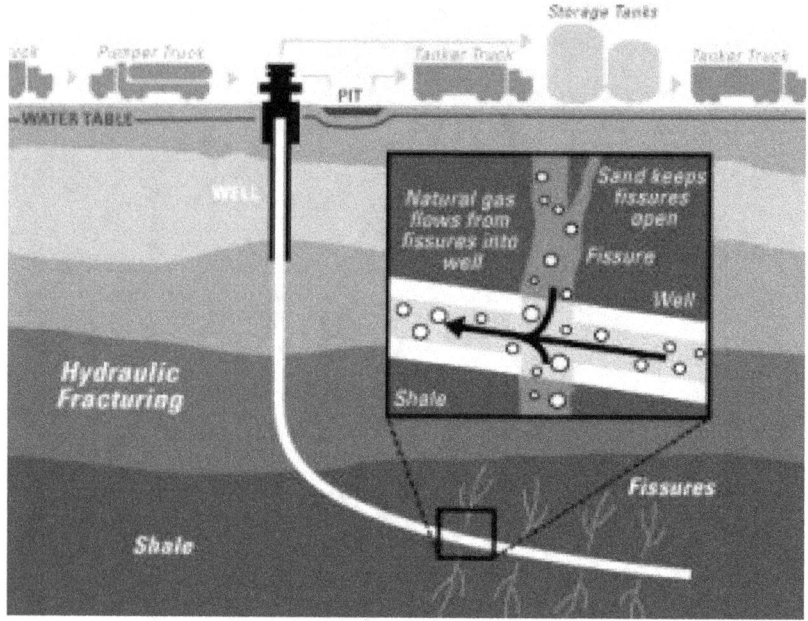

Fracking diagram

Every well is different, takes one to four weeks to complete, and follows this process:

- Scrape off an area the size of a football field.
- Set up a drilling rig.
- Drill 8,000 to 11,000 feet into the ground.
- Drive in 1,150 monster, 18-wheel or larger trucks filled with sand, 7 to 11 million gallons of water, and 900 undisclosed chemicals (hundreds are known carcinogens).
- Pump the water/sand/chemical mix up to 2 miles into the ground until there is so much pressure that it creates a small earthquake "freeing" the gas.
- Draw out half of the water/sand/chemical mix.
- Dispose of those 4-6 million gallons of toxic mix somewhere. The "Halliburton Loophole" exempts gas companies from regulation and frees up their options for disposal.
- The gas company gets their gas and the landowners and their neighbors can wait to see what they have to deal with.
- This process can be repeated up to eighteen times on every well.

The gas companies claim the chemicals can't get into the drinking water. After the wells are in, many people find they can ignite their faucets; make torches from bubbles on wet lands; and they, their children, pets, and livestock develop many serious medical problems. Additionally, they find the environment, including water, soil, air, vegetation, and wildlife is severely damaged, if not destroyed. The laws and agencies to protect the people have been gutted, allowing gas companies to deny that any of the new problems are related to fracking.

Neither the workers nor the bosses on the site had any idea what chemicals they were using. They were sure the fluids were safe "because the gas company sent them." Some workers had burns on their hands and faces, and were probably working with hundreds of carcinogens on their skin and in the air they were breathing during long workdays.

There's too much information in the film to be included in this book and this is one case where each picture is truly worth a thousand words. I sincerely hope you watch *Gasland* for yourself. Be careful if you try to pull it up on the Internet; you are apt to get a piece put out by the natural gas industry. The real documentary starts with Josh Fox, wearing a gas mask, playing a banjo, and walking toward the camera. There's a gas well in the background.

There are half a million unregulated toxic-carcinogenic-methane leaking wells on land owners' property, and as many as one hundred thousand on American's protected lands owned by the Bureau of Land Management. Most of these wells are in the western states, particularly Colorado and Wyoming, and along the Gulf Coast.

The frenzy continues, as gas companies scramble to develop the ocean of gas known as the Marcellus Shale in the northeast. They hope to put hundreds of thousands of wells in the northeast, especially in New York and Pennsylvania. It's only since the new Halliburton technology that the gas in shale can be "freed" (by a small earthquake). This is another example of carbon that should be left in the ground.

Gas companies have used fracturing to drill for natural gas since

1947; however, the method changed in 1998. Prior to that, gas companies where drilling for gas closer to the surface, which was easier to obtain and didn't involve the earthquake with nine hundred chemicals being forced deep into the Earth to free up deeper gas reservoirs. The older, more shallow drilling method was much safer. When gas companies claim they have a long history of safely drilling gas wells, that history is based on the old method used to drill over half a million wells from 1947 to 1997. It's the half million wells drilled since 1998 that we need to question.

Gas companies want to get gas out of the ground as fast and as cost effectively as possible. Laws were changed so that they can skip measures for safe drilling and capture. The current administration is running into brick walls built during the previous administration to prevent or slow inspection, information, regulation, correction, safe practices, or the passing of any law that could stop such drilling.

> **More than 650 of these products contain chemicals that are known or possible human carcinogens, regulated under the Safe Drinking Water Act.**
> **Additionally, 279 products are listed as "proprietary" or "trade secret" Material Safety Data Sheet (MSDS). How can they do "peer-reviewed scientific study" on these chemicals if they won't tell us what they are? They can't. Until that happens, we shouldn't allow it to be pumped into the ground, letting these chemicals into our ground water.**
> From the 2011 U.S. House of Representatives report on chemicals used in hydraulic fracturing.

The Halliburton Loophole in Bush's 2005 energy bill exempted gas and oil companies from the regulations of The Clean Air Act, The Clean Water Act, The Safe Drinking Water Act, and about nine other acts. One of those has to do with clean-ups. Cheney thought of everything. Realize that it just about takes an act of Congress to get our protection back. The "Brick Wall" is still in place.

Environmental Damage from Fracking

Some reports state that methane emissions more than offset CO_2 decreases. The methane loss in normal leakage of a gas well is 4%. Scientists and environmentalists claim that's because of the unsafe way the well is put in. Josh Fox compared the lack of safety devices and procedures in the way wells are constructed and operated to be similar to the difference between a car built in 1890 (with the seats not screwed to the frame) and one of today's cars. He mentioned many safety features that could be easily added and are common practice in industry. With no regulations, no oversight, and ethical thinking viewed as costly, gas companies are free to do whatever they please.

The fracked wells, which use the new technology, have only been going in for fourteen years. Information was withheld, eliminated from reports, denied, and ignored for most of that time. What is now known is that if you live within 3,000 feet of a fracked well, the methane in your drinking water is seventeen times higher after the fracking. This apparently gets worse instead of better, as the well deteriorates and is "refracked" up to eighteen times. In the fourteen years since fracking began, the cancer rate is up by 66% in people who live within half a mile of a fracked well. These statistics are from people in Colorado, who have had the exposure since early drilling of the new wells. What percent will there be after twenty-five years of exposure.

The first health study, though it was hindered because information was withheld by gas companies, was in Garfield County, Colorado, where there are five thousand fracked wells. Dr. Cleo Colborn worked tirelessly to determine what the citizens were exposed to. She tested water, patients' blood, and other substances, and came up with a long list of chemicals. She could never tie them to the gas drilling, because the list of chemicals used was protected under the law. She found benzene and arsenic in their blood. The symptoms that were rampant included excruciating and disabling headaches, dizziness, disorientation, pains anywhere and everywhere, inability to control limbs, peripheral neuropathy, and brain lesions. Once the peripheral neuropathy started, the brain lesions were already present. The gas company denied any responsibility, and without evidence of the chemicals used for fracking, there was no way to prove anything.

People have exorbitant medical expenses, some feel as if their lives are over, and many fear for their children's lives. It is no longer safe to allow the children to play outside because a cloud of chemicals hangs over the land and settles in yards and on playgrounds. Even when the air looks clear near the condensate tanks, infrared lights show a cloud of chemicals. Some of the chemicals in that air are at lethal levels. Many condensate tanks are next to schools. There are no regulations whatsoever. One mother said in despair, "And here we are supposed to be living in the beautiful 'green state' of Colorado."

People were tested and found to have arsenic poisoning. Patients were pulled aside and asked if they could think of a family member who might be trying to poison them. It's ironic that if a spouse poisoned his or her mate, the spouse would be sent to prison, yet the gas company can knowingly poison thousands or millions with no consequences, except profit.

> **The worst sin against our fellow creatures is not to hate them,**
> **but to be indifferent.**
> George Bernard Shaw

There were huge budget cuts and positions eliminated in the environmental protection agencies of state governments. In Pennsylvania, after the fracking started and complaints came in, the state's environmental agency budget was cut 25%, and 350 of their protecting positions were eliminated. That is one way to tie government's hands. When the government and EPA try to see what's really happening, the state agencies have minimal staff, and there are few reports to be checked.

VERMONT—WHAT A STATE!

The people of Vermont did their homework, demanded their water supply be protected, and in May 2012, Vermont became the first state in the nation to ban fracking for oil and gas. Citizens in Vermont weren't afraid to speak out. One reader wrote, "This needs to be taken to criminal levels. It's a crime against humanity; industrial terrorism. This industry is brutal and we need to call it what it is: a crime that kills. If I made my husband or child sick or dead with poison, I would be tried for a crime. Just because it's a business doesn't make their murder less criminal. This is like serial mass murder of generations, genocide. Get real."

Moratoriums are in place in New South Wales (Australia), Karoo Basin (South Africa), and Quebec, Canada, to stop fracking. People are protesting in many countries. Poland has so much fracking that the billions of gallons of water used for fracking and refracking of each well is depleting Poland's agricultural water supply.

I wonder what chemicals will show up in the vegetables grown using water supplies near fracked wells. Where did they dispose of the trillions of gallons of carcinogenic mix from the drilling process? Benzene and other toxins are in the blood of people in areas that have fracking. I guess that rancher's question in *Gasland* about what will show up on America's dinner plates when he sells his cattle has been answered. What happens when people eat benzene or other chemicals in their beef, grains, vegetables, and fruit? Can cooking destroy the poisons and carcinogens? They are not biodegradable.

The stream one rancher's cattle had to drink from smelled so strongly of a turpentine-like odor, the people could not tolerate having it near their nose for a fraction of a second. It is not the rancher's fault; he said he didn't know how the cattle could stand to drink the stuff. He had no choice but to let them drink, and he is sick about what it is doing to the herd and eventually to the people who may destroy their health by eating the meat. They can't sell their land. Who would want it?

People whose health, water, land, and peace of mind have been robbed say, "It seems as if no one cares." I hope you care enough to warn other people who are offered money for leasing their land to supply America with clean-burning natural gas. It sounds so noble. Well-meaning landowners may be signing papers that destroy their lives.

> **The best things in life are appreciated most after they have been lost.**
> Roy L. Smith

I do not want our children drinking, bathing in, breathing, or engulfed in poison. There should be laws against something done so willfully and deceptively that threatens thousands of lives. It is a crime; greedy companies are poisoning countless people and lying to everyone who tries to help. The thing I cannot tolerate is people from the gas industry testifying before Congress and telling absolute obvious lies, lies, lies, knowing they face no consequences. If an athlete lies before Congress, he can be imprisoned for perjury.

The victims of the gas companies' actions, who tried to get the companies to do something, were told, "There is no evidence our drilling is the cause of any problems. If you don't agree, hire a lawyer." What lawyer would sue gas companies who have so much power and influence that they can safely lie in sworn testimony to Congress?

When I think of Lilly and the world she will have, I wonder if she will drink water and eat food that causes brain lesions. No one is warned the water might be affected. Many of the people in the documentary had been drinking the contaminated water for several years, not realizing their medical problems were the result of being poisoned. Some of the worst carcinogens are colorless, odorless, and tasteless. Gas companies know before they ever drill what can go wrong. They deny responsibility and move on to a new area, quickly drilling thousands more wells. The wholesale price of natural gas has plummeted from seven or eight dollars per unit to three dollars over the past four years. Now, adding safety features to their drilling and wells is cost prohibitive. The commercials may advertise "clean natural gas," but there is a lot more to that story than the pretty blue flame it shows in the commercial.

If I hadn't seen *Gasland* and read more about the 4% methane leak from fracked wells, I would be breathing a sigh of relief. How many aquifers will be made toxic while the "frenzy" continues unchecked? Are there methane limits in any regulations? Is it possible to stop that methane release once the earth has been fractured and the gases freed?

Gas companies will do everything in their power to prevent "interference from big government." They make it sound as if "big government" is the enemy. I don't want layers and layers of bureaucracy, but I certainly want strong oversight on the gas companies.

We call fossil fuels "our natural resources." What if those resources were never meant to be ours? Today's population, demands, technologies, and release of the ancient energy may have created a situation that is violating laws of nature we are only beginning to realize exist. How can our country and our world get to renewables as soon as possible? We must direct subsidies and incentives in a way to make the switch to pollution-free renewables.

Our water supply is diminishing, and fracking may be systematically rendering watershed after watershed toxic. Glycol ethers in the water from people's faucets after fracking destroys the membranes of water purification systems, including reverse osmosis. It would be terrible for the planet to be forced to buy all bottled water. Could we be sure the bottled water doesn't contain the colorless, odorless, and tasteless glycol ethers? Where will we even get the water to bottle?

Josh Fox showed a thirty-five-mile-long stream, in which everything died, even the small animals nearby. The landowner drank the toxic water, developed pancreatic cancer, and died within two years. That had been a freshwater stream he safely drank from all his life.

New York, New York, It's a Wonderful Town

There's a plan to put thousands of fracked gas wells in the watershed that supplies New York City's drinking water. Over 6 million people drink that water from the largest unfiltered water system in the world.

City officials held meetings with one thousand people attending, and the state would not send one person from state government, despite repeated requests and demands. City officials called a press conference, and not one reporter came. Big gas was sending a message; gas companies have the power and will do whatever they choose.

> **There will come a time when the water will not be fit to drink from the streams. This will signify the beginning of the period of Great Purification, when the people will go through immense trials to purify themselves of the corrupt influences that have beset them. It will be a time of joy for those who understand, but one of great suffering for those who cling to their worldview and lifestyles.**
> Onondaga Indian Prophecy

ENVIRONMENTAL PROTECTION AGENCY RENDERED USELESS

The Environmental Protection Agency (EPA) was created in 1970 and is responsible for working with state and local governments to set standards that help control and prevent pollution and minimize the potential health effects of solid and hazardous waste and toxic and radioactive substances. The EPA was told by the Bush White House, "Don't investigate. Expedite things for business." Decision-making groups were loaded with big business members, so they always had the majority vote. Weston Wilson, a twenty-year employee of the EPA, stated that the Bush administration instructed the EPA not to investigate citizen's complaints. Wilson wrote a letter to Congress to protest what had been done to the EPA, but it did no good. He ran into a "Brick Wall."

It seems the more desperate we get to scrape, drill, blast, or frack for oil, coal, and gas, the more problems we create. After all that trouble to get the gas, and all the misery created for the people, the gas still has to be burned. Burn = CO_2 = global warming and disaster for Lilly.

> **Fearful as reality is, it is less fearful than evasion of reality.**
> Carlton Thomas

CHAPTER 9

NUCLEAR ENERGY

> **Nuclear fission could solve all our energy problems, but could also fry us in our tracks."**
> Alfred Crosby, author of *Children of the Sun*

Crosby was stating what many people believe. Nuclear fission splits the heavy unstable nucleus of an atom in a radioactive material, like uranium, into two daughter nuclei, releasing neutrons and a large amount of energy. One pound of uranium produces as much heat as 2.5 million pounds of coal.

I want to clarify a common misconception. Hydrogen fusion is a completely different process that also involves nuclei of atoms, and "fuses" the nuclei of atoms of hydrogen, deuterium, or tritium together in an extremely controlled method, producing helium and an enormous amount of energy. One gram of hydrogen converted to helium releases eight times the energy of one gram of uranium. Fusion is the process that creates the energy on our sun. There's enough deuterium in one gallon of seawater to make as much energy as three hundred gallons of gasoline. With both hydrogen and deuterium, there is no radioactivity and no possibility of a meltdown. We haven't been able to release this energy yet and the procedure involves temperatures of one million to one billion degrees Fahrenheit. We don't have the technology for the constant nanosecond precision required for this process. The research is very costly and hydrogen fusion is not a solution for today's energy needs.

Do not confuse this, as I had, with hydrogen fuel cells like those used for buses. Fuel cells convert water to hydrogen and water and produce enough electricity to run a vehicle.

> **No matter what else happens, this is the century in which we must learn to live without fossil fuel.**
> David Goodstein, physicist (2004)

KEEPING A PROMISE TO LILLY

If I had a magic wand, our Earth would have all the solar and wind energy generated that everyone needs. There is no wand, and the fact that nuclear energy doesn't emit greenhouse gases carries some weight. I don't favor nuclear energy use to produce electricity, but concessions may have to be made. So much of the greenhouse gas emissions can be stopped by people conserving (use those negawatts), developing and using more efficient technology, and making products that last (vs. single-use), but we are still left with a tremendous need for energy. The immediate threat remains that "overcoat" of greenhouse gases smothering Mother Earth. Therefore, I'm considering nuclear energy.

> **Those who cannot change their minds cannot change anything.**
> George Bernard Shaw

WHERE IS NUCLEAR ENERGY WORKING WELL? WILL IT CONTINUE WORKING WELL?

Vermont gets 74% of its energy from nuclear power; it has the lowest carbon footprint of any state, and it has the lowest electrical costs in New England. This is not problem-free; droughts caused reactors to be shut down four times in Vermont.

France gets 80% of its power from nuclear reactors. During France's terrible 2003 heat wave that killed tens of thousands, rivers were so warm that nuclear plants generating four thousand megawatts of power were shut down to prevent possible melt downs. Loss of power contributed to the death toll.

Prolonged heat waves, as global warming heats up, will limit the places where reactors can remain. It has to do with the temperature of the water used for cooling. The cooling water never mingles with radioactive material or water from the plant, but it has to be cold enough to bring the super-heated reactor temperature down.

In August 2012, Long Island Sound was so warm that a Connecticut nuclear reactor had to be shut down. On July 12, 2012, four giant reactors in Pennsylvania, Maryland, South Carolina, and New York were shut down during a heat wave. Michigan had the same problem. One-third of the nuclear power of the Tennessee Valley Authority was halted when the temperature of the Tennessee River was too high. This situation has repeated numerous times in France, Germany, and Spain. In 2009, Germany had to shut down eight nuclear reactors simultaneously.

Could such a thing trip our electrical grid and cause the mother of all rolling black-outs? Our infamous Northeast rolling black-out in 2003 got out of hand. A sagging power line touched a tree branch long enough to cause a short circuit. This over-taxed our grid, which was already burdened by normal demand. When one hundred linked power plants were affected, the grid turned the power off to a large portion of the Northeast. Some power was restored quickly, and all was on within a day or two. Millions of Americans got a taste of life without electricity. Even the water coming to the faucets and for flushing requires power at the water plants. What would our grid do if 10% or 20% of the power feeding the grid had to be shut down?

The United States gets 20% of its electricity from nuclear power plants. We have sixty-five commercial nuclear plants with 104 nuclear reactors in thirty-one states. Worldwide, there are more than four hundred plants, and they provide 15% of the Earth's electricity needs. China has at least 170 nuclear plants under construction or development, and some are very large. In 2013, India had eighteen with sixty on order.

Most countries with a fossil fuel supply have few or no nuclear reactors. Crosby had a clever way of explaining why some countries turn to nuclear energy. He said, "No oil, No Coal, No Choice." I wonder how safe plants are in poor countries that have "no choice."

Hot Water or Low Water Could Leave Us Sizzling

During many heat waves, reactors remained running when the temperatures of the cooling waters were above the safety limits. Permission was granted to exceed the design standards. Many countries around the world have experienced droughts or falling water tables due to excess irrigation. Nuclear power plants in the United States are well-regulated; that may not be the case in other parts of the world.

Bulgaria operated four nuclear reactors that were in dangerous condition. The country was asked to shut them down, but it refused. Finally, in 2002 and 2006, the four reactors were shut down as a requirement if Bulgaria wanted to join the European Union. If the United States and the world embrace nuclear power, what sort of construction and safety features will the poorer countries build into their plants? Safety features doubled and tripled the cost of nuclear plants in the United States, and increased construction time from a few years to ten or more. How are such projects financed in poor countries unless the cost is less and completion time is shortened so income can start? Bulgaria's decrepit plant did not melt down, but Chernobyl's did.

Things That Go Bump in the Night

In 1986, the worst meltdown in history occurred at Chernobyl, Russia. Everything that could go wrong, did. The plant was poorly designed, with safety containment barriers omitted; workers lacked training, and there was so much secrecy about anything nuclear that even nuclear plants didn't share information about problems. When the top blew off one facility, the radioactivity spread across the land and into other countries.

Japan's Fukushima nuclear plant disaster was the result of an earthquake in 2011, followed by a tsunami. The reactor was compromised, overheated, there was a meltdown, and the explosion released radioactive gases. A year later, a Japanese government report stated the meltdown was due to human error, because workers failed to respond to the danger and avert the meltdown. Environmentalists consider these events a wake-up call.

URANIUM HAS TWO BOOMS

Uranium can be used to build bombs or provide power. Early use was solely for bombs, and it can still be used for that today. There's an uneasiness about having uranium in the hands of all the countries that want to generate nuclear energy. Who will say "yes," these countries can have uranium, but "no" to North Korea, Iran, or any country deemed menacing? If we do say yes, what will relations with those countries be in twenty or forty years?

Heat waves in the last few years are less severe than the ones we can expect with increased global warming. Will countries follow safety procedures when cooling-water is over heated or the volume is too low for safe operation? The consequences of unsafe practices are meltdowns. Are nuclear power plants a security risk if terrorists target them? Because of our safety standards, terrorists could neither get into a U.S. nuclear reactor to blow it up, nor could they steal the uranium. What safety standards will be in nuclear reactors in other countries?

> **Nuclear power is too expensive and too dangerous. Wasting billions on more nuclear reactors would distract from the real task of developing renewables and reducing energy demands. Nuclear power is the ultimate unsustainable form of energy—for a little energy now, we would be condemning 10,000 generations to deal with the radioactive waste we would produce.**
> Andrew Lee (World Wildlife Federation, UK, 2006)

WHERE SHOULD WE INVEST OUR ENERGY DOLLARS?

I don't want money spent to build horrendously expensive nuclear power plants and be locked into that technology. A 1,600-megawatt nuclear reactor costs over 10 billion dollars to build and takes more than ten years to complete, before power is generated and money is coming in. Lending institutions are not interested in funding such projects. Nuclear power plants last forty years, at best. It costs as much to decommission each plant as it does to build it. Would taxpayers foot the bill? When the plant is decommissioned, everything is radioactive material, even the ground where the plant was built. Where do we put radioactive waste? Landfills emitting methane proved to be environmental disasters. Rather than safely making our discards go away, landfills are a leading contributor to global warming. The thought of burying material that will be radioactive for ten thousand years in salt domes or under the sea sounds ludicrous. What will they emit, how will we know if there was a leak, and who could we trust to inform and protect us? Can we learn to think and act differently before building nuclear power plants?

GRANDMA MEISTER'S HAPPY NEGAWATT HOME

I lovingly remember my two-week visits to my Grandma Meister during summer vacations in the late forties and fifties. I can still visualize walking through her home. We used one or two lights at a time, when needed. We had one radio or TV on for the brief time we used them. There was a small refrigerator, a hot water heater, a water pump, and a large freezer–that was it. Those weeks each summer were the happiest of my childhood. We lived simply. We didn't feel poor or deprived; we were happy,

Americans use ten times more electricity now than in 1956, and miss the joy of spending time together, talking with each other, doing things together, and building loving relationships. Kids today have more of an attachment to their electronic gadgets than to people. If mom and dad are out of town for a week, that is inconvenient. If the kids have no electronics for a week, there could be a meltdown.

According to a United Nations' study, the average per capita consumption of electricity in the year 2003 was:

United States	14,057 kilowatts
Japan	8,701 kilowatts
Equatorial Guinea	5 kilowatts
Cambodia	9 kilowatts

What did we plug in that caused our electrical consumption in 1956, to multiply five times over by 1990? What have we done since to reach ten times our 1956 consumption, and when does this over-consumption climb end?

Before we dot the Earth with nuclear reactors and radiation dumps, we need to use more negawatts. How close could you come to running your home in the "Grandma Meister" style? It was not Grandma's nature to leave anything electrical on when she finished using it. We turned on "the lamp" as opposed to "the lights," and in one room, as opposed to the whole house. Evenings were peaceful; we might watch one or two good programs, read, talk, play a game, and go to bed at a healthy bedtime. I recaptured some of the simplicity of that life while on Roatan. Wouldn't it be nice to relax? Visit Grandma Meister if you want to relax and enjoy someone's company—without interruption. It is unnecessary to use so much electricity that we are doomed to adding more and more power plants.

MORE PROS AND CONS

Power to Save the World: The Truth about Nuclear Energy (Cravens 2007) is pro-nuclear power. She did an indepth investigation, thinking she opposed nuclear energy. In the end, she thinks it can save the world. Other authors also backed her claims of nuclear power plants being safe. Cravens states, "We get far more radiation from everyday sources than from being near nuclear plants. American nuclear plants being built now are melt-down proof and terrorist proof."

Three Mile Island was not a meltdown, no one died, in twenty-five years the mortality rate in the area never went up, and the radiation exposure within five miles of the plant at the time of the problem was equal to one chest x-ray. Cravens also points out that not one American has died as the result of a nuclear accident, but that coal has a tragic death rate. We are used to mining deaths and accept it as normal. Cravens claims coal mining accidents have claimed the lives of one hundred thousand miners, 4 million more have been injured, and in 1969 fifty thousand miners had black lung disease.

The cons against nuclear power are substantial. It would take one thousand additional nuclear reactors to put a dent in the CO_2 emissions in an amount that would slow global warming. Each plant requires so much cement for construction that the cement production will raise the CO_2 level in the atmosphere and add to the problem.

When will uranium run out, and how expensive will it become as the supply dwindles and worldwide demand increases? If the uranium supply ends abruptly, perhaps because the amount of uranium remaining was not disclosed and many plants were built based on faulty information, could we quickly convert to a good alternative energy? Why go down another wrong road and lock ourselves into that technology for forty years, when our efforts could be directed to wind and solar?

> **Doing what's right is not the problem; the problem is knowing what's right.**
> Lyndon B. Johnson

CHAPTER 10

AMERICA, WE'VE BEEN "BIO-FOOLED"

Fuel + Burn = CO_2 = global warming means we should not use bio-fuel for long, but in my naïve brain I thought they were a better option than the fossil fuels. I was in for a surprise. A new concern for Lilly's future surfaced, and a present crisis for millions of children's survival emerged to stare me in the face.

WHAT I FOUND IS SICKENING

We use corn to make ethanol for our gas tanks; thus, one billion people who need grain to survive receive less. Two and one-half billion people live on less than two dollars a day, and 800 million exist at the very lowest level of Maslow Hierarchy of Needs, where they struggle daily to have enough food to stay alive. I want to be a person who reaches out to help instead of taking the last bite of food. Most of us have no idea what we are doing when we use ethanol. The industrialized world created global warming, but our poorest brothers are suffering the deadliest consequences. Scoundrels exploited the oil crisis to turn a profit, knowing that using corn to make ethanol costs millions of innocent lives. They pitched their venture to sound noble and good for the planet. We bought their story.

America is the world's largest corn producer and exporter. On the surface, the use of corn to decrease our dependence on oil seems like an ideal solution. Agribusiness leaders like Archer Daniels Midland (ADM) and Cargill pushed for this since the 1970s. They donate millions to political campaigns and get billions in subsidies as returns on their Washington investments. Ethanol production started small but has grown and worsened a world crisis. In 2007, ADM nearly doubled their capital spending to $1.12 billion to increase their bioenergy projects. In 2011 they had 270 plants worldwide with a net income of $2.036 billion.

Cargill is the largest privately owned U.S. corporation, based on revenue. The Cargill family owns 90% of the company and in 2011 had a net income of $4.24 billion. It has 140,000 employees in sixty-six countries, is responsible for 25% of U.S. grain exports, supplies 22% of U.S. domestic meat, is the largest poultry producer in Thailand, and all eggs used by McDonald's in the U.S. come from Cargill's plants. They produce biodiesel in the poorest countries in the world, and the profit is not going to the locals—it is destroying the locals.

In 2007 statistics show eighteen thousand children were dying of starvation and related diseases every day. Eight hundred and fifty million people in thirty-four countries, do not have enough to eat. Their incomes are so low they can no longer afford to buy food, even if it were available. Many who raised their food in the past had their land taken from them by big agribusinesses.

The United Nations World Food Bank has funds to feed only 90 million people. As the price of grain goes higher, the U.N. gets less grain for their money. Soybean and wheat prices also increased, because more profitable corn crops lead farmers to switch to growing corn.

The United States and the United Nations have issued an advisory warning of the continuing rise in food prices and the world hunger crisis this is producing. The primary cause of this crisis is the use of agro fuels. American agribusinesses are increasing global warming, while capitalizing at the expense of mankind's poorest.

Quick! Jump Out of the Frying Pan—Ouch!

When America embraced the ethanol solution, we launched headlong into production. Congressional bills passed, subsidies were given, and ethanol went into our gas. In 2005 only 10% of U.S. corn was used to make fuel. By 2007 more distilleries had been built, and 25% of the crop went into our tanks. Grain prices skyrocketed. In 2012 ethanol used 40% of U.S. corn, 40% went to feed cattle, and 20% was for food and the many products, especially beverages containing corn sweetener. As an incentive to grow and sell more corn for fuel, Congress granted a $6 billion a year subsidy to reduce the cost of ethanol by 45-cents a gallon and imposed a tariff of 54-cents a gallon on imports.

The only ethanol with a measurable benefit to the environment is made from sugar cane and comes from Brazil. Fuel from sugar cane provides more than eight times the energy it takes to produce; however, the rainforests are burned to plant sugar cane plantations.

U.S. ethanol made from corn takes nearly as much, if not more, energy to grow, fertilize, harvest, distill, and distribute as the energy it provides. CO_2 emissions are a mere 20% less. It provides 33% less power than gas, so we get fewer miles per gallon. Many people knew this when they made the big push to sell the idea to the U.S. government and the American people. The business's profit is the 45-cents-a-gallon subsidy the taxpayers hand them. Money beckoned; ethics be damned.

With the subsidies in place and corn production boosted, in 2011 the U.S. produced so much we exported 397 million gallons overseas. Yes, we exported a subsidized oil replacement, while importing costly foreign oil. Did taxpayers pay the 45-cents a gallon subsidy on every one of the 397 million gallons exported?

> **The ethanol programs encouraging America to use corn for fuel is**
> **an example of government policy run amok.**
> Steven Rattan, political advisor

This isn't giving us energy independence; it is making Cargill,

ADM, and others richer while more people starve. We pay higher food prices for everything grain-related, and we get fewer miles to the gallon, because ethanol is in all our gas.

THEY SAID IT WAS A SILVER BULLET, BUT THEY USED IT TO SHOOT US IN THE FOOT!

A 2007 energy bill mandates the U.S. to produce 36 billion gallons of ethanol a year by 2030, up 300% from our current 12 billion gallons. This is a recipe for disaster. Farmers have stopped rotating the corn and soybean crops every other year, which used to replenish the soil. Corn is a very nutrient depleting crop. Soybeans are now planted every third or fourth year. Staggering amounts of fertilizer and pesticides are used to make up for the nutrients not replenished by crop rotation. These chemicals are not a natural part of the soil. When chemicals are sprayed on crops, they run off, contaminate the water supply, get into streams and rivers, and travel downstream. This pollutes the Mississippi, and there is a 7,900 square-mile dead zone in the Gulf of Mexico the size of Delaware and Connecticut.

The U.S. Government Survey reported 90% of our streams and rivers have reduced water flow, degrading the ecosystem and resulting in a loss of native species. The report listed "nutrient pollution" as one of the top three causes of degradation of U.S. streams and rivers. The widespread concentrations of nitrogen and phosphorus remain two to ten times greater than the levels recommended by the EPA to protect aquatic life.

If you live in a corn producing area, the symptoms to watch for if you have fertilizer nitrates in your drinking water are spontaneous miscarriages, birth defects, and ovarian, uterine, and bladder cancer. Forty percent of the fertilizer in the U.S. is used to grow corn.

Fertilizers contain nitrogen and phosphate, which promote the oxygen-depleting algae blooms that kill fish. To produce three times as much ethanol by 2030 will require more fertilizer and pesticides, impacting our fishing industry and food and water supply. In 2007, The Ecological Society of America called the pollution and dead zones "the most widespread water quality problem in the United States and many other countries." Is fracking on their radar yet? We could have a race to see which will do the most damage to the world's water supply the fastest.

The 40% of our corn we converted to fuel in 2012 could have fed 412 million people. When the U.S. incrementally reaches the 2030 mandate, we will have tripled this year's amount and will be converting the corn to fuel that could feed 1.236 billion people. An increase from 12 to 36 billion gallons of ethanol or from 40% to 120% of the amount of corn produced today will hurt billions of people, while businesses get away with murder. Taxpayers subsidize this insanity. In 1995, ADM was called the most prominent recipient of corporate welfare in recent American history.

There are things in life we all could do but never would because our behavior could harm others. We make good and moral decisions every day. It's appalling how big businesses suspend doing what is right for profit.

WE ARE OUR BROTHERS' KEEPERS AND OUR BROTHERS ARE DYING

The options for keeping the population from climbing to more than 9 or 10 billion by 2050 are having either a lower fertility rate or an increased mortality rate. The American ethanol plan starves millions of people. If we use our land and crops to fuel cars instead of feed people who cannot get food elsewhere, what have we done? If an SUV had its tank filled with 100% ethanol, that uses the same amount of corn it takes to feed one person for a year.

If 100% of our corn crop were used to make ethanol, it would only replace 12% of the gasoline Americans consume. Think about that—no corn to give us burgers, steaks, pork chops, chicken nuggets, cheese, or ice cream. Does that get people's attention? It might, even if a billion people starving has not. Big business does not want this murderous consequence known; that information would not be good for business. We might conserve energy and cut into profits.

Americans can easily reduce their gas consumption by more than 12%. Our car cut ours by 67%. Similarly, our daughter went from her minivan (18mpg) to a Ford Fiesta Fuel Saver (40 mpg), cutting her consumption by 45%. Plan right now, how your family can drive or consume 12% less. This is doable.

For the first time, China, in 2012, couldn't grow enough corn to feed all of its people. China will buy a few billion tons of corn from the United States. China holds bonds on trillions of the U.S. national debt, and if they want to buy corn from us, they buy corn from us. Their needs will increase in years to come. Global warming will cause more rapid desertification, greater water shortages, and the rising sea level in China, India, Viet Nam, and many more countries in Southeast Asia will flood delta-croplands.

Disruption of the normal ocean and air currents is a consequence of global warming. I don't know if America's horrible drought affecting thirty states in the summer of 2012 was caused by global warming. The Weather Channel explained the drought was the result of the jet stream not dipping south toward the Gulf of Mexico to pick up moisture. We saw what a growing season without the normal air currents could mean.

Americans' wallets suffered. Corn futures went up 60% on the Chicago Exchange, with similar climbs in the price of wheat and soy. We see higher food prices and sub-Saharan Africa sees more children die.

Here Come the Godfathers With Offers You Can't Refuse

Agribusinesses such as Cargill and ADM are going worldwide with their biofuel production. When they go into a poor country with weak and/or corrupt leaders and no laws to protect the people, they have a field day. Once they are operating outside the United States, one might ask, "What goes on behind closed doors?" As far as Cargill, ADM, and their friends that do their dirty work are concerned, if exploitation, robbery, slavery, and worse are not against the law or laws aren't enforced, they can be used to further their business, growth, and profits. To allow others to do dastardly things on your behalf does not leave your hands clean.

There are two kinds of biofuels. Ethanol is made from plants that have sugar or starch (corn, sugar cane, or sugar beets). Bio-diesel is made from oils or fats such as, palm oil, soybeans, or rapeseed oil (which we call canola oil).

Sugar cane and soybeans grow in the tropics. Rainforests or other forested lands are burned, sending huge quantities of greenhouse gases into the atmosphere. Human rights are ignored, and the working conditions can be worse than slavery.

A United Nations' study estimates that 5 million indigenous people were displaced in Indonesia to increase palm oil plantations. Columbia's poorest people are suffering the same fate on top of ten years of civil war. Columbia now ranks second, behind Sudan, for displaced people. Landowners had their property taken illegally by the plantations without anyone speaking to them. Columbian authorities plan to double the palm oil production. Greedy American companies pay corrupt officials, and millions of people are pushed off their land.

Cargill's unchecked profiteering is for palm oil in Indonesia, Papua New Guinea, Africa, and South America. Cargill wants Americans to believe they are interested in helping the planet. Brune wrote that the worst assault on the planet from agribusiness is in Indonesia, where the peat forests are drained and burned to plant more palm plantations. The fires emit up to thirty-three tons of CO_2 for every ton of palm oil harvested. We thought we were protecting the planet with bio-fuels, but agro-fuel businesses have been destroying one of Earth's best tools to protect the planet. Palm oil production is one of the fastest growing industries in the poorest and most exploited tropical areas. The burning forests can be seen from outer space. ADM destroys tropical rainforests in Malaysia to put in these plantations.

The land is often taken from the indigenous people by what I would call "The Godfather Method"…an offer they cannot refuse. Brune describes some of the ways people's land is taken. One man refused to sell his land, he was stabbed seven times, his neck slit ear to ear, and his throat was pulled out. The family immediately fled. Plant the palm trees! Another man went to his field one morning and found all his crops had been cleared. He had no way to support his family and moved to a city. Plant the palm trees! Another strategy is to tell the man to negotiate with them or they will negotiate with his widow. Plant the palm trees!

The orangutan population in Malaysia is reduced by 98%, deliberately. Plantation owners pay twenty dollars for the orangutan's right hand, because the animal's diet includes young palm trees or sprouts. ADM isn't just in Malaysia; they're world-wide.

> **Agrofuel is a crime against humanity and I believe there should be a moratorium put in place until there is some way to eradicate the many problems it creates.**
> Jean Ziegler, United Nations reporter

The Cerrado, South America's forested savannah in parts of Brazil, Paraguay, and Bolivia, is being cleared at the same rate as the rainforest to plant soy plantations. Cargill and ADM like such areas. Some protections are now in place in the Brazilian rainforest, but not in the Cerrado. A representative of the indigenous people said, "Agribusiness is having a party, but not inviting the rest of us." ADM declined to sign an anti-slavery pact to prevent forced labor in Brazil. Brune said ADM was asked how many more meetings they would have to attend before they decided slavery was bad. ADM signed the pact a month later, under pressure. However, there is little enforcement; bribery is a part of doing business and included in the payroll.

The bio-diesel fuel production is plagued with infractions against millions of indigenous people, horrible destruction and burning of tropical forests, and the destruction of the habitat for orangutans, Sumatran tigers, the Asian elephants, and other species. When the burning of the forest is considered, palm oil puts ten times more CO_2 into the air than burning oil. Additionally, the soil in the rainforests has a bacteria in it that, when disturbed, releases nitrous oxide for two years. That greenhouse gas is three hundred times as damaging as CO_2 and lasts one hundred years.

There is a heart-breaking tragedy beyond our comprehension when indigenous people have their land destroyed. They believe to the depths of their souls that they are here on Earth to care for the Earth and that their god has entrusted them to pass on a well-loved Earth to their children. If we had that awareness, our children would have a safe future.

> **God gives His instructions to every creature, according to His plan for the world. He gave His instructions to all things of nature…**
> **Our instructions are very simple–**
> **To respect the Earth and each other.**
> **To respect life itself.**
> **That's our first commandment, the first line of our gospel.**
> Mathew King, Lakota Elder

Germany produces 50% of the world's bio-diesel that is from rapeseed oil, without violating human rights or destroying tropical forests. The European Union is developing standards that will not allow importing of agro-fuels that do not reduce greenhouse gases and do not protect ecosystems. According to Brune, U.S. policy is, "Just grow more as fast as possible."

America needs to know what disasters we put in play by turning to bio-fuels. Instead of using food for fuel, destroying our environment, and starving and displacing millions, we need to use less fuel. We need to build and use mass transit. Plug-in hybrids and electric vehicles are a big part of our solution, and they need to be plugged into a green grid. Contact your congressional representatives, senators, and the president.

Burning biomass, such as garbage, wood, wood pellets, or agricultural-waste, still adds to global warming. They may replace coal plants but might also produce as much or more CO_2. New Hampshire converted a coal plant to a fifty-megawatt plant that burns wood chips. Some plants in Hawaii burn wood waste. Check outside: Is there sunshine or wind in the area that wouldn't have to be burned?

You may have heard about using switch grass to make ethanol and solve our energy problem. It can grow almost anywhere, is fast growing, and doesn't require irrigation. The problem is, no process for converting cellulose to fuel has been discovered. It's like our digestive systems; our bodies can digest and use oil, starch, and sugar, but cellulose doesn't break down to convert to energy. If you hoped this would solve our problems, it won't and it would still be burned.

Now I want solar and wind power more than ever!

CHAPTER 11

NON-POLLUTING RENEWABLES

Are you ready for some good news? I feel as if I just crawled across a desert having to write all that garbage, but that garbage is what we must face. My thinking has changed dramatically. Spending a month on Roatan and remembering visits with Grandma Meister during my childhood summers helped open me to change. I think my sister's unexpected death in 2011 also made me realize that if there is something I can and want to do, I'd better get on with it.

I'm willing to examine deeper the idea of my "cluelessness." Alfred Crosby, in *Children of the Sun*, makes perfect sense to me, and I hope that after reading For Lilly this far, you can grasp his point. Read it three times; let it sink in. Crosby says,

> **"We of the richer societies, who have had access to more energy than we have the experience to wield intelligently are making decisions we are not qualified to make almost every time we enter the voting booth, go to the grocery store or step into a car show room. We do not know what is 'normal.' Because our whole life and in some respects a generation or two before us have only known this era of fossil fuel exploitation and resource grabbing; we call this normal."**

The last one hundred years have been an anomaly. The fossil fuels were discovered, developed, used, caused untold damage, will run out, and their use must be stopped before the consequences of releasing the CO_2 back into the atmosphere destroys the planet. This one-hundred-year ride brought many changes, good and bad. Now man must make some informed and intelligent decisions. We blindly went on this wild ride and believed it was normal. We have never known any other way, don't want to see another way, and at first, might think we couldn't manage any other way. We are like the rich children after dad invested all his money with Bernie Madoff. The ride we were on is over, life goes on, life is good—but different. The way we went through the Earth's resources was our "Madoff." The fossil fuels probably never should have been spent, at least not the way we let them go up in smoke.

In 2014 we need to become qualified to make better decisions when we vote, about what we eat, and how we feed our family of 7,000,000,000 plus people. We must use sustainable energy to live and prosper; we need to stop piling more overcoats on Mother Earth; and we need to reverse as much of the damage already done as possible. We need to understand the laws of nature and the limits of nature. We're no longer the rich and indulged children of wealth. Today, we must take a true account of our assets, liabilities, options, obligations, and desires, in order to formulate lives that truly can carry our children and us safely and happily into the future. Today we must come out of our cocoons. Welcome to the real world—welcome home.

WELCOME TO THE REAL WORLD—WELCOME HOME

The sun is shining and the breeze is blowing here in beautiful Naples, Florida. This sunshine and breeze isn't just lovely, it's an endless supply of energy for everyone on every continent. It was always there waiting for us. We were sidetracked for a few generations. Now, we turn to the sun and the wind for our energy, and there will be no damage done to our atmosphere miles above us or to the air we breathe in and out eighteen times a minute for as long as we live. I can hardly wait to see the good that will come of this. We might be able to pack away the children's nebulizers, return grandpa's oxygen tanks that he needed on bad-air days, and our allergy prescriptions can safely be sent for disposal with other toxic chemicals.

Figuring out how the economy adjusts to the shift from fossil fuel is beyond me. I hope the people who were exploited by big business can lease their land for wind farms, let their health repair as much as possible, and, for once, be the ones getting profits. The people in the Appalachians can tell their kids how the miners used to die of black lung disease, but then tell them they'll never get the disease that killed so many generations of their friends and relatives.

> **We are like tenant farmers chopping down the fence around our house for fuel when we should be using Nature's inexhaustible sources of energy sun–wind or tide.**
> Thomas Edison

I don't know how long it will take to convert to renewables, but the resources for our electricity surround us, in abundance and are endless. Not once will we have to exploit a fellow human to get our sun and wind. The U.S. National Academy of Sciences reports a wind-generating potential on land that is forty times the current world consumption of electricity from all sources. Michael Brune and Lester Brown claim forty minutes or one hour of sun shining on the Earth has enough energy to power the world with electricity for a year. Either figure sounds great.

> **If Not Now–When?**
> Zen saying

I read a remark by Eric Schmidt, the CEO of Google, and felt relief. He called for the replacement of all fossil fuels with renewable sources of energy in twenty years. That's the thinking we need. In the book

Greasy Rider, the authors told of their visit to the Google complex. The organization is green in nearly every possible way, and the employees are treated wonderfully. Imagine an employer that allows you time at work to play, tend to some of your personal business, sends in a masseuse, and gives you fine dining on the job. Going green didn't sound like a hardship at Google. They have their own solar panels for power, and they grow their own organic food the chefs use to prepare healthy gourmet meals for their employees. Shuttles bring employees to and from work, and the company provides electric-powered cars if employees need to go off-campus for an appointment. Google composts, recycles, and uses carpeting that can be refurbished rather than replaced. The place is a study in how we can live at our best, and it's good for business. Schmidt and other entrepreneurs go for it, and if you become the richest people on Earth from developing green technologies, I couldn't be happier!

WIND–WIND–WIND

The world uses 5,000 gigawatts of electricity per hour and will use 8,000 by 2020. Many countries will have the power turned on in people's homes for the first time. Those 5,000+ gigawatts are what we must produce without damaging the planet, and it can be done. The measurement of electrical production and use is PER HOUR.

Lester Brown, my expert, considers wind to be the centerpiece of our energy solution. The technology is already on the market for an advanced wind turbine that gets more energy from one turbine than from an aging oil well. Brown gives an example of how affordable the wind energy could be by describing the cost to run an electric vehicle using wind-generated electricity and charged during off-peak hours. It would be like buying gas for less than $1 a gallon. In that one example, Brown used a clean and unending fuel source, charged it at a time when power companies would have a surplus of energy, and he puts it in a car that doesn't pollute the atmosphere. I hope to have a similar arrangement in my life within a very few years.

"Off-peak" power is often wasted by the utility company when energy use is low. Power plants have to generate enough electricity to meet the demand when the requirements are greatest. They can neither gear up nor gear down as needs change hour to hour, nor can they store the excess during off-peak hours. Researchers are working to develop a battery or other device to store the extra electricity, but for now, extra power is wasted. A few hydroelectric plants use the extra power to pump water from below the dam, back up into the reservoir in the middle of the night. We can cut overall energy needs by running the washer and dishwasher during off-peak hours. High-peak hours are 1pm to 5 pm, low-peak is 10 a.m. to 1 p.m. and 5 p.m. to 8 p.m.. The off-peak hours are 8 p.m. to 10 a.m. This is something we can do to reduce energy requirements. It may not lower your electric bill, but remember that our new priority is to reduce global warming.

> **I long to accomplish a great and noble task, but it is my chief duty to accomplish small tasks as if they were great and noble.**
> Helen Keller

In mid-August 2012, the United States marked a milestone. We are producing 50 gigawatts of wind power and lead all other countries in the world for generation of wind energy. That energy output is equal to forty-four coal plants or eleven nuclear power plants and provides enough electricity for 14 million homes in the U.S. It saves as much CO_2 from going into the atmosphere as taking 14 million cars off the road, and it uses no water to generate the electricity. America's gigawatt output from wind has doubled in the last four years and added 75,000 jobs, of which 30,000 are long term and high paying. That's also $15 billion dollars invested here in America, rather than paid out for foreign oil. Our progress in adding more energy from wind is threatened by pressure from big business.

Senator Harry Reid is a longtime supporter of wind energy. He condemned Congress for continuing to subsidize the rich oil companies and refusing to extend the Production Tax Credit (PTC) that has helped stimulate this surge in wind-power production. The tax credit is repeatedly at risk of losing funding. The fossil-fuel industry lobbies to prevent anything that would help America switch from burning fossil fuels. Because of the possible loss of the tax credit, wind companies let workers go, and the industries change to manufacture other products.

The old fossil folks rush to get the coal and natural gas power plants up and running as fast as possible, locking us into using their fuels longer. The power players also invest millions for lobbyists to get their people into public office, on committees, and into agencies that make our energy decisions. If enough big business members are appointed to a committee, the majority vote will always be in favor of big business. Cheney's energy task force was such a group.

These are old figures, but I think you will get the picture. In 2006, while energy companies were earning historic profits, oil companies received $39 billion in subsidies, $8 billion went to coal, and $2 billion went to efforts to encourage conservation. I don't think the people making the decisions wanted conservation. America could easily conserve enough energy to shut down all of our oldest and most polluting coal plants this year.

California spent $2 billion on an energy efficiency program and was able to close their dirtiest power plants. They saved 2.5 gigawatts of power and cut energy costs to customers by $5 billion. Imagine if the United States government were to be equally as interested in conservation of energy. Why wouldn't the federal government want such results? There's no way to be really sure why Washington would spend so little for conservation, but oil companies invested $574 million for lobbyist and political contributions between 1998 and 2007. This may seem like a lot at first, but when you consider that oil received $39 billion in subsidies in 2006, you see they received good returns on their investments. If Washington planned to slow global warming, we would have a large portion of subsidies going for conservation, and for wind, solar, and geo-thermal development.

When land is leased for a wind turbine, everyone wins. The landowners can still raise a crop, graze their cattle, and receive royalties of $3,000 to $10,000 for each wind turbine. The landowner doesn't have to put out any money, none of his water is used, and there is no pollution.

Other countries are turning to wind power. China is working feverishly to generate wind energy. As of 2011, China only had 26 gigawatts of wind power, but has a new "Wind Based" program that is creating seven wind mega-complexes totaling more than 130 gigawatts of power. The new "Wind Based" program is the equivalent of a new coal plant every week for two and one-half years. China's prosperity and the sheer number of people and industries clamoring for more power means all avenues are pursued. Sadly, the building of coal power plants continues.

Europe is aggressively turning to wind power. Developers are planning 140 gigawatts of off-shore wind generation, primarily in the North Sea. There's enough off-shore wind generating potential to meet Europe's electrical needs seven times over. Scotland has increased its wind projects and plans to get 100% of its electricity from renewables by 2025, mostly from wind. This tells me it is possible for a country to switch to 100% renewables.

Unlike Scotland, America has an abundance of sunshine, so we have two fronts we can work on simultaneously. We have the wind, and it is on land. It's much cheaper to develop wind energy from land area than building turbines in the oceans.

> **The 20th century was the time when the world turned to use of fossil fuels and the 21st century will be the century of the renewables.**
> Lester Brown, Earth Policy Institute

Countries like China, India, and Brazil are scrambling to bring electricity to more than a billion people. They use wind and solar, but too often coal and other CO_2 producing plants are built even faster. If wind and solar energy production were the main sources of America's electrical power, the industry would be geared up and there would be mass production. Prices would be lower, technological innovations would be enhancing the efficiency, and we would have production and delivery of a totally clean energy that would never run out. Stop to think about it. This is more urgent than the mass production the United States had to muster as we entered World War II. This time the entire world is in danger and 7 billion people's lives depend on rapid change. Could the U.S. be the leader that gets the world up to speed on the fight to save our planet? We could make trillions of dollars and create enough jobs to significantly reduce unemployment.

The sooner wind and solar become the main source of energy the better. Billions of people who want electricity are not about to wait. A man in Brazil made that point very well. He said, "We are not going to stay poor because the rest of the world wants to breathe." Electrical power is key to industrial development, and they use whatever fuel and production methods will move them into prosperity for their people. The United States took more than one hundred years to industrialize; countries like China, India, and Brazil are trying to industrialize with billions of people in one generation. That takes energy in amounts we have never known.

Some countries are making wind the centerpiece of their energy future. They will be free of dependence on foreign oil and their electrical supply will not contribute to global warming.

> **The difference between what we do and what we are capable of**
> **doing would suffice to solve most of the world's problems.**
> Mahatma Gandhi

Denmark built the world's largest off-shore wind farm in 2001. They have since built more and larger turbines. The pioneering Danes are exporting the technology, supporting 20,000 jobs, and creating one of the country's largest and most profitable industries. The U.S. population is fifty-six times larger. New long-lasting renewable energy jobs are good for our economy. What are we waiting for— an available work force?

Eighty-three countries use wind power commercially. Countries getting significant amounts of their power from wind are Denmark with 21%, Portugal 18%, Spain 16%, Ireland 14%, and Germany 9%.

WHAT CAN AMERICA DO RIGHT NOW?

Twelve Midwest and Rocky Mountain states have enough available wind to produce 2½ times the electricity the United States uses. The switch to wind energy can be made rapidly and wind energy is low cost.

I'll review what watt, kilowatt (KWH), megawatt (MW), and gigawatt (GW) means. In our homes we use watts (like 29 watts to run a fan one hour). Our light company bills us by the KWHs (which is 1,000 watts). Power plants produce large amounts of electricity and usually tell how many MWs they produce per hour (1,000,000 watts equals one MW). One MW is able to power 300 homes. One GW is one billion watts. China's addition of 2 GW of power from coal every week is frightening. The world is generating about 250 GW from wind power of the 5,000 GW the world is using. The good news is that we have the technology and the wind to supply all our needs. Think what we could do in the U.S. with just half the fossil fuel subsidies.

Some people live in areas where the wind is steady and has enough speed that they can have their own wind turbine on their land. They can remain on the grid, so they also have electricity from the grid when needed.

American homes have become what I would call "obese." Homes need to be built to meet our needs, not our wildest and most extravagant dreams. There are Leadership in Energy and Environmental Design (LEED) certified architects who design homes to be very energy efficient. These homes are properly oriented to the sun, are shaded on the northern side, have the correct window exposure to allow heat in during cooler weather, and often include solar water heat and a wind turbine for power. The expense is part of the mortgage, and the energy savings can be enough to result in a lower mortgage payment than a similar home without the energy saving features. As electrical rates go up, these wind turbines and solar water heaters go beyond paying for themselves; they save money every month. When you build such a home, you have "green-proofed" your biggest investment.

Wind doesn't blow all the time in any location, but with many wind turbines in different locations feeding into the grid, there will be power in the system. In some areas, sunshine is the more abundant resource and is an important part of our energy solution.

SOLAR—YOU ARE MY SUNSHINE

Solar power has been used for many years. Jimmy Carter had solar panels installed on the White House, and Reagan had them removed. New panels that are more efficient capture a higher percentage of the sun's power. The total solar power used around the world is difficult to estimate.

Solar hot water is in more than a million Chinese homes, and more are installed as fast as the product can be manufactured. Additionally, millions of people in many other countries now have solar hot water and solar cooking long before there is electrical service to their communities. It's cheaper to provide the small amount of electrical power for the modest homes in developing countries by installing solar panels than to try to create the infrastructure and large power plants to put in electrical service.

Commercially provided solar power increased 20% a year from 2002 to 2006. There was an 89% increase in 2008. The world's commercial solar energy supply tripled between 2009 and 2011, and it's now the fastest growing energy technology. As of December 2011 the solar generating capacity world-wide was 67,000 MW at peak sunshine. That is only .5% of the world's current energy needs. The growth potential for the solar industry is unlimited. No one is counting my solar oven or all the solar panels and the millions of solar water heaters people use every day.

Solar Use is Spreading

Solar panels are mandatory on all new buildings in Spain and used in more than one hundred countries on rooftops, walls, and in pastures. When a family uses a solar oven, they greatly reduce the amount of wood and other fuels they burn to cook their food, and air is not polluted with smoke. Once all the wood is burned for fuel, land erodes and is often washed or blown away. When the top soil is poor or gone, food supply suffers. Children's lives are saved when solar ovens are given to people and to villages in sub-Saharan Africa.

The United States has seventy-seven commercial photovoltaic or solar thermal power plants working, or under construction and development. This represents 13,200 MW. The photovoltaic panels (PV) are the ones we are accustomed to seeing, and until recently were only used in small operations, in homes, or on the roof of a business. A solar thermal power plant concentrates and focuses the sun's energy on a liquid; steam is generated, and the turbines turn to produce electricity. The newer technologies have panels tracking the sun. Innovations in design and shape capture a greater percentage of the available heat. Once there's a strong competitive market, this will generate many jobs. Solar energy provides four times more jobs than the fossil fuel industry. They are American jobs. A solar plant near a community means local employment, cleaner air, and no fuel cost to operate the plant, plus using solar power slows global warming.

California is putting in many solar plants. Once the cost of the materials and installation is paid, these folks can look forward to a future of affordable energy. Oil embargos will not dim their lights. Germany is the solar leader. They had 10,000 MW of the photovoltaic panels installed and producing power in 2011, which provided 15% of their electrical needs. As of December 2011, China had the largest solar plant, 200 MW. We are just starting to see the larger MW plants developed.

Saudi Arabia has more sun than oil and very little water. To provide drinking water for the country's residents, the country is building thirty new solar-powered desalinization plants. Before the switch to solar, Saudi Arabia was using 1.5 million barrels of oil a day to desalinate its water.

DeSoto County, Florida, built a 25 MW solar plant to power 3,000 homes. Counties and cities building solar power plants to provide their electricity sounds promising. That may be why "brick walls" stand between solar and wind and the billions of dollars in energy subsidies that are doled out every year!

> **Use of solar energy has not been opened up because the oil industry does not own the sun.**
> Ralph Nadar

My Florida Power and Light installed a 75 MW solar plant to feed heat to an existing steam power plant and cut the use of natural gas. Yeah! That also answers one of my questions about how locked into one fuel we would be if we build a coal or natural gas power plant. Maybe, when solar is cheaper and the technology improves, China can convert their coal plants.

Lester Brown says India has the potential to meet most of its future electrical energy needs with solar. Brown favors wind energy in most areas. However, in the case of India, the Great Indian Desert could handle hundreds of large concentrated solar power (CSP) plants to supply most of the electricity. India is a relatively compact country, and loss of electricity during cable transit wouldn't be too great. Within two decades, India will be the most populous nation on Earth. If there were a country to go solar, India would be a good choice. Its land, air, and water are so degraded and polluted, the last thing the country needs is one more layer of smoke and chemicals. Let the sunshine give them energy.

DAM TRUTH—THERE ARE CONSEQUENCES

Perhaps years ago, billions of people ago, before man ravaged our waters in so many ways, dams looked like a good idea. Dams provided America with much of her energy in years gone by. Today, there are too many negative consequences to continue this route. They prevent fish from traveling up stream, fish are caught in the turbines, and sediment builds up behind the dam, decreasing efficiency. Dams prevent the natural cleaning cycles for the waterways, they restrict water flow to areas downstream, and they displace people when land is flooded. Loss of the land destroys habitat and wildlife in the areas. Old dams can become a serious risk for people living downstream, and dams are expensive to remove when they become unsafe. International conflict erupts when a country constructs a huge dam. The lives and economies of the nation or nations downstream are threatened.

The world's biggest dam and hydroelectric plant is China's Three Gorges Dam on the Yangtze River. Of the 1.4 million people who were displaced when the waters rose to form a 410-mile long reservoir, the government says, "Many have failed to rebuild their lives." The reservoir has become the "repository for waste from cities and industries." The sheer weight of the water behind the 600-foot high dam has caused landslides and increased the danger of earthquakes. The government doesn't believe the dam caused the 2008 earthquake that killed at least 87,000 people. Downstream, the water table has changed. Crops are failing, 400,000 people lost their drinking water, and many ports along the Yangtze River can no longer be reached by ocean-going vessels. Many feel the dam is unsafe. If you see a headline reading, "Millions Swept Away in Flood as Dam Bursts," you know the background.

Geothermal Power

There are places in the world where geothermal power is abundant. Iceland gets 90% of its power from the heat of the earth. The "ring of fire" in the eastern Pacific Ocean has the potential to provide many nations with power. The Philippines gets 26% percent of their power from the heat of the earth.

Many places in America have the potential to heat their water and much of their home using geothermal energy. The largest geothermal heating and cooling system in the world is in Ft. Knox, Kentucky. In 2006 they upgraded to geothermal. The system is a tremendous success. The temperature is constant, mold is reduced, and the air is cleaner. Ft. Knox saves 76,700 metric tons of greenhouse gases from going into the atmosphere every year. That includes a savings of 67 metric tons of the dreaded nitrous-oxide gas.

> **Modern civilization is a product of an energy binge.**
> **Binges often end in hangovers.**
> Alfred Crosby

Mary's Alterative to Energy Supply

Before we drill, fracture, mine, build more power plants and refineries, extend pipelines, or use corn to fuel our cars, could we try to conserve energy? We do not need to turn our water into a carcinogenic agent, kill more wildlife, make our land toxic, and our air a choking-asthmatic-respiratory fume. We must not send the CO_2 racing past 500 ppm. Before all that, please join me in my alternative to all of the above. My alternative is to conserve.

If America modestly conserved, in ten years we would save more energy than we would gain by opening up and damaging Alaska's North Slope. I don't want to be just modestly conservative; I want to be boldly conservative. Think of being conservative from a different angle, one that is more motivating than money. What I really care about is how much CO_2 I put into the atmosphere. Can you think how, in your home, you and your family use so much more power than families in other countries? I get it; we do, but how?

Last night I left a ceiling fan on all night in an unoccupied room. A little voice said, "That probably didn't cost more than a few cents." How many times have I thoughtlessly wasted energy because the cost was simply irrelevant to my budget? Then it occurred to me, that fan takes 40 watts per hour. If I left it on for 11 hours, I, for no reason, put 1 pound of CO_2 into Lilly's atmosphere. There are 8,760 hours in a year. Plug in the number of watts some of your conveniences use per hour and multiply the 8,760 hours in the year. If you leave a 40-watt fan on in a room 24/7, you use 350,400 watts or 350.4 KWH, .3504 MW in a year. As an FPL customer, I put about 2,000 pounds of CO_2 into the atmosphere for every MW I use. That one fan could put over 700 pounds of CO_2 into the atmosphere a year.

In Florida, many people feel the need to keep the air circulating in the bedrooms and the family room; some do it in all rooms, just for good measure. The ten cents a day it costs to have one fan run continuously is "not that bad" to many of us. That isn't the real cost, the one that is destroying our planet. I calculated the price the planet pays when you use 100 watts 24/7. That is 1,752 pounds of CO_2 per year going into the atmosphere.

Many of the conveniences we have don't tell how many watts they use, especially when the power switch is turned off. Why should "pennies a day" even matter? The "phantom energy" used by all our appliances and electronics to remain on stand-by keeps tallying. Wally and I invested in some surge protector power bars with off switches, so we aren't leaving everything on stand-by. We have cut our annual energy use by 84% of what it was three years ago and we live in the same house and are both now home all day. Three years ago, I was conservative by most American standards. Conservation makes an enormous difference. Image if we could do that in 50 million homes across America. The steps we took are listed in chapter seventeen. I don't expect everyone will tackle it with the determination we did. However, when you learn what is at stake and you look into the eyes of the little ones in your life, your conservation efforts might be quite remarkable. Oh, if you really love a person: "Honey, DON'T leave the light on for her."

Clean energy from wind and solar will someday power our cars. We can stop using food to fuel our cars and let the hungriest among us eat. Water and air won't be as polluted. We can stop spending our money on foreign oil; conflicts to get the oil can simmer down, and we won't have to build armies to fight for oil. Many of the respiratory problems that plague our citizens, even babies, can be put to rest. I saved the best for last: solar, wind, and geothermal will give Mother Nature a fighting chance to hang in there for my sweet Lilly.

CHAPTER 12

LAND DEVASTATION AND A POPULATION COMPLICATION

> **The very spot where grew the bread that formed my bones, I see.**
> **How strange, old field, on thee to tread, and feel I'm part of thee.**
> Abraham Lincoln

Is to "feel I'm part of thee" a knowing lost generations ago? We treat the land and all its resources as something we can take from, use any way we want, and abandon it in whatever condition we please. Our land is scarred. Coal companies have blown the tops off mountains. Beaches, lakes, ponds, and rivers where I swam and fished as a child have signs posted warning that the waters are hazardous. People with respiratory problems cannot leave their home because of air pollution.

> **I think the environment should be put in the category of our**
> **national security. Defense of our resources is just as important as**
> **defense abroad. Otherwise what is there to defend?**
> Robert Redford

NUTRIENT CYCLE AND TOP SOIL

It took millions of years to create the top soil that fed us for thousands of years. First, wind eroded the rocks and fine grains supported the first minute vegetation. A cycle began with plants protecting the soil from wind and water erosion. Vegetation provided more organic matter to make more fertile soil and grow more plants. Topsoil is often only inches thick. As long as it is not depleted faster than nature's nutrient cycle replenishes it, all is well. Man started crossing that line in the 1800s, as people spread across the land to till virgin grassland and cut forests. Today, one-third of the farmable land is degraded; nature cannot make new topsoil as fast as it is depleted. Like the gradual and unnoticed tire wear on your car, it can have disastrous consequences if ignored too long.

> **Soil erosion is the silent global crisis.**
> Stephen Leah

Topsoil stores 2,500 billion tons of carbon; our polluted atmosphere holds 760 billion tons. We need to replenish the topsoil we have lost, in order to grow food to eat and to keep the carbon from further polluting our atmosphere. Soil erosion was reversed in the past. Is that even possible today, when we need to provide food and materials for over 7 billion people?

Fertilizers and pesticides destroy earthworms and other organisms necessary to decompose organic matter and turn it into top soil. Once earthworms and other organisms are gone and nutrients are depleted, the land is dead. Agribusinesses rob the soil of all it has and move on to ground that is more fertile. The farmers who rented their land to big business are left with dead and useless land, and often the water supply has been exhausted as well.

One California valley found even the songbirds are gone, and in their place they have a new clinic to treat all the children with cancer. What had changed in the environment? Their land was farmed using great amounts of chemicals and heavy irrigation.

The United States exports banned pesticides to third world nations.

If pests become resistant, the chemical companies develop stronger and more expensive chemicals. Workers in third world countries walk through fields while spraying poison; they have no protective masks, gloves, or boots.

Species that overpopulate stress their environment until land and water are no longer able to produce the food they need to survive. Their numbers and health decline, and eventually they become extinct. We are destroying the land and water needed to feed all the people. One-third of the Earth's plant and animal species are in danger of extinction at a rate that is a total anomaly in Earth's history. Species that had been on Earth thousands, millions, even billions of years are becoming extinct at rates 1,000 times faster as the result of man's stewardship of the Earth in the last one hundred years. We kill them for their meat, feathers, hide, fur... and we destroyed their habitat. Many species, especially plants, are unable to adapt to global warming's rising temperatures. Plants can't pull up their roots and migrate north. When vegetation dies, ecosystems change, ending the area's normal nutrient cycle.

DESERTIFICATION

In their quest for profit, agribusinesses mine our farmlands, and we lose topsoil because of their unsustainable farming practices. In China and sub-Saharan Africa, there is such a tremendous loss of soil that deserts are claiming their land. The initial degradation starts from over grazing by cattle, sheep, and goats. When the human population rises, there is a similar increase in the number of animals. China has the same amount of farmland and cattle as the United States. However, the U.S. has 9 million sheep and goats, while China has 281 million. Sheep and goats pull up the roots, stripping the land of protective vegetation. This sets a process in motion that reverses soil building. The ground is unprotected; global warming's higher temperatures dry the surface, and winds blow away the finer soil causing terrible dust storms.

China's dust storms are monumental and travel as far as Pennsylvania and North Carolina. Much of the dust falls into the Pacific, damaging the ocean. Once the finer particles are gone, the wind picks up the courser material and cause devastating localized sand storms in China. The land between existing deserts is disappearing and forming one large desert. In other areas, new deserts are appearing. China is at war against expanding deserts, but their loss of land also places a great burden on the U.S. China turns to other countries for grain. China is our banker and the United States is becoming China's farmer.

It's a nightmare for China to be dependent on the U.S. for food, but there is no other choice. They use land in places like Sudan to grow grain, but that doesn't cover much of their needs. Since 1950, sand dunes have claimed or partially claimed 24,000 villages and their cropland in northwestern China. Millions of Chinese farmers drill wells deeper and deeper, and the water tables are falling under the North China Plain. The growth of cities and industries also claims water and cropland. In 2009, for the first time, the Chinese people purchased more automobiles than Americans bought. For every million cars added, 50,000 acres of land are paved for highways and parking lots.

China produced 14 million tons of soybeans in 1995, enough to feed the people. The same amount is produced today; however, China eats 69 million tons of soybeans. The U.S., Brazil, and Argentina are the main growers of soybean and 60% of the world soybean exports go to China. When selling food to China, we are dealing with an economic competitor and a creditor holding about a trillion dollars' worth of U.S. Treasury securities. If China pushes U.S. food prices higher, tensions between the two countries could climb. Americans think cheap food is our birthright, and we may press Washington to place restrictions on exports to China. If we limit grain sales to China, might the Chinese limit their monthly purchases of Treasury Securities? Our huge deficits of the past thirty years restrict our bargaining power.

China's food prices are climbing and their supply is dropping. The Chinese government is auctioning off some of their grain reserves to slow runaway prices for food. Leaders remember the Great Famine when 30 million people starved to death between 1959 and 1961. As a kid, my parents told me to eat all my food because children were starving in China. Children really were starving, but forcing me to eat more did not save one life.

China has the money and power to demand America sell it corn, wheat, and soybeans. The desertification problem is just as severe across the middle of Africa, except the people of Africa have no money and no power. Americans may be stressed when we have to meet China's demand for food, but where does that leave the people in Africa? We need to do whatever we can to retain fertile land and get food to the people most in need.

To put this in perspective, as many as 15,000,000 children and adults die each year from starvation and diseases related to malnutrition. This is a chronic and growing trend in sub-Saharan Africa. This is not just from drought; topsoil is gone. Governments are too weak or corrupt to distribute aid. Grain prices have soared. People caught in conflict struggle to stay alive. There is enough food for all if it is distributed to the poorest and not diverted to gas tanks, cattle, and other animals and crops that leave the soil depleted. The hungriest people are trapped in a downward spiral of poverty and death. They have no money for food, so they become malnourished, weak, sick, and unable to work. This continues until the person and the family die.

> **Ultimately, the human being is in the mercy of nature.**
> The Dalai Lama

RAINFORESTS AND OTHER DEFORESTATIONS

Cleared tropical rainforests change from incredible climate

controllers into deserts in a very few years. The warmer water temperatures of the Gulf of Mexico heat the climate enough to kill large trees. Rainforests act as air-conditioners and are the push behind wind currents that carry moisture from the evaporation of water in the rainforest. An Earth without rainforests is like a man without lungs, and an Earth with shrinking rain forests is like a man with shrinking lungs.

We clear virgin forests for lumber. However, a bigger problem may be the single-use paper products and all the new wipes. We must not turn trees into single-use items and trash. I've used cloth dinner napkins for forty years. Paper plates, cups, and towels are banned, and we have a nice supply of cleaning rags from old towels and wash clothes. We use cloth handkerchiefs, which are gentler than blowing your nose on a tree. If you think that sounds gross, you are brainwashed–get over it. Americans are convinced to buy single-use items because they are handier, safer, healthier, and neater. Manufacturers want products that are disposed of after one use so they keep making money over and over and over. I won't buy recycled paper plates etc., either. I don't need them and I don't want them in my home. They are signs of a country gone mad.

We cannot afford unnecessary deforestation. When lumber companies clear cut a forest and replant saplings, it is little more than a public relations ploy. They claim this is sustainable. There is no way a young sapling or small tree could begin to do the work of a mature tree, which sequesters huge amounts of carbon, purifies the air, provides shade, and gives animals food and a place to live. Trees stabilize soil, prevent erosion, and limit flooding. Forests can be maintained when appropriate timber is harvested and a perpetual forest lives on to provide benefits to the land and animals.

Haiti is 98% deforested and the country has little hope of recovering from the 2010 earthquake. The country cut down their trees, lost their top soil, and no longer has a way to produce enough food for their 10 million people. People will be trying to survive their next hurricane in tents. Haiti is near the top of the failing states list and will be remaining there indefinitely.

ACID RAIN

> There are nations that resist, voices that attempt to diminish the urgency or dismiss the science, or declare, either in word or indifference, that this is not our problem to solve. Well, let me tell you, it is our problem to solve...
> To the reticent nations, including the United States, I say this: There is such a thing as a global conscience.
> Paul Martin–former Canadian Prime Minister (2007)

The United States ignores the harm we do to our country and to our neighbor to the north by not addressing global warming. Canadians struggle with the spread of disease, more droughts in the prairies, melting permafrost in the north, longer and more intense heat waves, smog, and rising coastal waters, all related to global warming.

When our government acts as if China needs to stop building coal plants and the problem would be solved, it makes it easy for Americans to not hear, not understand, not take responsibility, and to allow the status quo to continue unchallenged. We sound like such heartless people. We are not heartless, just ignorant due to lack of information.

LANDFILLS

> The throwaway economy that has been evolving over the last half-century is an aberration, now itself headed for the junk heap of history.
> Lester R. Brown

Landfill liners leak toxins into the soil and water table, but not in the back yards of the rich and powerful. Children along the roadways leading to dump sites have extremely high rates of asthma and other respiratory illnesses.

William McDonough (godfather of green design) said, "Pollution is a sign of design failure." By recycling, we can save energy, land, and prevent toxic water and air. Recycled steel requires 26% as much energy as making steel from iron ore. The energy required to recycle other common items are 4% as much for aluminum, 20% for plastic, and 64% for paper. This saves resources and reduces chemical pollution.

Landfills bury our garbage, and greenhouse gases form when trash breaks down without oxygen present. In my first hour of reading *Harmony*, when this all began, I read about a United Nations report that said, "The United States alone buries 222 million tons of household waste a year. As the rubbish degrades it gives off landfill gas, 50% of which is methane and up to 40% is CO_2. Landfill sites are one of the biggest producers of methane gas in the world."

We recycle in our home, but other ways in which we try to cut down are not buying more than we need, repairing what we have, and buying used. We know that whatever we purchase requires resources to produce, and in the end, many items end up in the landfill.

Earth's Carrying Capacity

Countless things are presented as good ideas to an uninformed public, but create disastrous results. That's the case with the soil and water depleting, higher profit, big business methods of crop production and meat-factory farming. People who once raised some of their food were marketed to become consumers of processed food. The sheer number of people, 7,000,000,000 plus and climbing at the rate of 8.3 million people a year, changed the food production picture. The population, because of the way a few billion of us eat and live, has passed Earth's "carrying capacity." I heard about Earth having a carrying capacity for various animals nearly twenty years ago and now there is strong evidence that man is facing that issue himself.

The statistic of 18,000 children dying every day from starvation or related diseases was the death rate in 2007 before grain prices started skyrocketing. The poorest people could no longer buy food, and they had no land where it could be grown. Charitable organizations' dollars are stretched to the limit and are able to feed fewer and fewer. More recent figures range as high as 14,560,000 children and adults dying of starvation or related diseases each year. Millions of people dying each year from lack of food is a sign that we are nearing Earth's carrying capacity for the human species. There is enough food, but it does not reach the people most in need. The limited land is used in inappropriate ways and food now goes into our gas tanks.

> **Nature's standard operating procedure, pairing a population explosion with a population crash.**
> Alfred Crosby

FAILING STATES

Every year since 2005, Foreign Policy Magazine and the Fund for Peace has studied, ranked countries at risk, and published the list of failing states. Factors considered include ineffective central governments that have little control over their territories, non-provision of public services, widespread corruption, involuntary movement of populations, refugees, and sharp economic decline.

Lester Brown had difficulty believing that food could become Earth's weakest link and most immediate threat when it came to the collapse of human civilization. Starvation problems compound when governments are too weak or so corrupt that food and other aid cannot be distributed. Grain prices soared when the United States started using more of our corn crop to go into our gas tanks in the form of ethanol. This happened as a response to the rising gas prices after hurricane Katrina. As more ethanol refineries went on line, even more corn went not to starving people, but to our gas tanks. Agribusiness seized the opportunity for greater profit by growing corn for fuel, knowing that it would increase starvation. They also knew it does little to decrease our dependence on foreign oil, because fertilizers that are used to grow corn require petroleum. They told the public a feel-good story and we bought it.

Countries at the top of the failing states list receive food from the United Nations' World Food Bank. More could if grain prices were not so high. A problem these countries share is their land is deforested and the top soil is gone. Weak or corrupt governments allow citizens to be exploited, so even if there is fertile land, rich and greedy companies take the people's land, and their water with it. Global warming adds to the problem when higher temperatures dry the land. Tonight's 11pm news is forecasting the latest dust storm from Africa will reach Florida on Friday.

IS SEA LEVEL RISING OR ARE RICE PADDIES SINKING?

The answer is, "Yes."

Lester Brown is not an extremist and does not base his calculations on the worst-case scenario. Scientists offer predictions with a range of three outcomes. The mid-range is most probable, if we work to correct the way we use the environment. The most favorable outcome possible is if man radically corrects his behavior immediately and acts to reverse what damage we can. The worst-case scenario is if man continues with business as usual. There will be a 6-foot rise in sea level this century, using mid-range predictions. Brown tells what happens with a 3-foot rise in sea level within Lilly's lifetime, maybe even mine. Conservative scientists who write the IPCC reports state that current findings exceed their previous worst-case-scenario predictions. Therefore, I believe Brown's estimates of damage done by a 3-foot rise in sea level are conservative. The mid-range assumes man is doing something to correct his course, which we are not.

We are causing a 3-foot rise in sea level and reaping the consequences like a domino chain reaction. The Greenland ice cap is melting so fast it triggers minor earthquakes when large chunks of ice weighing millions of tons break off and slide into the sea. Thousands of square miles of ice from the Western Antarctic Peninsula fall into the sea and melt. Temperatures rise much faster in the Arctic. Instead of the 1 -1 ½ degrees rise most of the Earth experienced in the last century, the temperature rise in the Arctic is 4-7 degrees F. and insures the Greenland ice sheet will melt even faster. A 3-foot rise will reduce Bangladesh's Gangetic Delta rice land by 50%, and leave a country of 164 million people with half as much rice. Viet Nam's Mekong Delta, which produces half their rice, will have many parts submerged and Viet Nam will lose its export income. The twenty countries that buy rice from them will be forced to find rice elsewhere. Other Asian rice deltas will be submerged. Brown summarizes, "Ice melting on a large island in the far North Atlantic could shrink the rice harvest in Asia, a region that grows 90% of the world's rice."

Over population, land degradation or loss, and global warming are mixed together like the ingredients in spaghetti sauce. Try to separate them; you cannot.

> **When we try to pick out anything by itself, we find it is hitched to everything else in the universe.**
> John Muir

ANOTHER WAY TO ACQUIRE LAND

Wealthy countries with their land degraded and their aquifers drained shop for foreign land to buy or lease. After the oil embargos in the 1970s, Saudi Arabia felt vulnerable, and worried that countries like the United States might retaliate and cut grain sales. They decided to grow their own wheat using oil-well technology to drill deep enough to get water from an aquifer. They poured fertilizer and pesticides on their land and grew wheat. Thirty years later, the land is a lost cause and the aquifer is drained. Saudi Arabia has plenty of money and now buys or leases land to grow its wheat. That may sound like a good plan, but the countries or leaders who make these deals are either desperate, corrupt, or both. Saudi Arabia uses the land, and therefore water, in the Sudan and Ethiopia to grow its food. The countries are third and seventeenth on the list of failing states and have millions of starving citizens. They are on life support and get food from the United Nation's World Food Bank. Ethiopia leases land for a dollar an acre. That land will soon be dead and the water gone.

China leased 7 million acres of land in the Democratic Republic of the Congo (DRC) to grow palm oil for food and fuel. The DRC has 68 million people. Many are starving and depend on the U.N.'s World Food Program to survive. The DRC has civil unrest and this adds to the problem. Humanitarian agencies had to evacuate their staff from the DRC, and an unprecedented number of refugees are fleeing. One refugee camp in Uganda received more than 30,000 Congolese refugees, adding to Uganda's lack of food and water for its own citizens. Relief workers face a starving population within another starving population who view the refugees as competitors for distributed aid. Workers have to deal with conflicts between the citizens and refugees. Additionally, they face the issue of what to do with the children who arrive without parents. Some are orphans; others were separated from their parents as they fled. Protection and care of these children is an enormous responsibility for aid workers with no lasting solutions. A camp in Rwanda reports tens of thousands of refugees in the camp and more than 500 new refugees every day. All refugees arrive severely malnourished, and most of the babies die. Citizens from countries receiving refugees sometimes become refugees in another neighboring nation, thus there is a ripple effect across Africa.

Ghana is a coastal nation with natural resources that can sustain its people. The government is not corrupt. Under their current president, Ghana has improved tremendously; however, refugees from all five of its neighboring countries overwhelm the nation. Ghana lacks the resources to feed the refugees and meet their needs.

South Korea leases land from several countries, including the Sudan. India is a poor country, and their water and land are shrinking. India grows grains in Ethiopia. This is a story of the "haves and the have-nots." Sudan is the country receiving the greatest U.N. famine relief. Yet other countries grow grain on what little tillable soil Sudan has and send the grain out of Sudan. The grain used to produce fuel for the cars of the world is a compounding factor. This sounds so cruel, thoughtless, and greedy, as if we pull food from the mouths of the starving. I think of how American companies, like Cargill and ADM, are acquiring land to grow palm oil and soybeans for bio-diesel. Aren't they doing the same thing and aren't we buying their products? The "haves" are using up the land of the poor and exploitable. When Lilly is forty years old, what will the world look like and how will this affect her daily life?

A GLIMPSE AT LIFE IN LILLY'S LAND

In 1900, 1.6 billion people lived on Earth in a seemingly sustainable manner. Land was plentiful with millions of unused acres. Some people may have gone hungry because of unequal distribution, but the land was not in short supply. Nature replenished the topsoil as it had for billions of years. The nutrient cycle was nature's script for feeding its people in the "Play of Life" on Earth.

Act I of the play moved to the next fifty years of the 1900s. As the population climbed, farmers in the United States opened unused land to increase production. Rotation of crops and animals grazing in pastures returned nutrients to the soil. Crops, like corn, use great amounts of nutrients, but farmers planted soybean or peas to replenish the nitrogen. Manure dried in pasturelands, keeping fields fertile.

By the mid-1900s, the population doubled or tripled, with billions of bushels of grain grown and transported to feed people around the world. Farmers boosted production with fertilizers and pesticides, applied new technology to drill deeper wells for irrigation, and developed better seeds. Man may think he can take over nature's job, but his interference in the nutrient cycle is getting troublesome.

As Act I closes in the "Play of Life," the audience doesn't sense a problem. They look forward to more progress and an exciting life ahead for their children.

In Act II the plot twists. The progress that made the play an adventure has dark clouds on the horizon. The path is crowded with people and the land has been taken from Mother Nature's care. Huge corporations plant monoculture crops using genetically modified seeds. The rotation and natural nutrient enrichment that rebuilds the soil is replaced by dumping chemicals on the ground. Even if they are plowed under, the chemicals never become part of the soil. When it rains or heavy irrigation systems are turned on, the chemicals wash into streams, rivers, and the water supply. They contaminate drinking water and damage ecosystems that were never meant to be bathed in chemicals.

The agri-businesses raise larger crops faster and make more money quicker, but land is mined of its nutrients while Mother Nature is pushed aside. "It's not nice to fool with Mother Nature." I think that may be one of the most basic laws of nature. For thousands of years, Mother Nature sustained the Earth with an ideal climate, fertile land, plentiful clean water, seas abundant with fish, and fresh air to breathe. Pushing Mother Nature aside may be one of the dumbest things we arrogant humans have ever done. Now we want to deny there is a problem or say, "It's not my fault." This attitude leaves little chance to improve the situation; we need to face the real world–NOW!

Will there be an Act III with Mother Nature playing a leading role in saving the Earth for mankind, or will we keep doing what we're doing and let the final curtain drop? Lilly, I'm sorry I didn't know what was happening, but now I'm trying to find ways to help. Your life will be very different from what I expected. In some ways, it may be happier once the focus is off having every new item business can think up.

As the Earth warms and winters are milder, many old and new diseases are already affecting areas that never before had those "bugs." Trees are dying across the northern forests, because such bugs as the pine beetle are not killed off by winter temperatures. Mosquitos reach farther north and higher into the mountains, spreading malaria to new areas. Diseases thought to be eliminated are reappearing.

Lilly, have a good life and live within Earth's ability to provide. Your family may have some adjusting to do. Enjoy a small home and grow some of your own food. Don't buy more "stuff" than you need. Let your life be "unencumbered." There is comfort in not being mortgage poor, and there is joy in having time to spend with the ones you love. Don't be "clueless" like Great-granny's generation. Maya Angelo's words will always be true, "When we know better, we do better."

When you are in your thirties, the richer nations will have many elderly who are no longer able to produce what is required for their own needs. The poorest nations will have many more young people. They will need food, clothes, education, and jobs by the billions. This will be unlike anything Great-granny has ever known. All people need to be well fed, to be educated, and to know how to live within the laws of nature.

Find your joy in people and nature. All the possessions people from 1960 to 2015 worked so hard to acquire didn't make them happy. I hope you know the freedom of leaving the "have to have" obsession behind and walk out into a world where you feel a part of nature. There is so much beauty in our world. Protect it and let nature provide for you as you give back to Mother Nature. She is a wise and beautiful lady. I can promise you beautiful sunrises and sunsets nearly every day. I hope you can walk barefoot in the grass, swim with fish, and sleep under the stars. Your life may be very different from what I assumed it would be when you were born. It could be better.

CHAPTER 13

WATER

> **Water and air, the two essential fluids on which all life depends,**
> **have become a global garbage can.**
> Jacques Cousteau

GREENLAND'S ICE SHEET AND
ANTARCTICA'S WESTERN PENINSULA ICE SHEET

Temperatures are rising faster at the poles. The Greenland ice sheet and the Western Antarctic Peninsula ice sheet are melting at unprecedented speeds, causing a rise in sea level around the world. They are not just melting into the oceans; they are forming large lakes on the surface of the ice. Scientist now realize these lakes have water, like raging rivers, called moulins, going down through the depth of the ice caps and ice sheets(over land) and ice shelves (extending out over water). Moulins make the ice porous and huge chunks of ice break off sliding or collapsing into the ocean. The Larsen A ice shelf on the Western Antarctic Peninsula collapsed in 1995 letting scientist know this could happen. In 2007, the 700-foot-thick by 150-mile-long and 30-mile-wide Larsen B ice shelf collapsed and disappeared within days. Scientist thought the Larsen B shelf was stable for another century. Shortly after that, 2,000 square miles of ice broke off the Thwaites Glacier. In 2012, ice the size of Rhode Island broke off the nearby Ronnie-Filchner ice sheet. When ice sheets and shelves, which had been acting as barriers, collapse, the ice caps behind them advance faster and faster to the ocean and slide into the sea.

The world's largest ice cap covers the continent of Antarctica, is up to 10,000 feet thick, and is stable. NASA monitors the cap by satellite and knows it melts at a rate of 31 billion tons of water a year. As threatening as the situation is at the southern end of our world, scientists have the gravest concerns for the Greenland ice sheet, where temperatures are much higher.

> **Saving Greenland is both a metaphor and a precondition for saving civilization. If its ice sheet melts, sea levels will rise 23 feet. Hundreds of coastal cities will be abandoned. The rice growing river deltas of Asia will be under water. There will be hundreds of millions of rising-sea refuges. The word that comes to mind is chaos. If we cannot mobilize to save the Greenland ice sheet; we probably cannot save civilization as we know it.**
> Lester Brown

How much loss of land, lack of food and water, overpopulation, and weather catastrophes can governments manage before becoming failing states?

In 2012 the Arctic had a heat wave and the Greenland ice sheet melted thirty times faster than ten years ago. The lakes of ice-melt and the moulins raging to Greenland's bedrock make the ice porous and puts the skids under the Greenland ice sheet. The moulins scientists are seeing on the Greenland ice sheet are identical to the ones they saw in Larsen B before it disappeared in 2002.

The North Atlantic, where the fresh water melts off Greenland, is also the area of the Thermalhaline Pump, which powers the ocean currents. Scientists had not believed the pump would stop due to melting of Greenland's ice sheet. Their concern has increased, because in the summer of 2012 the surface area ice-melt went far above any previous year and nearly reached the summit. The similarity with the ice cap riddled with moulins begs the question: "Will the Greenland ice sheet suffer the same fate as the Larson B ice shelf? Is that possible?"

Sea level is rising at double the rate it was twenty years ago, but it is still minimal compared to what we might see in the near future. The U.S. National Research Council suggests a possible sea level rise in this century between 22 and 79 inches. Events that could hasten that rate in sudden and staggering amounts are the ice sheets and ice shelves going into the sea. Slowing and eventually reversing global warming is the only way to have Earth's climate "right enough" to keep man as Earth's main tenant.

The rising sea level shows up in subtle ways for some and tragic ways for others. In 1986, London built barricades on the Thames River to prevent flooding from the sea. Before then, the water was encroaching but had not flooded into the city. At first, they used the barricades one or two times annually. Now they close them a dozen times a year. By March 2011, the barricades had been used 119 times for high tides and storm surges. Some places have a far less subtle situation.

TUVALU, MALDIVES, KIRIBATI, MARSHALL ISLANDS, PAPUA NEW GUINEA, ETC.

> As for my own country, the Maldives, a mean sea-level rise of 2 meters would suffice to virtually submerge the entire country of 1,190 small islands, most of which barely rise over 2 meters above mean sea level. That would be the death of a nation.
> President of the Republic of Maldives to the U.N. General Assembly, 1987.

The Alliance of Small Island States in the Pacific has 39 countries that are in danger of losing some or all of their land. Islands have been evacuated, because the rising saltwater has destroyed their drinking water and made land unfit to grow food. Tuvalu had a population of 10,000, but 30% of their people had to be relocated to New Zealand under an arrangement with the New Zealand government.

The Maldives has 300,000 citizens, and the president is trying to buy land in another country to provide a place where fellow countrymen can remain together. For now, the government is moving citizens off the lowest islands onto the highest. Eventually, the nations of Tuvalu and the Maldives will no longer exist.

People from Carteret moved to the island of Bougainville in Papua New Guinea. There is a documentary on the Internet describing how they set out in a boat in search of a place where their people would be welcome. Sea-rise refugees are unwelcome where food and water is in short supply.

Some countries will cease to exist and the membership of the United Nations will drop. No one has determined when the countries are no longer U.N. members. Is it when the government no longer exists or is it when the last spit of land goes under the water?

Coastal areas in the United States will need evacuation, and the people will never be able to return. At least we have higher inland areas for our sea-rise refugees.

Mountain Glaciers

Mountain glaciers existed before agriculture began. They have been called "the reservoirs in the sky," and are an intricate part of Earth's fragile balance. These great fresh water supplies are disappearing everywhere: the Andes, the Rockies, the Alps, the Himalayas, and the Tibetan Plateau.

Peru's Quelccaya Glacier melted at 20 feet a year in the 1960s. By 2007, the rate was 200 feet a year; in 2009, melting claimed 550 feet, and the rate accelerates every year. Lima, Peru, with a population of 9 million people, is nearing a crisis. When the glaciers are gone, so is the water during the dry season. A United Nation's study calls Lima "a crisis waiting to happen." The 53 million people living in Peru, Bolivia, and Ecuador depend on the water from the glaciers during the dry season to produce their food and half their electrical power. This threatens the political security in the region, as the battle for the dwindling water heightens.

> **If you run out of water, you run out of life.**
> Uzbeki saying

Profiteers pounce on opportunities to exploit others' extreme misfortune. Bolivia is the poorest nation in South America. Ten percent of the children die before the age of five, and 40% of the population is under the age of fifteen. In the 1990s, inflation soared and the government was unable to maintain needed services. International financial institutions and the World Bank advised the Bolivian government to sell its assets: railroads, mines, electric, airlines, and the water systems. In 1999, San Francisco's Bechtel Corporation, through a multinational consortium, bought the water system of Cochabamba, Bolivia. They agreed to increase service and make much-needed repairs. Instead, they raised the rates so high the citizens could not afford water. The people of Cochabamba revolted and the army battled civilians for three months. Six people were killed and dozens were wounded. An American activist living in the area put information on the Internet and finally the revolt got some news coverage. *The New York Times* reported, "The world is running out of fresh water and the fight for control has begun." This put enough pressure on Bechtel to persuade them to leave, but they sued the Bolivian government for $25 million in compensation. Citizens now run the water system, but there is no money for repairs and the water is running out. This is an example of what people do when their water supply is threatened. What will happen when there is no water?

> **People think the only place where there is potential for conflict over water is the Middle East, but they are completely wrong. We have the problem all over the world.**
> Kofi Annan, former Secretary General of the United Nations

The hope for "peace on Earth, goodwill to men" in Lilly's future seems threatened from all directions. The Himalayan glaciers are melting twice as fast as they were a decade ago. In addition to the higher temperatures, the newly exposed mountains absorb more heat. The reflective ice is gone and the rate of melt gets faster and faster. We cannot stop this process. Global warming causes the massive glaciers to melt faster. Flooding kills tens of thousands, washes away villages, destroys crops, and carries off precious topsoil. Floods are devastating, but temporary.

The long-term and unending problem is the loss of water that has always been stored in the glaciers. During the yearly dry season, the glaciers supply water to the seven major rivers of Southeast Asia: Yellow, Yangtze, Mekong, Indus, Salween, Brahmaputra, and Ganges Rivers. Without water, crops will fail and millions of people will suffer malnutrition, die of thirst, or starve. Industries and hydroelectric plants that depend on the rivers will suffer.

> **If there is one area where equity is crucial and essential, I think it should be the issue of water.**
> Kofi Annan, former Secretary General of the United Nations

Conflicts arise between the countries that depend on the water from the rivers and their tributaries. When India built the Baglihar hydroelectric project, water flow into Pakistan was restricted. As the rivers receive less water from the receding glaciers, and each country struggles for water to generate power, raise crops, and provide drinking water for their people and livestock, the potential for conflict builds. The rivers fed by the Himalayan glacier melt provide more than half of the drinking water for 40% of the world's population.

> **War over water would be an ultimate obscenity.**
> **And yet, unfortunately it is conceivable.**
> Queen Noor of Jordon

Maslow's Hierarchy of Needs is stamped on this issue. When people's food and water supply is cut off, nothing else matters, and their only priority is to get what they need to survive. Billions of people facing that struggle paint a picture of a world unraveling.

AQUIFERS 101

We get our surface water from rivers and streams. Underground water is in aquifers. When we dig a well, the depth where the top of the water in the aquifer is reached is called the water table. Rechargeable aquifers fill when snowmelt and rainwater filter down through the soil into the aquifer. This cycle goes on indefinitely, as long as water is not removed from the aquifer faster than it can be recharged. Rechargeable aquifers slowly release water into streams, rivers, and surface soil.

The other type of aquifer is the fossil aquifers. They are usually deeper under the ground. The water has been there for eons, and they cannot be replenished. When the water is gone, the aquifers cease to exist.

After World War II, diesel-powered pumps replaced windmills. The new equipment went deeper, pumping greater volumes of water. In West Texas, the number of wells for irrigation went from 1166 in 1937, to 66,000 in 1971. The area provided food, exports, and fed 40% of our nation's grain-fed beef. By 1980, the water table was down ten feet. In the central and southern high plains, the decline was over one hundred feet. The U.S. Geological survey started monitoring 7,000 wells for annual water level changes. Water use had a 500% increase from 1949 to 1974. Some farming areas were withdrawing four to six feet of water a year, but nature can only recharge at the rate of ½ inch per year.

In the late 1970s, Saudi Arabia used high-tech oil-drilling equipment to drill deep under their deserts to a fossil aquifer to irrigate land to grow wheat. That aquifer is finished–gone. They now raise wheat in Ethiopia and Sudan. Impoverished countries or corrupt leaders are selling what little cropland they have– and therefore the water under it– to dry countries with enough wealth to pay.

Yemen is the poorest Arab country and has no money to buy land elsewhere. Their aquifers that replenish are over-pumped and inadequate for the soaring population. The deep fossil aquifer is draining rapidly, and the water table is dropping more than six feet a year. It is expensive to keep drilling deeper. The country is in crisis and ranks eighth on the list of failing states. The capital, Sana, has tap water one day in four, and the city of Taiz has tap water one day in twenty. Oil peaked long ago in Yemen and that income is shrinking. There is no other industry. Yemen imports 80% of its grain, not enough to feed the people. Nearly 60% of the children are chronically ill and their growth is stunted by malnutrition. These thirsty and starving people are at the bottom of Maslow's human needs chart. The government cannot provide for them. In the struggle to get food and water, warring starts between different factions and spills into Saudi Arabia along an unprotected border.

Overpopulation, poverty, and food and water shortages (exacerbated by global warming) are leading this country into collapse. Lester Brown sees this scenario as a distinct probability for many of the poorest countries of Africa and possibly some in Southeast Asia. Once the water is gone, crops fail, food and water are unavailable, people die, and those who live struggle to get what they can. The United Nations' funds to buy grain and water are limited. The world food shortage became overwhelming when food crops were used to make ethanol and bio-diesel fuels for cars. Corn grown to produce ethanol requires a tremendous amount of water. During America's souring temperatures and drought in the summer of 2012, non-irrigated cornfields lost their crop. Global warming will bring even higher temperatures to more areas, droughts in some places, and floods in others. The air and ocean currents that worked so well to keep our climate "just right" are flawed, due to man's activities.

Most of the countries in the top ten failing states are facing poverty and overpopulation, and the majority of the citizens are under the age of twenty. They lack education and jobs. Deforestation, depleted soil, crop failure, lack of food and water, people in terrible health, and governments too poor and disorganized to provide services means there is not enough humanitarian aid to prevent hundreds of millions of deaths. Who will fund the aid? Only .5% of Americans contribute to humanitarian efforts on a regular basis. Global warming is global; all countries face some part of the consequences.

> **We never know the worth of water till the well is dry.**
> Thomas Fuller

The three top grain-producing countries in the world, raising one-half of the world's grain, are the United States, China, and India. All three face aquifer crises.

The largest aquifer in the world is the Ogallala fossil aquifer under America's high plains from South Dakota to the Texas Panhandle. It had 4 trillion tons of water, but 13 million gallons of water a minute goes to more than 200,000 wells irrigating 8.2 million acres of cropland. In 2007, the water was more than half-gone. The shallower southern part and some of the wells in the Texas Panhandle are drilled to the bottom and going dry. Irrigated farmland in Texas peaked at 7 million acres in 1978, but has decreased to 5 million today. Twenty percent of America's grain comes from irrigated land.

Historically, people have grown crops using rainwater. Later, man added canals, dug shallow wells to get to the water table, and used windmills to pump water. There are more than four times as many people living today as there were in 1900. Land expansion is complete; new lands where crops can flourish on natural rainfall are gone.

Rivers dammed for power projects reduced water for irrigation below the dams. People dug deeper wells and used pumps to irrigate fields. This is wasteful and inefficient, but their harvests increased. They used new oil-drilling technologies to bore deeper into aquifers. Rechargeable aquifers are over pumped, running dry, and in danger of collapsing. The fossil-aquifer drilling goes deeper and deeper if people, companies, or governments can afford the cost. The frenzy is called, "the race to the bottom."

In many areas water is too costly to use for agriculture. Farmers who are able to drill deep enough to reach the water table sell to cities and no longer grow crops. It takes 1,000 tons of water to raise one ton of wheat. The fossil aquifers have a bottom of impermeable rocks and other material. Once it's reached the aquifer is empty forever and may collapse. In some areas the farmers can still "dry land farm," but the crop yield is lower. Water is no longer a "right," unless you have the money to reach the ever-deepening water table. Only the rich can stay in the game.

There is a lot on the internet about people and multinational corporations like Royal Dutch Shell, Monsanto, and Nestles trying to buy water rights in the United States and other countries. T. Boone Pickens is a man with the money and the deep-drilling equipment to get what he wants. The following paragraph is from "There Will Be Water," an article by Susan Berfield in the June 11, 2008, *Bloomberg Businessweek Magazine*."

> **If water is the new oil, T. Boone Pickens is a modern-day John D. Rockefeller. Pickens owns more water than any other individual in the U.S. and is looking to control even more. He hopes to sell the water he already has, some 65 billion gallons a year, to Dallas, transporting it over 250 miles, 11 counties, and about 650 tracts of private property. The electricity generated by an enormous wind farm he is setting up in the Panhandle would also flow along**

that corridor. As far as Pickens is concerned, he could be selling wind, water, natural gas, or uranium; it's all a matter of supply and demand. 'There are people who will buy the water when they need it. And the people who have the water want to sell it. That's the blood, guts, and feathers of the thing,' he says.

Wherever Pickens or some mega-corporation has water rights, the neighbors might as well not have rights. Once the big boys start pumping billions of gallons from many wells, the water table will go down so far no one else will be able to afford a well deep enough to get the water they need. The neighbor becomes a customer. Pickens sees water as the gold mine that oil once was.

I suggest a good financial investment, to reduce water requirements, might be low-flow faucets, 1.6-gallon tank toilets, or the odorless composting toilets if you can.

When aquifers are depleted, the next step is to import water from distant sources. It could be in the hands of corporations looking for the highest possible profit. This has started. Water rights are being purchased, pipelines are going in, and ocean-tankers to haul water are being built. Water is not toxic, so tankers do not need to be the great double-hulled behemoths used for oil transport. One tanker design reminds me of sausage casings that are filled, leaving enough air so they float. A long line of them link together to tow ice-melt from polar-regions. I thought the "Oscar Mayer Express" would be a good name.

It sounds as if people who can afford it will be able to have water. I'm not sure how much food will be grown or how much it will cost. There will have to be new technologies developed so that water is recaptured in a loop for agriculture. This method is used to raise fish, herbs, and vegetables in one circulatory system. I found designs on the Internet for "grow towers" that recirculate run-off and grow skyscraper-like gardens. I didn't see where that would replace fields of grain. Any method providing water for people or crops will be a method that has corporations making money to deliver their product. Water is moving from something we thought of as a "right," to a product that is for sale—if you can afford it.

Desalination is only an answer for the rich. It is extremely expensive because it requires an enormous amount of energy for the process. It took 1.5 million barrels of oil a day to process the water in Saudi Arabia's thirty desalination plants. They switched to solar energy so they could sell their oil. Desalination produces one gallon of useable water from three gallons of seawater, leaving polluted brine that is a problem for safe disposal. This is not on option for use on a scale to meet the needs of millions or billions, even if they were wealthy.

The other two countries that are the world's leading grain producers are in more trouble than the United States, which produces 20% of our grain on irrigated land. Sixty percent of India's grain is grown on irrigated land, and in China, the figure is 80%. The northern half of China is very dry and relies heavily on irrigation. The North China Plain produces half of China's wheat and a third of its corn. They use what surface water is available, are over-pumping the one shallow rechargeable aquifer, and have drilled deep into the non-rechargeable fossil aquifer. Once they deplete these two aquifers, all farming will revert to rain-fed crops. The northern half of China receives very little rain. The fossil aquifer was dropping at the rate of ten to twenty feet a year when measured in 2000.

Beijing's 23 million people, receive 75% of their water from the aquifer. In 1990, they drilled 200 feet to reach the water table; in 2010 they drilled 1,000 feet. China's expanding industries take water once used for farming. The World Bank's report on China's water situation contained a harsh warning. It foresees "catastrophic consequences for future generations" unless water use and supply can quickly be corrected. Lester Brown's *World on the Edge* (2011) tells the scope of the problems around the world and is a great resource for the person who wants to know the facts.

India is poorer than China, and wells are going dry all across the country as water tables fall. The two large grain-producing states of Punjab and Haryana yield most of the surplus grain India uses to feed the low-income people in its massive food distribution program. When food production is artificially high for a few years while the over-pumping of water is possible, it creates an unsustainable level of production. This artificially high production is called a "food bubble," and India's food bubble is about to burst, as has Saudi Arabia's.

Brown's book describes many other countries that are nearly out of water or are losing their food supply. This is happening in many places at the same time. Water has peaked in over half of the countries of the world, often in overpopulated areas. Jordon's 6 million people import 90% of their grain, because their harvest is only 20% of what it was when the population was lower. Israel imports 90% of its grain.

> "In the Middle East, where populations are growing fast, the world is seeing the first collision between population growth and water supply at the regional level. For the first time in history, grain production is dropping in a geographic region with nothing in sight to arrest the decline. Each day now brings 10,000 more people to feed and less irrigation water with which to feed them.
> Lester Brown

Afghanistan and Pakistan are nearing a water crisis. A World Bank report says, "The survival of a modern and growing Pakistan is threatened by water."

Mexico's 111 million people face rapidly-dropping water tables. More than 50% of the water has been extracted from their aquifers. The large aquifer that irrigates the wheat-growing state of Senora used to reach water at 40 feet. They now have to drill more than 400 feet. The growing population and industry is pulling water from the farming area, as well. Mexico City, with a population of 21.2 million, will run out of water as early as 2015. As they continue to pump the remaining pockets of water under the city, empty pockets collapse, and the city is subsiding (sinking) at the rate of 20 inches a year. This crushes water pipes and other structures underground while damaging architectural treasures. However, for corporations set to provide water from afar—what a market! Millions will be desperate for water to drink!

And Every Drop for Sale (Rothfeder 2001) and *Blue Gold* (Barlow and Clarke 2002) point out many aspects of the water shortage. As I read Rothfeder, I kept thinking that the large corporations irrigating in the most wasteful ways and turning billions of tons of fresh water into carcinogenic toxins every minute aren't that concerned. They are the ones designing enormous pipelines and transport methods to sell water to the thirsty world. Water is no longer treated as a "human need" to which each man has a "human right." Thirsty and starving people are a rich new market. The poorest, not having money, will not make the purchase.

In *Blue Gold*, Barlow and Clarke state, "Alberta, Canada, uses 204 billion liters of water every year, mostly from aquifers, to pump into oil wells to enhance production. This is enough water for 70,000 people for 20 years. When the oil is gone, the water remains and is unusable. It is so contaminated it is good for nothing including nature." Does this mean water extracted from fracking will never again be useable and should be stored as a hazardous liquid? What happens to the water from a million fracked wells, each using 7 million gallons of water to drill and 7 million more for each of the eighteen re-frackings per well? The gas companies extract half of the carcinogenic water and the other half remains in the ground. What is this doing to our water supply over time? Fracking is not regulated, and the documentary *Gasland* showed a landowner's home movie of a Halliburton tanker pumping the extracted production water into a nearby stream. Is that dumping legal? Is Halliburton and its business friends multi-tasking, drilling for natural gas and oil while at the same time building a water market? No wonder they aren't worried about contaminating the water shed that supplies New York City. It might provide a new market for bottled water. Will people need a new source of water for cooking and bathing?

> **There is no technological 'fix' for a planet that has run out of water.**
> Barlow and Clarke

Montana may get 25,000 coal-bed methane wells that would pull 13 billion liters of water a day from the aquifers, lowering the water table thirty-four feet in ten years. Barlow and Clarke warn, "At some time in the future, we will be fresh-water bankrupt."

> **Stopping global warming is not just about saving the environment for the hunters, fishermen, hikers, and the other outdoor enthusiasts of today and tomorrow. Global warming is a matter of national security. Will we live in a world where we must fight our neighbors for fresh water and food?**
> General Wesley Clark

DAMS

Damming rivers and streams was a method used more in the past. Dams were built to provide hydroelectric power, and reservoirs behind the dams stored water that could be used for irrigation. This damaged ecosystems downstream. Waterways have a natural "turning cycle" to clean themselves and distribute oxygen to the fish and plants living in that habitat. Reservoirs silt-in, dams deteriorate, and at some point become a huge risk for people living down river. The 35-year-old dam that supplied water to Mexico's Sonora region is bone dry.

Dams are often a source of conflict. Turkey is building dams at the headwaters of the Tigris and the Euphrates rivers. This reduces the water Iraq and Syria depend on to feed their people. Grain harvests dropped in both countries, and they are over-pumping their aquifers. Brown suspects their food bubble will burst sooner due to Turkey's dam building project.

Many dams have problems. A 2010 report states Lake Meade, the reservoir behind the Hoover Dam (built in the 1930s), was only 41% filled and dropped 130 feet since 1999. There is a 23% reduction in hydroelectric generating capacity. If drought conditions persist in the Colorado River Basin and high water use continues, there might not be enough water to power the dam's generators. Without power from the Hoover Dam, millions would need a new power source. The expense could create havoc for the economy. It's time to rethink how we use our precious water, and perhaps install solar panels or wind turbines.

Mindfulness at Home Pays Off

I came across someone's calculation of how much water would be an Earthling's fair share. The magic number for Wally and me was twenty-five gallons a day, total. That seemed reasonable; surely, we were within those limits. I had not been reading the water meter. Our water bill comes every four months. The July 2011 bill showed we used 160 gallons a day. I have no idea how we used so much, but you guessed it, we changed our evil ways. First, we checked for leaks and found that a garden hose had the tiniest leak where we screwed it onto an outside faucet. I don't know how much was being wasted; all I cared about was stopping the loss. For a while, I read the meter every day and went into an ultra-conservative mode.

We were already catching our rainwater in clean bins to water plants. We decided to try to get down to the Earthling quota, so I carried water into the house for flushing the toilets. I felt like such a good pilgrim and realized I was grateful I was able to do that. Our use for the next twenty days varied from eight gallons to fifty-three gallons a day, but the average was twenty-six gallons. We have a high efficiency washer, so that did not account for the few high days. Fifteen of the twenty days were between twenty and thirty gallons. It became apparent that company with kids who left the faucet running while washing their hands could add an extra five gallons within a daylong visit. We told people what we were doing, so they were on their best behavior. Quickly turning the faucet off is the type of fine-tuning Earthling quotas require. It was interesting to learn how water is wasted.

Now I'll confess a relapse. Our rainy season ends December 1. There is little rainwater available until June. However, we did not use rainwater for flushing again. The novelty wore off; plus, I hadn't given it any thought, until I compared the 2011 and 2012 water bills. At first, it looked great! Instead of 19,510 gallons, we used 5,910. I was ready to pat myself on the back until I calculated we were averaging 50 gallons of water a day and had been gone nearly five weeks of that time. I was sure we were using near our Earthling quota. When I think about it, some of our lightning-fast faucet action is sloppy and maybe we are occasionally a little frivolous with our showers. We have the lowest flow faucets and showerheads, and when we shower, we briefly get wet, turn off the water, lather up, and quickly rinse. I can't account for the 50 gallons a day, but I am returning to daily water meter readings; I have a mystery to solve, and Wally comments, "Here we go again."

Many books say to read your electric, gas, and water meter every day. This taught me a lesson. If I don't pay attention, old habits slip back in drop by drop. You might find a reality check enlightening and enjoy the challenge of reaching the quota of an average Earthling.

It would be a wonderful gift for children to teach them to be water-friendly Earthlings. Someday, the cost of water may rival the car and mortgage payments. If your bill already rivals those payments, that could mean your municipal supply comes a great distance. Some of those remote sources are drying up. Future costs could really skyrocket. Corporations know there is big money in water and that rights can be purchased.

Growing up in the country, using well water, meant we didn't waste it, or we could find the well was dry. I have reclaimed some of my old country habits. One inch of water in a glass is all I need to brush my teeth. I dip the brush into the water, brush my teeth, rinse with half and use the rest to clean the toothbrush and rinse the sink. Such a nitpicky thing seems trivial, but it can save thousands of gallons a year.

THIS IS A VERY UN-AMERICAN LESSON

When I say rethink something as trivial as a different way to brush your teeth, is there something in you that says, "Wait a minute. Why should I have to do such a thing? I don't use that much." Well, yes you do. Water shortages are threatening many people. It is already being purchased from farmers for residential use in California, making it unavailable for crops (our food). They make more money selling their water than they can from farming.

There may be information in this chapter that you have never heard. Do your own checking. You might be willing to start a new brushing routine. Instead of saying, "Wait minute. Why should I have to do such a thing," ask yourself, "What would be so difficult about changing the way I do a few things, and why am I so resistant?" Our automatic defense is to say, "That's a bunch of hooey," and with that we wipe our hands of such a notion.

Remember the Ogallala Aquifer, the largest in the world, the one under seven U.S. breadbasket states? Ogallala is a fossil aquifer and it is being drained. What terrible news for our children and grandchildren. The water to grow their food will be limited to rainfall amounts. Many of the glaciers that put water into America's rivers have melted and the few remaining are rapidly receding. The Amazon rainforest that provides precipitation to the southwestern United States is being slashed and burned. Higher temperatures evaporate more water from the soil, and the trees and grasslands that slowed run-off so that rain could soak into the ground are ravaged. Rethink, and say to yourself, "It may not be much to brush my teeth in a different way, but I can do that. It's a start." What else are you willing to try?

Study how much water you can save, rather than waste what our children and grandchildren need to be able to brush their teeth with just one inch of water. When put into practice, not only will you learn a new way to think about living responsibly, but you will also be a part of saving many lives.

Change the saying, "It's a big world," to "It's a small world with an unprecedented number of people to support." Drink the eight glasses of water we all need each day, but do not waste a drop. We didn't know water was limited. Now we do, and when we know better, we do better. Apply this improved attitude to your bathing, dishwashing, laundering, lawn watering, hand washing, and dumping half-filled glasses and bottles of water down the drain.

We have never faced the challenge of 7 billion people, an atmosphere heating up, ice melting that has been frozen since civilization began, water and land over-utilized, and world food production dropping. Americans do not like bad news, but we do not want to be left in the dark when it comes to our children's future. To those who would say, "Stop. I can't deal with this right now," my response is, "If you think it's a problem now, give it a few years!"

Lilly's world will be different from what I thought in my clueless days. Americans have been living in an artificial reality, thinking the way we lived caused no harm and could keep getting better and better. With the changes we make, we may have a happier and more relaxed way to live. All the stuff we buy requires energy to make, water to produce, and our hard-earned money to buy. I enjoy my simpler life, and our retirement savings last much longer.

CHAPTER 14

FOOD FOR MOTHER EARTH'S FAMILY OF SEVEN BILLION

> **The impact of climate change will fall disproportionately upon developing countries and the poor persons within all countries. It will therefore exacerbate inequalities in health status and access to adequate food, clean water and other resources.**
> Rajendra Pachauri, chair of the IPCC, July 2005

COULD FOOD BE OUR WEAKEST LINK?

Lester Brown resisted that idea, but once food was used to make fuel and the number of people who starved to death each year approached 15 million, that qualified as the weakest link. United Nations' resources are inadequate to prevent countries from turning into war-torn battlegrounds with tribes, sects, or other factions struggling for food and water. Desperate refugees seeking food cross borders and are threats to countries they enter.

The industrialized world caused global warming, but Africa is our "canary in the coal mine." If Africa's sorrow wakes us up, we can save Lilly's world. Africa's rivers are lower and animals are disappearing, endangering Africa's main industry of tourism. Will we notice global warming is causing the extinction of some of the great animals of the world? If we pay attention, Africa's tragedy may encourage us to work with nature, rather than knock nature off balance.

FOOD BUBBLES

Food bubble is the term for the temporary and artificial expansion of the food supply the world briefly experienced in the last half of the 20th century. The last of the tillable soils were opened, modified seeds and chemicals produced higher yields, deep drilling into aquifers provided access to new sources of water for irrigation, and technology aided mass production and distribution of food. We thought this growth would continue, little realizing that instead we were destroying our means of food production. The catastrophic effects of overpopulation colliding with decreased resources are localized in pockets, primarily in Africa and Southeast Asia. There are indications areas in the Middle East, island nations, and Central and South America may soon lose access to enough food and water for their growing populations.

Hurricane Katrina inadvertently pushed the food shortage issue to the forefront, as something that could lead to the collapse of our way of life. I'll recap how fragile food supply issues had become before Katrina even hit. The CO_2 in the atmosphere was approaching 400ppm, and the temperature of the Earth's oceans, land, and air was rising. Earth's oceans and air currents were changing, creating extreme and unpredictably harsh winters, heat waves, droughts, and floods. Crops didn't adapt to climate change and food production suffered. Plants ceased pollinating at certain temperatures. With each degree above average temperature, 10% more water was needed for crops to grow. The low-lying islands of the world had saltwater invading their crops, making it necessary for some people to abandon their island homes. The sea level rose as ice-melt went into the oceans. Thermal expansion added to the higher sea level. Environmental refugees needed food from elsewhere. One billion people were malnourished and had no way to grow or buy their food. Farmland was lost to population expansion, as homes, roads, parking lots, and buildings took up more of the land. Fish stocks around the world were collapsing from over-fishing, pollution, and loss of habitat. Rivers, rainfall, and aquifers were declining, and farmland was abandoned.

More people were eating beef, which takes the grain that would feed seven people to provide one person with one serving of beef. The meat we eat is raised on factory farms called "Concentrated Animal Feeding Operations" (CAFOs), and instead of keeping the waste in the nutrient cycle, it is managed in ways that increase global warming. There are few regulations to protect our land, water, air, or food when it comes to the CAFOs. Half of U.S. agricultural land was devoted to livestock, mostly cattle. There is grassland available to raise cattle that would not require the staggering use of water or the hormones and antibiotics. Contented grazing cattle do not grow fast enough to turn the higher profits Archer Daniels Midland and Cargill seek. Regulations were passed that make it extremely difficult for the small farmers to get their cattle slaughtered.

Land was being lost to desertification, at times due to deforestation of the rainforests. Other causes of the loss of topsoil and desertification are over-use of chemicals, over-plowing, and over-grazing in areas with growing populations.

Things were at crisis level before Hurricane Dennis hit the Gulf of Mexico in July 2005. Katrina filled the Gulf in September, causing gas prices to jump to over three dollars a gallon. The food conglomerates had urged the government to develop ethanol since the 1970s, and this time the government bought this ill-conceived plan. Before the ethanol craze, 70% of U.S. grain was used to feed livestock. By 2012, only 40% of the grain fed livestock, and ethanol got 40%. We do not have more land available, so corn replaces other crops. At that crucial moment in history, we made a fatal error. Rather than converting food to fuel, Americans should have been urged to conserve by driving vehicles with better gas mileage. This would have motivated automakers to increase fuel efficiency. Subsidies should have gone to development or increase public transportation rather than ethanol production.

The switch to ethanol was not for the purpose of energy independence, as we were told. Conservation would do more for energy independence than all the ethanol we produce. The real purpose of making ethanol was for higher profit from billions of tons of corn. Agri-businesses knew this would raise grain prices, and they knew the poorest people would be denied food.

Some of the biggest food companies played the grain markets, bought up the grain, and stored it a few months until prices doubled and even tripled. For the most ruthless, this was an opportunity too good to pass up. They could squeeze the last possible dollar from desperate people. In Mexico, one agri-business, from the U.S. bought one million tons of corn at $123 a ton, stockpiled it in warehouses, and sold it as high as $320 more per ton than they paid for it. American owned Cargill bought corn at $160 a ton, stockpiled it for two months, then sold it for $320 a ton. Cargill controlled the ports and the silos and was able to create a desperate situation and turn a rapid profit at the expense of our neighbors to the south.

This is one reason I have concerns for Lilly's food. How much more ruthless could a company be? Cargill is one of our largest food providers. Lilly and her mommy live on a tight budget, and when corporations contrive to drive up prices of food and water, life could get tough without warning.

In 2007, "Tortilla Wars" in Mexico drove people to the streets in protest after corn became so expensive the poor couldn't feed their families. Agri-businesses are no less than monopolies and control all aspects of the distribution. They have so much influence in the Mexican government that the politicians supported the exploiters instead of their own people.

Americans need to find out what elected officials are more supportive of agri-businesses than the people in their home states. Agribusinesses have been deeply involved in politics for many years. Cargill's past leader wrote the $25,000 check to pay for Nixon's Watergate operation. Policies must be changed. It does not seem mathematically possible for the U.S. to meet the future mandate to produce three times as much ethanol. Three times the 40% of our corn crop that goes to ethanol would be 120% of our crop. That is an agri-business's dream come true. Sell the corn at the high price for fuel as mandated, create a shortage of corn, stockpile millions of tons of corn for a few months, and really turn a profit. I'd like to think our government would protect us, but look what corporations are allowed to do. The loopholes exempting Halliburton's fracking from the Safe Drinking Water Act, the Clean Air Act, and the act to clean up carcinogenic pollution in our land, air, and water are still written in our laws. So is the mandate that will create the shortage of corn. These are terrible, greedy, and dangerous laws, but Congress passed them and continues to subsidize these ethanol and fracking fiascos.

Where will the price of meat, dairy, and poultry go when the amount of corn to make ethanol increases—doubling and then tripling? Do not take too much comfort in the stability of other crops; fields of vegetables may become cornfields.

All our gas stations pump a gas-ethanol blend, and carmakers are building "flex" vehicles that can burn up to an 85% ethanol blend. More distilleries are planned. This is an example of food companies making decisions for higher profit, knowing it will hurt the average American and add to the number of people starving to death in the world every day.

By 2009, the U.S. corn crop going to ethanol was enough to feed 340 million people. Put another way, in 2009 the U.S. took the food that could have fed 340 million people and put it in their gas tanks. Now you know. Agri-businesses knew it all the time but failed to mention it to the people filling their tanks. If you are wondering how you can make a difference, how quickly can you cut your gas consumption by 20-50%?

We cut our use of gasoline by 75% between buying a fuel-efficient car and being more mindful about unnecessary use. That solution is doable for many. Other solutions are much more complex. Food bubbles are bursting as water tables drop, land is degraded, and the population increases.

REDUCING FERTILITY RATES

There is no doubt that the world's population continues to increase, with the best-case scenario of 8 billion in 2042. The more likely figures are between 9.2 billion and 10.5 billion by 2050. Most of the growth will be in the poorest countries and the people will face a lack of food, water, education, health care, and employment. The population could pass Earth's carrying capacity. Lester Brown writes about solutions that are effective and humane. Educating females about health care, abstinence, and family planning reduces the fertility rate. In some countries the TV and radio soap opera dramas have characters who decide to learn about family planning. This was an effective tool in Mexico and Ethiopia, although there are places where a TV or radio is unheard of.

People are starving to death every day and women live in fear of their next pregnancy. Many babies die in the first year, and the children that survive are often physically and cognitively impaired due to malnutrition. One of the most effective approaches to lowering fertility rates is school lunch programs because girls are sent to school. This is especially true if a ration of food is sent home with the child for other family members. This gets food to the preschool age children, so that they will be healthy enough to attend school and be cognitively able to learn. The longer girls attend school, the later they marry and the fewer babies they bear. They learn about health and family planning and are better able to care for their children. With fewer people in need of services, governments and relief organizations are more able to provide food, water, education, health care, and security for the people still in need. The poverty level and all aspects of life improve and governments have a chance to become more stable.

The population topping at 8 billion in 2042 requires the 280 million females wanting access to health care, family planning, and contraceptives, have this made available. The United Nations and charitable organizations would like to provide these services, but to serve 280 million women who lack any resources is costly.

Another way to decrease starvation is to improve water quality. The dry composting toilets have become lifesavers. They keep pathogens out of the water and put nutrients back into the cycle. Many babies die of diarrhea or parasites from filthy water. Their tiny bodies cannot use what little nutrition they get. Providing people with an inexpensive sieve to strain water prevents many infant deaths by removing a deadly tapeworm from the drinking water.

One study found that the single best way to reduce the fertility rate and lift people out of poverty was for females to receive a secondary level of education. Another sobering statement was that illiteracy is becoming a bigger threat to our civilization than terrorism. Millions of hungry, illiterate, unemployed, and angry youth in a country that is unable to provide the most basic services is a recipe for civil unrest. Once chaos breaks out, it is more difficult to get aid to the people, and the spiraling violence spreads as people become more desperate.

Brown and others suggest that since this represents a threat to world and national security, industrialized countries re-allocate some of the money spent on military defense to address the issues of poverty, illiteracy, hunger, and overpopulation. A world with growing numbers of failing states is dangerous to everyone and expensive to defend against. I don't want a world where each month, millions are starving to death and it is too late to do anything about it.

We can't feed them all, but I wish corn wasn't going into my gas tank. Food is a weak link and a threat to Lilly's world. That was a surprise to me. We will be indulging China's demands for corn; they are unable to produce enough to feed their people and have let the United

States know they will buy some of our crop. China is our banker and we can't "just say no" to them. Supplementing China's corn shortage could send our grocery bill to dizzying numbers in the near future, especially when you consider all the food we eat that contains corn syrup solids, high fructose corn syrup, or corn oil. Check the labels in your kitchen; you will see we aren't just talking about corn-on-the-cob. How large of an increase in grocery expense can your budget accommodate?

I hope Lilly and her mom like some of my vegan specialties. They are more affordable, leave more food for others, and are much healthier. Eating lower on the food chain is one of the most beneficial changes a person can make on an individual level. Perhaps one day, Lilly will even be able to grow some of her food. That is a more sustainable lifestyle. A tomato plant might be a start. The best I can do is to provide an example to follow.

How Does Your Garden Grow?

I wish schools had classes on food gardening. I love that Michelle Obama has a vegetable garden at the White House to show children where food comes from and how to grow their own food. Florida Gulf Coast University, near us, has a half acre "food forest," with native trees that produce fruit. They also grow heritage vegetables. The goal is to teach the principles of regional sustainable agriculture. They believe it is important for people to know where their food comes from and to understand what can grow in our area. They distribute the harvested "fruits of their labor" on campus. I plan to visit the college and learn the best seeds for my tiny backyard venture. Are there programs that teach a person to garden in your area? Some county extension services offer classes on the proper use of rain barrels and sell them at a low cost to people who take the class.

When I was a kid, we grew much of our food. We learned gardening at home by planting, weeding, watering, munching on things like tender peas, and finally picking the vegetables for dinner. Americans lived a more sustainable life style in the 1950s and 1960s. Many of us can do that again. Today's families are smaller and a well-planned garden can produce an amazing amount of food.

The Okinawa Program described the diet and lifestyle of people who live active and healthy lives past the age of one hundred. One of the main exercises recommended was gardening. I thought about how that could increase longevity. Fresh organic food and the peacefulness we experience when we take time to enjoy nature are important benefits. They also make a point about the need for stretching and remaining flexible throughout life. The bending, reaching, and squatting I do while tending my plants is not something I do in any other routine activity.

> **If I'd known I was going to live this long,**
> **I'd have taken better care of myself.**
> Eubie Blake

I was a good gardener in northern New York, but south Florida is different. I didn't take up gardening when we moved here. There are restrictions to the point that it seemed as if the community rules meant, "Thou Shalt Not Garden." Now, it is near the top of my list of things I really want to do.

I have had marginal success in the two years since I retired, but I am still a novice in Naples. The garden goes in around October 15, and we can continue planting vegetables through February. I have good luck with Swiss chard, a delicious vegetable full of calcium, vitamins, fiber, protein, and iron. I keep snipping off the larger outside leaves for several months, so growing it is a productive use for several of my beautiful pots. It is sad that Americans turned over the growing of their food to the unsustainable methods of big business. We gave up a wonderful natural family activity. It used to be a happy part of our lives. At the dinner table, we ate what we helped grow and talked about how soon the strawberries or corn would be ready. There were big family gatherings or community socials to enjoy fresh strawberry shortcake. Can any of you remember those gatherings?

George Washington is one of my favorite forefathers, and I love to visit Mount Vernon. He was an excellent farmer and believed farming had to be self-sustaining. He kept "everything" in the nutrient cycle, including the waste from all animals—that would be from people, too. He had "necessaries" (fancy outhouses) all around the property. Slaves removed the slide-out trays, emptied the contents into wheelbarrows, and took it to the compost pile near the stables. Animals take in nutrients and energy, and the waste produced is a source of nutrients for the ground where the food originated. The thought of throwing animal or plant waste into the Potomac or burying it in the ground would have been unthinkable to George Washington.

Today, we pull many nutrients from the cycle and turn them into pollution, toxins, methane, etc. Then we use fertilizer which contaminates our streams and destroys ecosystems. We need to relearn the way nature really works and adopt those principles.

Thomas Jefferson is another favorite forefather. In 1811, he wrote to a friend,

> **No occupation is as delightful to me as the culture of the Earth, and no culture is comparable to that of a garden.**

Other occupations Jefferson had were writing the Declaration of Independence, Governor of Virginia, Minister to France, third president of the United States, founder of the University of Virginia, architect, scientist, inventor, and musician. Above all those activities, his favorite was to garden. Perhaps we should try it; we might enjoy gardening, too.

Our SAD Diet

SAD is the abbreviation for the "Standard American Diet" and is it indeed SAD (sickening and deadly). We are addicted to fat, sugar, and salt. Our country faces the consequences of the SAD daily and holds the world records for obesity, heart disease, diabetes, and a list of cancers related to the way we eat. The SAD is also draining our personal retirement savings and crippling the Medicare system. Our children are developing SAD diseases at an earlier age, and it's robbing them of years of health, productivity, and financial security. Americans are killing themselves with food, while millions of people in faraway lands are starving to death.

MOTHER EARTH, HOW CAN I HELP YOU?

I know both ends of the food problem are real, but I have no world-changing plans to offer. I hope readers start eating in a more sustainable way. The average American adds four tons of CO_2 to our atmosphere, based on their food choices alone. The more processed a food is, the worse it is for people and the planet. We are hooked on fast food and refer to ourselves as "fast food junkies."

> **The chains of habit are too weak to feel until**
> **they are too strong to be broken.**
> Samuel Johnson

Could we try breaking the chains that are killing our children and us? There is a tremendous benefit to the individual, the people of the Earth, and to the climate when a person eats more from a whole-food plant-based diet. I've been doing that for more than three years and I can truly say I now feel very fortunate to be vegan. If you think breaking some of our most unhealthy eating habits is too complicated, it is anything but complicated. Living with heart disease, strokes, diabetes, or cancer is complicated. The immediate health benefits alone help uncomplicate our lives. A favorite question I ask myself is, "Am I willing to let this be easy?" If you think people won't understand when you change the way you eat, skip that thought. Don't make it complicated; let it be easy. When someone wonders about what I'm eating, I say, "I'm a vegan." It's part of who I am, lucky me! Surprisingly, many people say, "I wish

I could be vegan." I admit that at first it was a challenge to find the recipes I liked best. That is a matter of time and a little testing. I can serve an all vegan meal to company and they love it. If there ever was a right time and an important reason to cut down or cut out eating meat, I think we've reached that time. To feed nearly 3 billion more people, more food has to be produced in the next 50 years than was produced in the last 10,000 years. How much can Mother Earth produce and for how long? Who gets the food when supplies are more and more limited?

> **When a needy person stands at your door,**
> **God Himself stands at his side.**
> Hebrew proverb

EATING LOCAL

That is an excellent idea, but so far my efforts are marginal. I notice where food comes from. This week grapes were on sale, and I knew I wouldn't buy them if they were flown from Chile. They were labeled "product of USA." I almost missed that the oranges on sale in Florida came from South Africa. I can wait for something a little closer to home. Grapes and oranges or any other produce flown halfway around the world for me to buy has to add to global warming. Things like that add up to Americans using seven times the energy and creating seven times the pollution as the average Earthling.

Take a world map to the grocery store to give the kids a geography lesson and teach them how to help save the planet at the same time. Once we are aware, many of us will gladly buy food raised closer to home. I pointed out to a man who was putting the oranges in his cart that they were from South Africa. He hesitated, but decided he really wanted oranges. When someone does not realize the fragile state our world is reaching, why not get oranges from South Africa?

If 300,000,000 Americans shopped in an Earth-friendly manner, it would make a real difference. Does that sound like too much of an inconvenience, or does it leave you feeling deprived? I understand. We are used to seeing something and knowing we can have anything that is within our budget. Putting travel restrictions on our food is a change, but see what you can do. I think I will appreciate my Florida oranges a little more when I get them. If we ate foods that were in season and local, can you imagine how special that first tomato or orange would taste? Every little change we make goes into the big pot of things we are doing better and comes out of the pot of the worst way of having our wants met.

Notice I said our wants met. We do not need everything we want. That was a Roatan grocery shopping lesson. I had my list as I headed for the store, but I was not necessarily going to find everything on the list. I survived very well. Remember, global warming adds to food shortages. Our grocery choices can contribute to a child starving in sub-Saharan Africa. You may think that is melodramatic, maybe so, but it is also true.

Magic Dirt

> LAWN CLIPPINGS AND LEAVES
> SHREDED PAPER
> FRUIT AND VEG SCRAPS
> WAIT SIX WEEKS AND YOU MADE MAGIC DIRT

I have to mention composting; it is the right thing to do for the planet. It's surprising that composting works the way it does. Look up the right amounts for what you will be using and with the ingredients listed above you really have beautiful dark brown dirt. My magic dirt has provided me with some mystery squash that turned out to be cantaloupe. When seeds sprout, I move them to a good place to grow and those are my volunteers.

Where I live, you cannot have a compost pile, so I never thought I could make my own dirt. Then I read *The No Impact Man* and learned there are boxes for sale to use in city apartments. Fruit and vegetable scraps, lawn clipping, and paper are all meant to stay within the nutrient cycle so that our garbage continues to work for us as new dirt. When garbage is buried in a landfill with no access to oxygen, those same items form greenhouse gases and become part of a toxic soup mixed with all the other discarded items. This toxic ooze gets into drinking water and pollutes streams.

There is something fun about making dirt. When a friend calls and asks what you are doing, you might be able to say, "I'm mixing up a new batch of dirt." Can you grow some of your own food? This is one of the nicest and most beneficial ways to connect with nature. I want to serve Lilly food I grew for her to eat.

I have to garden like a city dweller because of restrictions in our community. Beautiful pots contain salad greens, a tomato plant, a cucumber vine, six swiss chard plants, four kale, and seven herbs? I am still looking for a "garden-guru" who can tell me how to have each plant be highly productive. Eventually, I will accomplish that goal and can teach it to my grandchildren and to Lilly. Any volunteers that pop up in my magic dirt are well-treated. My daughter calls the volunteers "God's gifts" from the gardens. It feels good to respect and work within the laws of nature and appreciate the gifts we receive.

The world is not ours.
It is a treasure we hold in trust for future generations.
African Proverb

CHAPTER 15

VEGAN ANYONE?

WE'VE OUTGROWN MOTHER EARTH

Sustainability and eating or not eating meat didn't seem related. We buy it, eat it, and it's gone. There is plenty of meat. Americans eat meat at an ever-increasing rate and see no apparent problem, so what's the big deal? We know technology, science, and human ingenuity can fix any problem man faces, including feeding the billions of people who show up for dinner.

Mother Earth has a "carrying capacity" and man goes beyond it year after year. How much can science, technology, or human ingenuity do to give us a bigger Earth? In 1980, we crossed the line where one Earth was enough for 4.5 billion people. By 1999, we needed 1.2 Earths to provide for 6 billion people, then 1.5 Earths to live the way we were living in 2007, with 6.5 billion people.

I hope this isn't coming across as blaming; I was as clueless as anyone. In January 2011 a weird chain of circumstances caught me at a time when my mind was open a crack. After totally enjoying living a no-frills lifestyle for a month, I was looking forward to seeing Lilly. That book I forgot I ordered was waiting for me. I paid nearly $40.00 for it. If I weren't such a penny-pincher, I might not have read *Harmony,* and nothing would have changed .

I had paid little attention to what was happening to our planet. It's not all progress. Now, I wonder what we have "progressed" ourselves into. When did food become a tipping point? Sometimes the darnedest things happen when nobody's looking. I'm glad *Harmony* landed in my home six months after I became a vegan.

In the 1920s, Hoover campaigned for the presidency, boldly promising the time would come when every Sunday "there will be a chicken in every pot." The world population was less than 2 billion and a family of six or seven in America was dreaming of the day when every family could have one chicken a week. Times have changed. Americans are eating or wasting half again as much meat, per person, as we were thirty-five years ago. We didn't notice the serving sizes getting larger. The obesity epidemic didn't happen overnight. Quadruple bypasses are a common part of many middle-aged Americans' health histories; when did that start?

We can afford the dollars to buy the meat and have all the beef, pork, chicken, and fish we want. However, every time we do that, there is something else going on. It takes seven-four-two times as much grain to raise each serving of beef-pork-poultry, respectively, as it takes for one serving of grain to feed a person. That is what we cannot afford. A healthy serving size is three to four ounces of meat. We may be a little off course there, too.

We use the land to grow grain to feed people and to raise the animals we eat. Land and rainforests are cleared, overgrazed, and some turn into desert. A United Nations study reports that within the last fifty years, one-third of the world's farmable soil has become degraded. This is despite, or because of, the ever-increasing use of petro-chemicals. Fertilizer and pesticide run-off pollutes our streams and destroys the eco-systems where fish spawn and grow. Insecticides kill nature's helpers, like bees and earthworms, and wasteful irrigation drains rivers and squanders our aquifers.

Sustainability started taking on new meaning when I read what Prince Charles wrote: "Sixty billion farm animals are raised for food, using one-third of the world's farm land, eating one-third of the world's grain harvest, and are responsible for 18% of the greenhouses gases causing global warming."

> **One billion people get less nutrition a day than the average**
> **American house cat.**
> Fred Pearse

IF YOU WOULD LIKE TO BE VEGAN, MAY I HELP?

Let me help you love being vegan. It saves as much greenhouse gases as switching from an SUV to a Prius, and it is something an individual can do for the planet.

Would you like to cut your risk of heart disease, reverse existing heart disease, avoid or cure type 2 diabetes, and cross many cancers off your risk list? Then there are those who are truly starving and are grateful you leave a little more for them. Veganism is not for everyone, but consider checking it out.

I promise I won't send the food chain police. I'm not the enforcer. My job is to give you information and motivation. Perhaps you can occasionally join me at the bottom of the food chain. My husband, who still eats some meat, enjoys many vegan meals, and his favorite restaurant is vegan.

You may buy a burger off the dollar menu, but when the real cost is charged to our children and grandchildren, it's going to be hard to swallow. A world of 8 to 10 billion people with billions starving, water scarce, and land depleted is not what I plan to leave for Lilly.

> **How could I look my grandchildren in the eye and say,**
> **"I knew about this and did nothing."**
> Sir David Attenborough, Naturalist and Veteran Broadcaster.

I keep thinking of Maya Angelou's kind observation, "When we know better—we do better." I'm not asking everyone to swear off beef, pork, poultry, fish, eggs, and dairy. That's what vegans don't eat; we eat nothing that comes from something with a face or a mother. I will ask you to consider smaller and fewer servings of meat. Try one day a week with no meat, like the "Meatless Monday" mentioned on TV. Stop buying more than you'll eat; that's a huge help. If you have two little kids who leave half their fast-food order, perhaps you could you buy one order to split. It's a variation on the old "Eat everything on your plate; there are children starving in China" theme. The difference is that you saved it for the children in Africa instead of eating more than you need.

It's time we stop trying to get kids to eat more. Advertising has that covered. Many of us struggle to find a way to avoid overeating. We are killing ourselves. There are many personal benefits of being vegan. Medical concerns gave me my instant vegan conversion. I ask people what made them interested in environmental issues, global warming, or eating vegan. Reasons for becoming vegan differ and are often a bit strange.

A vegetarian I met had a different reason for warding off meat. She was driving her car when a truck hauling pigs to slaughter passed her. She doesn't know how it happened, but she made direct eye contact with a passing pig. They looked into each other's eyes and she started to cry. She knew she could never eat another piece of meat again. A brand new vegetarian was born in an instant. She's lucky to have had a conversion experience. Dr. Dean Ornish, the doctor who reversed heart disease in his patients, says it is much easier to quit cold turkey, than to try slowly changing to a vegan diet. He sees cutting back on unhealthy food as an approach with a lesser chance of success.

I would suggest to the serious future vegan, get ready, and just get up one morning and say aloud, "A brand new vegan is born." Let it be easy. You might pick a meaningful day. If I weren't already a vegan and it was near Lilly's birthday, that would be the day. I'd do it for Lilly in a heartbeat. If you find yourself over-thinking the switch, there is a bit of Alabama country advice I heard at a workshop by Edwene Gaines. I believe she attributes this to her grandfather. If you're going to kiss a frog, it's best not to look at it for too long.

Follow your doctor's advice, but don't stick with a doctor who instantly says it's dangerous. Read *The China Study* and feel really good about the many things you're doing to live better and longer—and maybe saving your children's lives.

Eating vegan is budget friendly; in fact, it's cheap. Our bodies adjust to beans. If you experience some brief difficulty, eat small amounts, and soon your body will build up the enzymes and bacteria needed to digest the added fiber.

Now, how I became a vegan. I retired in 2010, was overweight, and I had high cholesterol. My doctor convinced me I had to go on three medications. I'd put it off as long as I could, thinking I was going to lose weight. That never happened. One of the meds kept my heart rate low. I felt exhausted if I tried to do something strenuous. Sometimes I felt lightheaded. I pleaded my case to my doctor, but she was not going to back down. She finally had me on the medications she had been trying to get me to take for two years; the subject was not open to debate. I dragged along, trying to enjoy my retirement, but feeling a medication-induced twenty years older.

In July 2010, we went on a five-week vacation to northern New York. We decided to help family do some remodeling while we were there. I did a lot, but I was not the help I hoped to be. I felt like a wimp. Wally was also pushing himself and needed to take more pain meds for his back and neck problems. Because he needed pain meds, I did most of the driving. The problem was that my prescriptions made me feel lightheaded. I did not feel safe driving. So I stopped all my pills just before we were starting our 1,500 mile drive home. Stupidity can be inspiring. My reasoning went, "Something in my medications makes me a geriatric mess. I'll stop them all and just to be safe, I'll be a vegan." A brand new vegan was born.

I avoided going to my doctor. I had no choice but to remain vegan and add gym workouts. Later, I chose a new doctor and told him of my brainstorm that had now been going on several months. I had lost twenty pounds and felt much better. He patiently heard my case and explained why I must take something for my cholesterol and high blood pressure. The labs showed my cholesterol was forty points lower, even off the meds. But, it wasn't where it should be. He prescribed new drugs that didn't leave me disabled.

The doctor praised me for being vegan. I asked about getting enough protein and he assured me there was no problem. The full lab work-up for my most recent visit was the best report I've ever had. My doctor said his thirty-year-old patients would love a report like that. My weight was going down slowly. I'm still on some medications, but my goal is to lose the weight and get off them entirely.

As a vegan, I find I'm not eating something that doesn't agree with me. There's a "rightness" about my food that I can't explain. I feel as if I'm respecting my body, improving my health, and I'm pleased to leave a portion of grain for a hungry person. Others can choose to eat meat, but I feel lucky to have been able to let it go.

I, in my impulsive act, didn't stop to tell myself it would be too hard to give up meat, dairy, fish, and eggs. I just did it. A great question that invites a person to do something–without the soap opera is, "How would I be doing this differently, if I were willing to let it be easy?" Gandhi said, "In a gentle way you can shape the world." I feel as if that is exactly what I am doing and it feels good.

Millions of Americans are trying one scheme after another to lose weight. I found, as I read *The Okinawa Program*, that practicing Hari Hachi Bu (not eating portions that stretch your stomach and leave you stuffed) made sense. I notice people who naturally practice Hari Hachi Bu. If I grew up eating only until my stomach was 80% full, I would be healthier physically and emotionally. I would have been free of years of self-consciousness about my weight.

Another lesson I learned about eating in the Japanese style concerns Shojin Ryori. The food is presented and has five colors in the meal. This helps combine the full balance of nutrients, because each color stores different vitamins, amino acids (for protein), and other important nutrients. I use beautiful small dishes to serve our meals. Visit a Japanese restaurant and start experiencing the ritual of admiring each part of the meal and appreciating the color, flavor, and texture.

If you don't mind reading a book that is clinical, *The Okinawa Program* has helpful and motivating ideas. I wanted books that had nothing to do with another fad. In graduate school I learned to respect good scientific research, and when it came to finding out what was the best way to eat, I wanted that accuracy. Everything in that book agrees with *The China Study*, Dr. Ornish's *Eat More, Weigh Less,* and Dr. Joel Fuhrman's *Eat to Live.* These four books are like a short college course on how the human body was meant to thrive. I follow their guidelines and believe I will have a long, healthy, and active life. I want to live long and die short, free of the lengthy debilitating diseases the SAD so often brings. I would highly recommend everyone read *The China Study.* It will improve the quality and length of your life.

EATING OUT

Quite a few vegans and vegetarians are eating out, so don't make it into a soap opera. Salad and vegetables work; you can have some protein when you get home. That's the worst-case scenario. There's usually something on the menu that can be put together. Burger King has a veggie burger. Wally's favorite restaurant is vegan. Their serving sizes are smaller than many American cuisine restaurants. Last week Wally and I treated ourselves to lunch. Before we entered, we decided to practice Hari Hachi Bu. We split our favorite entree and were surprised that it felt just right. That is so different from our former habits.

"Sweet Tomatoes" is a fantastic salad (and much more) buffet restaurant chain that is great for vegans. It is a certified 2-star green restaurant serving local fresh vegetables, and everything is made from scratch daily. For the non-vegan, there are homemade soups with meat, pasta dishes with cheese, and salads with meat and tuna. I want to support a place that does the right things for the environment. They even compost their fruit and vegetable scraps.

One of the challenges people worry about when they become vegan is finding foods with the required nutrients. Vegans get plenty of calcium, protein, and iron with no problem. I have looked up the nutrient value of what I eat several times and it is always fine. Getting the perfect lab report at my last physical, after being vegan for years, has put my concerns to rest. It's the SAD that lacks nutrients and is filled with deadly addictive sugar, salt, and fat.

VEGAN KITCHEN FOR EARTHLINGS

Organic brown rice is the rice with all the nutrients. It takes 40 minutes to cook, but the white and instant stuff is nothing but calories. Rice cookers are convenient. The small cookers make three cups, or you may prefer the larger size. Cooked rice keeps well in the refrigerator or freezer, and it heats perfectly in the microwave. Be sure to read the labels on noodles; some have no protein per serving and some have as much as fourteen grams. Whole grain noodles are what to look for. I find the best variety at Oriental stores.

I try dishes from other countries, and when I have a delicious vegan meal at a restaurant, I ask the chef for pointers to get that great flavor. Many dishes from Central and South America, the Middle-East, and Southeast Asia don't use meat and are seasoned with herbs and spices rather than piles of salt.

Dr. Joel Fuhrman strongly recommends allowing our taste buds to adjust to no added salt to reduce the risk of the kind of stroke caused by a tiny blood vessel rupturing in the brain. He explains many health issues in his book. I am getting healthier by making changes he recommends, and the weigh continues to go down. I seldom feel hungry and no longer have food cravings. That is on my gratitude list. Dr. Fuhrman has great insight about ending food cravings.

Beans and rice or other grain are good protein sources. When we have company, instead of cooking something different for myself, I have a serving of black beans, put garbanzo beans in the tossed salad, and serve two cooked vegetables. I never worry about having "nothing I can eat" when we dine at someone's home. I let people know I'm vegan, but tell them not to go to any trouble. There are usually vegetables, pasta, salad, or something I can eat. I put a cooler in the car with an apple and some walnuts in case I feel I must fight off starvation. A quick look in a mirror tells me starvation is not knocking at my door. If you have young children who want to save the Earth, you might call some of your new meals, "Meals Eaten by the Earth Rescue Team."

I HOPE FOR SOME VEGAN BIRTHS!

CHAPTER 16

HOW COULD I NOT KNOW THIS IS HAPPENING AND WHY ISN'T IT NEWS?

There is a "cluelessness factor" infecting America. What I took as being aware, driving less, not buying bottled water, hanging my clothes to dry when I could–STOP, right there! What on Earth ever convinced me I could NOT hang my laundry outside? Americans don't realize how our thinking has changed in ways that harm the planet.

Some people remember the first time they heard of a clothes dryer. My mother could. In 1920 "can't hang the clothes out," meant you were paralyzed. Even lazy people did that. We are SO brainwashed. Where I live, lines are discretely hidden behind a tall hedge. Of the hundreds of residents, I am the only one who always uses them.

Why don't we know about global warming? Maybe there's something in us that doesn't want to be inconvenienced and willingly latches on to ideas like we can't hang out the laundry. Is that a hint as to why we are clueless? How much do we want to know? There is an inkling that if we knew more, we might feel we have to give up something. What I've read suggests, yes, we will have to change some of our ways.

Try using Mary Guay's Hierarchy of Happiness for an attitudinal adjustment. There are things in life that are ours to do. At the bottom level of the Hierarchy of Happiness, we HAVE TO DO, and grudgingly hang the laundry. Reframe that same activity and think why you would CHOOSE TO dry the clothes outside. Maybe it feels good to reduce the stress you cause to the environment, or it's quiet and the fresh air is calming and pleasant.

The next step requires you to reframe the same activity and feel something beyond willingness. There is a sense of purpose or honor. You may find reasons deep inside why you WANT TO hang the clothes out. Enjoy the fresh air and imagine how well your children will sleep as they nestle in line-fresh sheets. You may feel energized. It gets even better with the next step.

This is the reward, "the good that is in every situation." Reframe again. Now, you LOVE TO DO it and there is a sense of gratitude and joy. You look forward to the quiet time in nature. What had been a chore now becomes a gift. You are grateful for your family and this opportunity to bless them with tender loving care. You appreciate the grass under your feet and the music of the songbirds. There are times your soul seems to sing with them. We absolutely have the power to change our attitude. Put it to the test and your life will change.

When you can take a task, stifle the moaning and complaining the mind throws at you, and "**You Use Your Mind**," rather than it using you, something changes inside. You claim your value and your power to reframe, take action, and be happier. This chapter asked, "How could I not know this?" You are now becoming a person who is ready, willing, able, and eager to know what is yours to do.

I have an artificial orchid in a pretty little jug on the windowsill above my kitchen sink. Wally loves and grows orchids, so they remind me of one of my special blessings. I read the words painted in lavender, on the jug, "I CHOOSE HAPPINESS." I choose happiness when I hand-wash the dishes. It has meaning to me far beyond doing the dishes. If I choose, and I use my mind in a good way, doing the dishes can feel as if it "feeds my soul." For some, that might sound (as Oprah would say) a little "woo-woo." OK, but oh my, does it feel good! Thank you, God. Thank you for the family, the food, the home, the honor to love and care for the people and things that I value so dearly. Life is good!

I would LOVE TO save the world for Lilly. This book is a huge part of my "divine purpose." Searching for the truth, working to do what is mine to do, and writing this book adds joy to my life. The more I know, the more I can do.

There are many reasons why I didn't know about the threat to Lilly's life called global warming. As I learn more, I do not stay at the bottom of the pyramid. I stifle thoughts that I am powerless to do anything. As I climb the pyramid, I am given power, guidance, energy, curiosity, help, and I ASK God for help. I don't beg; "Thou shalt not whine." I BOLDLY ask. Sometimes I feel as if I have unleashed a powerhouse in me. Imagine a 70-year-old, great-granny out to save the world.

Do you have loved ones you want to protect from harm? Let's see what power you can unleash. The crisis may be terrible, but it need not be overwhelming. Good can come from facing the problems that engulf Mother Earth. One personal gain could be realizing your own value. Remember the quote at the beginning of the book? It wasn't written just for me; it is for everyone who is willing to start on their path.

> **YOU are here to enable the divine purpose of the universe to unfold.**
> **That's how important YOU are.**
> Eckhart Tolle

I put the emphasis on "you." Can you do the same? An affirmation I like is, "I am responsible for the events in my life. I stand with God, doing what is mine to do." I might wake before dawn with an inspiration that something needs to be written right NOW. I accept the intuitive guidance and push the power button on the computer. I don't have to know what I am going to write; I will be guided. Hours later, when I finish, I feel wonderfully uplifted.

We are awesome! YOU are awesome! I can dream about all the good that will pour out when more and more people take action. That is a visualization, and it is powerful. See yourself as the capable and miraculous person you really are.

Years ago, I read a wonderful little book called The 100th Monkey about two far-distant islands, each populated by many monkeys. There was no contact between the islands. On one island, a monkey started washing his food a different and better way. Gradually, others started washing their food the same way. Then one pivotal day, when the 100th monkey did it the new way, the rest of the monkeys on the island started to use the new way AND the monkeys on the other islands also changed to the new method at the same time. The explanation for this phenomenon is that we really are interconnected, and when enough people or monkeys reach a critical mass, there is a shift in consciousness that affects all.

At a three-day workshop about realizing our dreams, I told everyone "I am an author." Until then I would say, "I'm a retired hospice social worker," and not feel qualified to say I am an author. The speaker asked us to claim our value and power and instructed us to write twelve goals and to make some of them BOLD. WOW! This did not come as a thought drifting by; the exploding breath-taking words slammed into my brain! "*FOR LILLY* IS THE 100TH MONKEY!" That still sits in my heart as a dream. I want it to be something, as I put it, "I Know–I Know–I Know."

Dear God, I ask that *For Lilly* is "The 100th Monkey," and that stopping global warming becomes the United States' primary focus. America needs enough people who learn about global warming and take action to reach a critical mass, so we quickly change our behavior. The U.S. will again be a world leader in the best possible way. I ask that much good comes from this and everyone is able to live happier, healthier, safer, and more meaningful lives.

I hope each reader will take corrective action and share this book and what they are doing with others. America needs to move from being clueless to suddenly "getting it."

Global warming is affecting us all, right now. Sooner or later, we will HAVE TO DO something about it. If we wait for the HAVE TO DO, hiding as long as we can, it might take an event as sudden and shocking as Pearl Harbor or 9-11 to scare us into action. If we remain like the lobster in the pot, not noticing the temperature rising, we allow ourselves to get deeper and deeper into hot water. Scientists agree that once a tipping point is reached, nothing can save civilization from collapse. For me, it is not an option to let this happen.

STIFLE–STIFLE–STIFLE your brain when it screams reasons you can't. Rolling over and playing dead while the Earth comes down around us HAS TO STOP. It's time to HAVE TO–CHOOSE TO–WANT TO–LOVE TO be powerful. Sooner rather than later is best. Later is like pretending you don't have cancer.

HAVE A LITTLE FAITH

People who have changed the way they live to reduce global warming say they feel freed from the hectic pace of working to pay for all the possessions they thought they'd earned, deserved, and had to have. The belongings did not bring them the happiness, convenience, or the prestige they sought. What if sustainable living feels more like a release from a prison than being deprived of all the stuff we've been programed to think we need? We resist personal change and label moves to a simpler lifestyle as severe or bad for the economy. We can be misguided and have set ideas that we do not want to let go. Do we even know where some of our steadfast ideas came from or who put them in our heads? If advertising is to blame, who paid for it and who benefits the most?

MARY'S MUSINGS–LOBSTER FOX

On July10, 2012, ABC News had a brief statement about the

United States government reporting global warming is serious. Each of the last 12 months has been the hottest on weather-keeping records and the Greenland ice sheet is melting 30 times faster than a decade ago.

Could that be newsworthy enough for a little in-depth information? Apparently, not. I turned to MSNBC, not a word. I checked The Weather Channel and again nothing. I considered Fox News and decided not to waste my time. If there is a plane crash, there will be coverage on Fox News. They don't consider global warming news and aren't even sure there is such a thing. Fox doesn't deny global warming could exist; they're just waiting until all reports agree. There are many conflicting reports with hundreds, if not thousands of different findings. Did 35,000−45,000−50,000 people die in the 2003 European heat wave? Numbers varied nearly 50%. Figures may differ, but scientists agree that global warming exists and is caused by man. Fox still waits until all reports agree.

Is that the way it is for the lobster? He's in water that is hotter and hotter and hotter. The problem is, we are not lobsters, and we are the ones in the pot. For Fox News Service to avoid knowing to the degree that seems to be their policy just makes them a Fox, not news, not service, just a sly fox.

I wish I knew who pulls the strings at Fox. I don't know who pulls the strings anywhere, but sometimes I think I recognize a puppet. When does not saying anything become a lie? That isn't a question for just Fox. It's a question for media, government, and citizens in general. When do they and we have a responsibility to the viewer, the voters, or our families to find out and take action? The stakes are life and death.

In fairness to Fox, other news services are lacking as well. We live in a hurricane-prone area in Southwest Florida, and keep an eye on The Weather Channel (TWC). They reports floods, record high snowfalls in the winter, drought in the summer, and record-setting extended heat waves covering large areas. Weekly series cover many topics. We have not, however, seen a program on global warming, nor has it been the subject of a special report. How can TWC and other "services" continually report record-setting weather events and not tie it to global warming? Is the topic too politically controversial for them? Who are their major sponsors, owners, or supporters?

Walter Cronkite, a well-respected retired newscaster is now free of any network control. He has an opinion about global warming: "The governments of the world have tarried long enough, and the United States is scarcely without doubt the greatest culprit among them." Newscasters are not on the air to give their opinions, but they have an idea of what is and is not news we all should know. When will global warming be newsworthy?

Colin Campbell described how industries manage to get people in positions of influence who then handpick people who make policies. Is that what's going on with the media of all kinds? Controlling, withholding, and manipulating information is a well-practiced practice, Maybe "practice has made perfect."

Oh breaking news, Tom Cruise and what's-her-face are not talking! More to follow! Being clueless has a lot to do with what is presented as newsworthy. What do we follow; what do our "inquiring minds want to know?" Would news programs covering global warming lose viewers to *Entertainment Tonight* for an update on some Hollywood break up?

We seem to drop everything for a good celebrity scandal, or another favorite, photogenic carnage. Global warming might be too boring. Our viewing choices make it easier for networks to skip over life and death information, and we don't seem to care. It is a convenient excuse not to investigate for ourselves. Surely, if it were important, it would be on the news or reported by our government.

We cannot trust TV or government leaders to tell us what we need to know. Even the politicians who want to address the problem have their hands tied. If the power-elite are not able to pull the puppet strings, they can render that wayward upstart powerless. Congress seems to be broken. Have you noticed their inefficiency? How many politicians are really representing the folks back home? What is going on?

Question: Do you know the name of the act opponents have dubbed "Obamacare"?

Answer: It's the Affordable Health Care Act. It was passed.

Question: How many times have our elected Senators gone through the process of bringing "Obamacare" to the Senate floor in an attempt to have it repealed?

Answer: Thirty-one times as of July 11, 2012.

Question: Does even one of those Senators believe they can get the Affordable Health Care Act repealed?

Answer: No. It has not passed the House thirty times. The President has assured them that if it were to pass, he would veto it in a heartbeat.

Question: Do you know the definition of insanity?

Answer: Doing the same thing over and over and over and expecting a different result.

Question: Why is it impossible to get urgent legislation through Congress?

Answer: They're insanely busy.

OK, no surprise, I'm in favor of the Affordable Health Care Act. I spent years working with dying patients who couldn't afford to pay for the follow-up biopsy, scan, or treatment that would have saved their lives. Many would have lived if we had Affordable Healthcare. I had too many self-employed patients who died each year. They were not eligible for Medicare or Medicaid. Private insurance was outlandishly expensive, too restricted in coverage that the person could afford, or needed coverage was denied. It was a choice between putting food on the table or paying an impossible premium. In the end, they lost everything.

I'm truly disgusted with the time stolen by the useless attempts to repeal the Affordable Healthcare Act. As much as I favor that act, my vote will go to the candidates who show a desire to do something about global warming. I am single-minded on that issue. No one will be healthy on a planet that cannot sustain us. It's scary to think of the control big money has over our elected officials. If the insurance industry can wield so much influence, what can big oil do? Now I wonder how much money and influence oil has put into slowing Congress by using healthcare as a decoy. The problem of global warming is SO big, yet it seems it barely exists when we look at Washington's actions.

Question: How many million voters does it take to equal the influence of big oil? The 2012 election was a nightmare for me. The candidates that favored big business got millions and millions of dollars for their primaries and the general election campaigns. Election years must be an exciting time for the power-elite. They have a chance to buy a new House of Representatives, a third of the Senate, and perhaps a president.

Recently, a workshop leader directed me to ask God if I really wanted something. Here is something I really want. Please give us a government with officials who are willing to do all they can to stabilize global warming and save the planet.

My disillusionment with Washington has ramped up since this search for truth began. The extent of the Federal Government ignoring global warming is far beyond anything I ever dreamed. The boldness of big oil and their power to pull strings is astonishing. It's especially noticeable to the people who know the problems.

On June 21, 2004, forty-eight Nobel-Prize-winning scientists accused President Bush and his administration of distorting science. Their statement reads in part:

> **By ignoring scientific consensus on critical issues, such as global climate change, President Bush and his administration are threatening the Earth's future.**
> 48 Nobel-Prize-winning scientists

The list of scientists is on page 269 of *An Inconvenient Truth*. This is beyond a political issue; it speaks to morals and integrity. I know the Bush administration is history, but it's not the specific person who is president that's the real problem. It's a system that has the very powerful people pulling strings from behind the scenes, having people placed in positions of power that control policy and create laws that favor the rich and powerful individuals and corporations.

Oh Captain—My Captain

The captain of the *USS Mighty Progress* and his circle of advisors were conferring on the bridge one dark night. On the horizon they saw an approaching vessel. A few minutes passed and the ship was still headed in their direction. The captain ordered that a message be sent telling the approaching ship to alter its course and gave the coordinates. Still, the vessel remained on the same course. Then, the *USS Mighty Progress* got an answer. "No. You must change your course." The captain was FURIOUS. The *USS Mighty Progress* was the biggest and mightiest ship on the seas. For some reason the other ship didn't seem to know who she was dealing with. The other ship was again informed that this was indeed "THE" *USS Mighty Progress* and this ship will remain on the current course. This was not a matter for discussion. The approaching ship was informed in no uncertain terms the *USS Mighty Progress* is more powerful and would not take orders from any ship. Quickly the response came. "No," you must alter your course "IMMEDIATELY!" The captain fired back a cutting response, "We will not alter our course! I am the captain and I am in command of the *USS Mighty Progress*!"

The final response was, "I AM A LIGHT HOUSE."

Arrogance can result in blindness and deafness when one thinks no one else's information, concerns, warnings, needs, or attempts to help are relevant. Refusal to listen or respond to messages of warning is never a good idea. Unfortunately, we have remained headed dead-on for disaster. The many messages and warnings that could save us are ignored, denied, and hidden.

How can so few, compared to the U.S. population, keep us on a course of disaster for our country and the world? Forty-eight Nobel-Prize-Winning scientists are ignored. The former Prime Minister of Canada, who angrily accused the United States of not having a global conscience, was ignored. Every other developed nation (132) in the world ratified the Kyoto Treaty and the United States arrogantly refused. The island nations of Maldives and Tuvalu tried to sue the U.S. for its part in creating global warming and its refusal to take any responsibility or corrective action. The United States acts as if we are above being asked to join in a worldwide effort to save our planet. What greed and arrogance it takes on the part of those behind the scenes to use their power and influence to line their pockets and turn their backs on humanity. Congressional representatives; Senators; people in the executive and judicial branches, even if your office or appointment was financed and backed by the power elite; could you please serve the millions of Americans who look to you to do what is right?

> **Go to your bosom, knock there and ask what it doth know.**
> William Shakespeare

Look deep into the eyes of your child or grandchild and vow, "With all my heart, I love you and I will keep you from harm." Do it for the ones you love. The world that lies ahead for our children and grandchildren is a world of ever-increasing losses of all they hold dear and need to survive. We are plundering their futures and destroying the Earth for everyone.

Be a hero; save our world. Could anything be more important? Leaders, have the conscience, caring, and courage to say, "In my heart I know I must do what is right." The power, influence, and control of the power elite runs deep, and certainly defying that control is dangerous for elected officials. Richard Lugar is an example of this, and elected officials are aware of what can happen if they step out of line. It would require great courage and personal risk to take a stand for your child, your grandchild, and your country. There have been many courageous Americans in our past; surely, there must be such people among us now.

WHAT HAS AMERICA PARALYZED?

The power of big business should not be underestimated. Sadly, eight vital years were lost during George W. Bush's presidency. He campaigned as if he cared about environmental issues. That wasn't a true representation to the voters. If he cared about global warming, who would he want to fill position of the chief of staff for the White House Environmental Office, and be in charge of environmental policy for the White House?

On the day George W. Bush was inaugurated, he hired Phillip Cooney. These were his qualifications for the job: Education: No scientific training, but he was a lawyer/lobbyist; Current employer and experience: 1995 to present, employed by American Petroleum Institute as lobbyist in charge of global warming disinformation. Cooney's Whitehouse duties included editing and censoring the official assessments of global warming from the EPA and other parts of the federal government. This information is from *An Inconvenient Truth* where the unbelievable is there to see. There is a picture of *The New York Times* article showing part of a report an inside whistle-blower from the Bush administration provided to the *Times*. It shows a report stating global warming is rapidly melting polar ice caps and mountain glaciers. It warned of danger to people, to the fishing they depend on, of flooding, and several other problems. In his duty to be in charge of environmental policy, Cooney, with no scientific training whatsoever, took a red pen, neatly crossed out line after line, and noted in the margin in his own handwriting, "Straying from research strategy into speculative findings from here." When the news hit the press, there was no defense. He resigned and went on the payroll of Exxon Mobil the same day. We are clueless because facts were withheld.

To understand how broad the issue of information being changed or withheld is, watch *Gasland*. I told you about this in Chapter 8. An EPA veteran admitted it's useless to go to the EPA with urgent environmental concerns. The Halliburton loophole has gutted past environmental laws. Gas company representatives are able to lie in sworn testimony before Congress and face no charges.

There were some candidates for the national election on the news who have terrible personal records, but someone liked them enough to fill their war chests and bombard the viewers with endless TV spots. How much money does it cost to air three consecutive political ads evening after evening for the same person running in a primary during the coverage of the summer Olympics? I DO NOT want that puppet for my Congressman. He may owe someone a great deal. Sadly, he was elected. There is another well-financed puppet in Washington. I never gave that a thought in the past. I'm suspicious about how and why this happened. In November 2013 he was arrested for cocaine possession and his political future is uncertain.

There are reasons we didn't know what was happening and why it's not news!

CHAPTER 17

THE BIG THREE: HOW WE SAVE 50,000 POUNDS OF CO_2 A YEAR AT HOME

EMMY SUE, OUR PRIUS

President Obama signed a bill on August 29, 2012, requiring American cars to get twice the mileage of today in twelve years. Several congressional representatives worried the cars will cost more and limit choices for Americans who want luxury. I believe there will still be some fine options available for those who cannot make the sacrifice. As far as it costing more, that may be true. Our Prius was more than some, but every month "Emmy Sue" pays part of her payment by saving on gas.

The van got seventeen mpg and the Prius gets triple that amount. Every gallon of gas takes us three times as far. Eventually it will be paying us. The family driving a car that gets fifty or more miles per gallon might be able to afford a fill-up. Our green investment will pay for herself in seven years, less if gas prices rise.

We hadn't planned to buy a new car. However, with every fill-up it became clear this was a significant way to reduce our carbon footprint. We still drive about 20,000 miles a year. Trips to Tampa to see Lilly and our older grandchildren, who are wonderful ballet dancers, remain a luxury we indulge in whenever they perform. Flying is so polluting we drive to see family in Washington, D.C. and northern New York. We wanted an American-made car, but none compared to the Prius for good mileage. It was the right thing to do for the environment and it supports a business that helps to limit global warming.

By April 2012, Japan had sold one million Priuses in the U.S. Those could have been American-made cars if our automakers were willing to build them. They preferred to focus on production of the high-profit cars, trucks, and vans. Millions are spent on advertising to sell their environmental disasters, and millions more are spent to prevent Americans from learning about and taking action to correct global warming. All that money spent for immediate profit with no thought for our children's futures.

Since the signing of legislation mandating better gas mileage, I have noticed more advertising for fuel-efficient American-made cars. I hope nothing happens to overturn the new mileage requirements. If that happened, I'm concerned American auto-makers would once again be unable to build the cars we so desperately need.

On our trip north, we were in a traffic jam for thirty minutes on I-95. We pressed the "EV" (electric vehicle) mode. The self-charging battery lasted the entire time, using no gasoline. It was low by the time traffic started moving again but recharged itself within five minutes.

When it comes to lowering carbon footprints, the car you drive and your driving habits can make a huge difference. Do every big and little thing you can to be part of the solution and stop adding to the problem. Don't forget to walk when you can. Our convenient and indulgent lifestyles are a health bomb that is exploding in our pudgy little faces. Walking or biking is often seen as something that is either too inconvenient or time consuming, when it could be a built-in workout.

Some of you may not have experienced the serenity of a quiet walk on a wooded path or the closeness you feel walking along a peaceful trail with a friend. It's a different type of companionship compared to going to the mall or sitting and texting to the person. There's a personal contact and richness we forfeit by always having to "do," "go," or "be entertained." See if you can start putting active and peaceful experiences into your life. Let the criteria be to use no gas, buy nothing, find a quiet place, and let it involve walking or biking for at least twenty minutes. The health benefits are instantly apparent. You feel energized, peaceful, and have more clarity to make decisions. If you feel worn out or winded, be grateful you discovered how deconditioned you are and that you have an activity that can restore your health.

Another big change we made goes hand-in-hand with reclaiming good health. We eat fresh food that has not been over-processed, stripped of nutrients, filled with sugar, salt, and fats, and chemically fortified. Many Americans eat a bizarre diet that's more manufactured than grown. We've been persuaded that the convenient, fortified, and labeled-healthy foods are good for us. People pay higher prices for food replacement products. Adding vitamins or calcium does not enrich food the way nature balances all the nutrients so that our body can use it correctly. Many added nutrients are flushed, because the fiber and other important parts of the original food have been refined away. Look at what people have in their grocery carts. I see carts full of health problems and unnecessary financial burdens. Eating food concocted in a factory is an American way of life that we can change and at the same time, improve our lives and help save the planet.

WHAT WE EAT MAKES A DIFFERENCE

I've been a vegan since 2010, so I was being good to the planet even before I found out how much trouble Lilly's world was facing. Wally eats more than half his food from the bottom of the food chain. His change is primarily for health reasons. Even the way I cook is helping the environment and entertains me at the same time.

Wally and I saw our neighbors' solar oven and tried to build one from instructions off the Internet. That wasted twenty dollars, cooked only a few things, and the contraption looked so hideous I had to hide for fear a brand new rule would be drafted by our ever-vigilant homeowner's association. Wally gave me a solar oven for Christmas. It has not lost its entertainment value. I cook our food in it on sunny days.

An example of eating that sounds different because we "don't eat that way," is corn on the cob for breakfast. Husk the ear, rinse it, wrap it in a clean wet dishcloth, and microwave for three to four minutes. Use little or no salt and margarine. Allow your taste to change and enjoy sweet and juicy corn on the cob. Manufacturers get seventy large boxes of cornflakes from a bushel of corn. There cannot be much nutrition in a bowl of sugared cornflakes, and it has far more calories than an ear of corn. When it comes to fruit, eat the whole fruit instead of fruit-like drinks.

People in other countries eat fresh fruits and vegetables for breakfast. Their pastries are not from a factory and do not have a list chemicals for ingredients. If you can breakfast on unprocessed foods, you have done one good deed for the day before even leaving the house.

Imagine you were born one hundred years earlier and the food you learned to cook was the most delicious in the world. We had incredible cooks in our family, and Grandma Meister made wonderful meals with fresh food from the farm and garden. During the winter, they ate food they canned and froze. Few of us will grow all our food, but remember that food not from a factory is healthier and costs less. I am not talking about "slaving over a hot stove." That is one of the phrases or images used to persuade us to turn to factory meals. If we can learn to prepare and eat chemical concoctions, we can learn to prepare and eat the real thing.

If you and some friends are reading this book, I'd like to suggest you support those interested in becoming vegan. You might have a book-club type group and start with *The China Study*. Then start sharing some easy vegan main dishes. Some might be so good that your family would like them. It's easy to spout out, "I could never be vegan," but that's not a true statement. Try restaurants with great vegan entrees, and see how close you can come to duplicating their delicious dishes. Try it with a buddy who would like to give it a shot. Be proud of being vegan. It's such a beneficial thing to do on so many levels. I still have family that chuckles about Grandma being vegan, but now they want to know what new dish I have discovered.

Our youngest daughter became a vegan because there are plenty of delicious meals she enjoys, and she has some truly American health issues that make it necessary for her to take better care of her body.

As you read the alarming information in the earlier chapters, you may have wondered how to make a significant improvement. When a family makes changes in the way they eat, there can be huge benefits to everyone's health, as well as the food supply for people in other lands, the environment, and local farmers. If a family of four goes vegan, you win the grand prize—many added years of healthy living on a healthier planet. Having lost both my sisters to cancer and my father to heart disease, I don't find being vegan inconvenient or difficult at all. Dying of heart disease and cancer is inconvenient and difficult for the person and the entire family.

The Electric Bill—Eureka!

Pricing solar panels was enlightening. It would cost many thousands of dollars for our home. Unless we reached a Biblical age, a solar roof would be a poor investment. With the possibility of a significant rise in sea level for Southwest Florida, the increase in property value did not carry much weight either.

The CO_2 generating FPL will still have our business, but not much! I have creatively cut every last KWH I can. I read my meter and chart the 24-hour and running monthly total on the kitchen calendar. I look forward with joyful anticipation to the arrival of the electric bill. When I checked my May 2012 bill, we had used one-eighth of the power we used a year ago and one-tenth of what we used in 2010 for the same month. This realization was one of those unexpected moments of pure joy. I don't see it as a drop from \$86 to \$16. I see 1,664 pounds less CO_2 going into the atmosphere.

The changes made around the house are ongoing and now require some thinking outside the box. I keep asking myself, "How did we drop from 952 KWHs to 119 KWHs?" This success was leaving me giddy. One thought that helped curtail our power-binging lifestyle was, *what can I do for myself instead of using electricity*? I've learned a lot. Let me joyfully share this list of things we do in our quest to stop the little black dot on the electrical meter disk from moving. Knowledge has power and in this case requires less power.

1. I know how to sweep my floors with a broom.
2. I know that my electric toothbrush, which the dentist says I should use, will charge in eight hours and the charge will last two weeks. It's unplugged most of the time.
3. I know I can read with only one light, and when I move, the light is turned off. Having lights on in the kitchen, dining room, bedroom, and bathroom doesn't improve my vision when I'm reading in the living room.
4. I know I can often walk into a room to get something without turning on the lights. It helps to have things de-cluttered so you know where everything is.
5. I know that locking windows and doors makes a tight seal and prevents heat or cold leaks.
6. I know when the breeze is more than two miles an hour and the temperature is four to five degrees lower outside, that windows go up and we have a glorious breeze wafting through the house.
7. I know how to lower blinds, close draperies, pull shades, and not turn on the A/C. The east and west ends of our home are all windows with a view of our sailboat in the canal to the east and the yacht basin to the west. We have double-pane windows tinted with sun and heat reflective film and have external manual

rolldown shades. The west windows are our Achilles heel. The homeowners' association is very strict, and our request to plant shade trees was denied. Negotiations ensued, an agreement was reached, and for Mother's Day, I received two new shrubs that were planted in front of our house. Although they are smaller and thinner than the trees we preferred, they will provide some shade for the west windows. I named them Eckhart and Lester.

8. I know we can give our shrubs a "tall trim" to shade some windows. Our bylaws state we must keep our shrubs and bushes trimmed.

9. I know how to cook in a solar oven. This is green-granny's entertainment center, and it doesn't heat up the house.

10. I know I don't have to heat up my house to cook. Many foods are delicious raw, and I have a microwave and cooking plate on our patio to use on cloudy days when my solar oven is not an option. The object is to keep the inside temperature as comfortable as possible and avoid turning on the A/C.

11. I know energy-saving tips for when I use the electric stove. Pull food from the freezer or fridge early so it reaches room temperature before cooking. Put a lid on the pots to keep the heat in. Use pots with flat vs. rounded bottoms, and use the smallest burner that will do the job. Turn the burner off early and let the pot remain on the burner to finish cooking. Don't preheat your oven, and turn it off early. When I'm finished cooking, I turn off the circuit to the stove. There are electronic timing devices built in that use energy.

12. I know if the forecast is for cold weather, I can roast a chicken or a pot roast. Wally still gets the occasional roasted meat dinner, and I get to experiment with oven-cooked vegan dishes. Then the leftovers are divided into three to four ounce servings of meat. An eight-pound turkey lasts a l-o-n-g time. In Southwest Florida, roasting a turkey can replace turning on the furnace.

13. I know that a separate freezer will waste more money than it saves, even with food on sale.

14. I know how to make wonderful vegan chocolate and strawberry shakes and fruit smoothies in my Vitamix. They cool us from the inside out.

15. I know that drinking ice water and sun tea helps keep me cool. When I feel hungry, I am often only thirsty. I've consumed many calories in the past, when all my body really needed was a cold drink of water.

16. I know that the freezer is most efficient when kept full, and the fridge does better when there is space for the air to circulate. We bought a smaller, more efficient refrigerator. The salesperson asked if we wanted an icemaker. I said, "No thanks, I know the recipe." I'm not sure how much energy an icemaker takes, but it is electric.

17. I know I do not need a garbage disposal. Ours died. We have put in four new garbage disposals since we moved here fifteen years ago. We decided to wait two weeks and see if we really needed one. Nope, do not need it or want it.

18. I know I can charge the cell phone and computer in the car while we drive.

19. I know I can walk to the telephone and stay there to talk. One day we thought we had everything electrical unplugged or turned off. All phantom energy drains were disconnected, the appliances unplugged, but that little electric dial kept meandering along. Wally checked every wall outlet, while I was stationed at the meter. When he unplugged the base station to the portable handheld phones, the meter stopped. Cordless phones became history!

20. I learned that I can leave the TV off when I am not watching it and that I don't need to watch it as much. When we checked how the electric meter moved, turning the TV off slowed the

speed of the dial. We had a 50-inch plasma TV. That thing used so much energy it could heat a small room. We rarely need any room heated. We gave it to my 92-year-old mother, who lived in a nursing home. Her poor eyesight made it difficult for her to enjoy her programs on a small screen. Both she and her roommate were delighted to have a large TV, and they were the envy of all the patients and staff.

21. I know how to handwash and dry the dishes and use very little water in the process.

22. I know how to put a pan of water in the solar oven and heat it for dishwashing. The hot water heater quit. Our home is an older manufactured home with a small hot water heater. At Home Depot the ten and nineteen gallon tanks both looked like the one we were replacing. In a courageous moment, we decided to buy the ten gallon model. It eats KWHs like a starving lion. Buying another, more efficient one is not in the budget, so we turned the circuit off and only use it in emergencies. That would be for company who think showers have to be hot.

23. I know that on a hot Florida day a shower in the afternoon feels perfect; 10 p.m. is poor timing if the water heater is off. That's when we resort to turning on the circuit. When I want a really hot shower, I can use the solar shower bag from the sailboat. Again, we use it when the sun is shining. That water gets so hot I can have a warm bath, because it takes cold water to get the temperature to a comfortable point.

24. I know my hair will dry by itself and rollers will make curls in my hair. This may require planning ahead or a change in routine. There are easy non-electric hairstyles. I call mine "pool hair." I can take a refreshing swim, shower off, and brush it to style my hair as it dries.

25. I know that bath towels can be used for a week, as long as they are hung up to dry after every use. Our grandchildren may not do

well with this at home, but the granny-police do not tolerate such frivolous behavior on these premises. We use small bath towels. I once tried a washcloth for a towel but found it quite inadequate.

26. I know that a small plastic bottle of frozen water tucked into a bra or top of a swimsuit is a great cooler. I learned that when I took bus rides from Ixtapa to Zihuatanejo, Mexico, where I wandered through the huge market bazaar. I was on vacation and definitely not as acclimated as the locals. I didn't trust the drinking water, so I drank the water as it thawed. By the time the vacation was over, I was packing three bottles of ice in my pockets. The big ice wraps for the back feel wonderful. It can be 95 degrees outside and I can sit in my own little climate, sipping ice tea, and enjoying a good book. Life is good.

27. I know how to hang clothes on clotheslines. I hang them early and take advantage of the shade provided by the tall hedge. Later, that little bottle of ice cools me while I take my laundry down. I always think of Grandma Meister as I hang the wash. I have reached the point that I will not use the dryer for any reason. I named her Virginia, the virgin clothes dryer, because she NEVER gets used. As I was enjoying hanging clothes today, I wondered what I'd do if I were unable to hang my laundry in my 90s. I decided I'd gladly pay someone to do my laundry and hang them rather than needlessly use electricity and put CO_2 in the air.

28. I know I can do less laundry by not washing clean clothes. One of my secrets is wearing dark print tops. If I wear a white blouse, it takes fifteen minutes to drop some blob front-and-center.

29. I know my coolest and warmest outfits and when to wear them. The A/C will not be turned on until I feel too warm wearing shorts and a tank-top, and I will be wearing many layers before I would think of turning on the heat. We didn't turn the furnace on once last winter.

30. I know those dark print tank-tops can be worn wet to cool me if

there's work to do.

31. I know I can acclimate to the temperature. I learned that in Roatan. I am not talking about being miserable, but I want to push the envelope a little. My goal is to acclimate to an 85-degree thermostat setting in the summer and be comfortable. That requires careful planning, but it is possible. The good news is that it doesn't allow us to do hard work on hot afternoons; we are sentenced to relaxation.

32. I know I can get my housework done in the morning when the house is coolest. As it gets warmer, my activities get more leisurely. I laughed when I read, "all day I do nothing and then I rest." Everything gets done.

33. I know putting water with a drop or two of peppermint in a clean spray bottle makes a refreshing "peppermint spritz." Kids like it, too. Just spray and be cool.

34. I know how to use a handheld fan, and when it gets really hot we can turn a fan on instead of the A/C. The only fan needed is the one in our immediate area, and when we leave, the fan is turned off. Medium speed uses half the energy as high speed.

35. I know it is cooler sitting in an armless wooden chair on hot days and that on cold days the big overstuffed recliner is warm and cozy.

36. I know what spots in my home are the most comfortable at different times of the day. The breezeway is usually the best place at 4 p.m. in the summer.

37. I know we can go to the small room (the east wing) overlooking the canal and boat and be cool in the evening with the windows open. If it does not cool down outside, that room has a window A/C unit. We will never again pay thousands of dollars to replace the large whole-house A/C. There are more efficient ways to cool our immediate area.

38. We tried running a vent hose into the master bedroom from the

east-wing A/C, but it wasn't very effective. I hate to cool the entire house to lower the temperature in one room, but that's what we do once the low is in the 80s at night. That would be almost every night in August. I chill the warm mattress with ice packs before going to bed so that we are comfortable with the A/C off or at a higher setting.

39. I know a refreshing dip in our community pool will instantly erase any feeling of being hot and tacky. Then we can sit comfortably in our breezeway, read, do research, talk on the cell phone, or write. All the while we are entertained by butterflies, fish jumping, birds singing, and a lesser-blue heron that comes over when I'm on the patio/breezeway or in my garden. We named him Azul and he loves raw shrimp. I know if there is any way to avoid turning on the A/C until after the setting sun is not beating on the front of our house, I'll try it. We do our shopping and visiting during the hottest time of day, so we're out of the house, and we have a clubhouse nearby where we can play cards, use the computer, or we can take a dip in the pool.

40. I know a visit to the cool public library is a great option available to many Americans. It is one of my favorites.

41. I know that reading the electrical meter daily is a great reality check and helps me find ways to save more energy. October through May, my readings are three to four KWHs most days.

42. I know we can bike at sunset, swim, shower, and be comfortable all evening.

43. I know we can plan outdoor activities like biking, swimming, or sailing with guests. This prevents the A/C running to accommodate others. When we have company and we're in the house, we adjust the temperature for others. Heaven help the people who think they need my A/C set at 72. I'd make them read this book first. If that didn't help, I might toss them in the pool.

44. I know I can suck the humidity out of our house with the A/C

from 6:15 a.m. to 6:55 a.m., when the outside temperature is lowest and the humidity is highest. It also happens to be the time my exercise program, Classical Stretch, is on TV. Perfect!

45. I know I don't need electric clocks and other devices that require power 24/7. We have the power turned off everywhere we aren't using it. The circuit is turned off for the range and microwave, because they have clocks and other electronic conveniences. Turning off main circuits at the breaker lets us see how many times we switched on a light we really don't need. Why we automatically turn on the light in the bathroom when it is light enough for everything but applying make-up is a mystery to me. Who needs stage lighting to tinkle? When we first started turning off circuits and going off the grid, even knowing we had the power off, we kept opening the fridge. When the light didn't come on we quickly shut the door.

46. I know the refrigerator can have the power turned off for six to eight hours on a regular basis with no ill effects. The secret is to let it run until the motor turns off. Go off the grid and don't open the door of the refrigerator or freezer until half an hour after we go back on the grid.

47. I know how to have my home independent of the need for electricity 24/7, so I can go "OFF THE GRID" hours every day. And I do! I don't know why, but there is a peacefulness we both feel when we flip the main circuit to "OFF."

Everyone's situation is different, but we do everything listed above. There are other things we tried that turned out not to be for us. On cool nights when we want to be off the grid at bedtime, as a joke we strap on little camping "miner's lights" and read in bed. I like that one. I hope this inspires you to try some for yourself. If you want more inspiration, take your last light bill and divide it by 2, 3, 4, or 5. Good luck. Be radical.

It takes time to put some changes in place. We had our roof replaced, trying to be as hurricane resistant as possible, so that added some insulation. Our clothes washer died, and we bought one that is energy efficient. Wally was especially impressed when we discovered the new front-loading model uses only fourteen gallons of water per wash, as opposed to the top-loading models that use about forty. Whenever we have a major purchase, we use the money we save to buy the most energy efficient model that is within our budget.

It's still hard to figure out how we cut our light bill to one-eighth of last year's bill, but we did it! I'm not done yet. This tells me we can do more. Our highest usage was for August 2010, when we used 1,831 KWH. My new goal is to use at least one KWH less than that for an entire year. We were short by 522 KWHs for 2012. Considering we cut our use by 10,289 KWHs when comparing 2009 and 2012, we might reach that goal some year. It would be a year when we are not home in August and September. We use one-third of our year's electricity during those two months.

Friends used to be surprised that our electric bill was always so much lower than theirs. I didn't bring it up, but someone would say, "I can't believe our light bill is over $400." Our highest bill was $202.62. I didn't say "only," because I thought $202.62 was outrageous.

When I look at the old bills, it is obvious that in recent years we tried more to cut our power use. We both still worked in 2009, and the A/C was set above 80 while we were at work. Once I retired, I always hung my laundry. We were home more, but even before the "Prince" got to us, our use was dropping. The drying clothes on the line was the main change from the year 2009 to 2010.

This is the annual KWH use and the monthly average for the past 4 years:

	Total KWH	Monthly KWH Average
2009	13,030	1,085
2010	11,300	942
2011	4,859	405
2012	2,352	196

In the entire year of 2012 we used less than 18% of the electricity we used in 2009. That's an 82% reduction. The potential for saving energy in America's homes is staggering and a big step toward energy independence and slowing global warming. Americans use so much and we have no inclination of how our consumption relates to the cost to the planet and the other citizens of the world. Pick some of the changes we made and see if you can cut your energy use by 25%-50% or more. Wally and I would not have believed our reduction was possible, but those are the actual number of KWHs we used for the last for 4 years. This granny is no longer clueless about electrical use. I can confidently say we have gone green!

CHAPTER **18**

WHAT CAN BE DONE ABOUT
GLOBAL WARMING?

Yes, I believe global warming is the biggest issue we have ever faced. Depending on what people living on planet Earth do, it could become the only issue. We could find ourselves at the bottom level of Maslow's Hierarchy of Human Needs, where the struggle for air, food, water, and shelter becomes all consuming, and every higher level, even safety, is set aside.

> **While there is a chance of the world getting through its troubles, I hold that a reasonable man has to behave as if he were sure of it.**
> H. G. Wells

SOME THINGS CANNOT BE CHANGED

Irreversible damage is already done: Earth's temperature is up; ice caps and glaciers, which were there for thousands of years, can't be un-melted; land and sea exposed after ice melts continues to absorb the sun's heat they once reflected; and warmer waters melt more ice. The remaining ice sheets, held in place by the massive amounts of ice, some of which has melted, are moving faster toward the sea.

CO_2 had been retained in the atmosphere in a specific amount that gave us our ideal climate. The ppm (parts per million) had not been over 300 in the last 650,000 years. Man has unearthed so much carbon in fossil fuels that the ppm reached 315 in 1958 and passed 400 ppm in 2012. Other sources of the CO_2 burden are burning of forests and peat bogs, melting of permafrost, and top soil loss. More than 7 billion people are exhaling CO_2 with every breath. Domesticated livestock raised annually for humans to eat exhale a significant amount of CO_2. As more people move up the food chain, eating more meat and less grain for protein, the number of livestock will increase further above sustainable limits.

The unleashed CO_2 remains in the atmosphere for one hundred years. Man dumped a comparatively small amount of CO_2 into the atmosphere in 1914. There were few cars, and few oil, coal, and gas powered electricity-generating plants, only 1.6 billion people exhaling CO_2, no passenger planes, and fewer factories used power from fossil fuel. That 1914 CO_2 is nearly gone today. The humungous amount of CO_2 spewing into the atmosphere today will be with us until 2114.

THANK YOU ECKHART TOLLE

Tolle's writings helped clarify things that I had not understood in my seventy years. I loved working with hospice patients, but the ever-increasing charting requirements for Medicare and the higher caseload due to budget cuts as the economy and donations declined made the job difficult. I was unwilling to shorten visits to my patients, so I saw patients all day and charted late into the night. I told management the size caseload I would accept. They agreed caseloads had become unmanageable and said they would hire more social workers. That did not happen. I read from Tolle's books each morning. One day this message stood out.

> **If I find here and Now unacceptable, I have three choices:**
> **1-Totally accept it.**
> **2- Change it.**
> **3-Remove myself from the situation.**
> **That is taking responsibility for my life.**

That day I framed and took that inspirational piece to work to hang over my desk. I stopped by my boss's office, who knew I had spoken to management weeks earlier. I repeated the size caseload I'd accept; it was a very large number. Just the drive time for some rural patients could take over an hour each way. I showed my boss the message, and I checked off number one. In six weeks, I had more patients. I took the framed message to my boss, checked off number two, and handed her my resignation. As much as I loved my patients, I had no doubt I was supposed to resign. I now believe it was to make room in my life for a new "divine purpose."

Do you have loved ones who will be in the prime of their lives with families in 2030 or 2040? I have eight. After what we have learned, let's review and use that clear message.

> **If I find here and now, global warming, unacceptable I have three choices.**
> **1-Totally accept it.**
> **2-Change it.**
> **3-Remove myself from the situation.**
> **That is taking responsibility.**

I cannot totally accept global warming for myself and never for Lilly. There is no way I could remove myself from this situation. There is nowhere to go. Rich or poor, our address is Earth. With one and three checked off, I don't just have to, or choose to, or want to, I'd LOVE to do all I can to help solve global warming and the related issues. Three choices—which will it be?

SOME THINGS CAN BE CHANGED

There's good news and bad news here. The bad news is that Americans are seven times as much of a mess-maker as other people. The good news is we therefore have the ability to make great improvements. Imagine how little power to change anything you would have if you were a starving mother holding a dying baby in the Sudan. What can families on one of the islands of Tuvalu or the Maldives do to stop the rising sea level from claiming their homes? Some of these victims have never heard of global warming; but their lives are torn apart because of it. Life was not easy before, but now what necessities of life they had are disappearing and their very survival is threatened. I do not like to use the word victim; it implies such powerlessness. However, in the above cases, it fits.

Americans enjoy lives of convenience, never realizing the consequences of our unsustainable prospering. Our government and big business keep us clueless. Some scientists started speculating about damage to the atmosphere in the 1940s and 1950s. By the 1960s, the increasing CO_2 in the atmosphere was recorded. Scientists realized the connection between a rise in the CO_2 level and a simultaneous climb in the Earth's average temperature once new technology to study ice cores was used in places like Antarctica. They debated the possible consequences. The public was not informed. Facts were ignored or hidden. Understanding the path we were on was further complicated by talk of a coming ice age due to lower temperatures after a 1970s event that briefly blocked some of the sun's rays.

Another distraction was the discovery of the hole in the ozone layer. Science and governments, in a cooperative effort, enacted regulations, eliminated most of the offending chemicals, and the hole in the ozone is slowly closing.

People whose accumulation of wealth could be slowed chose

to use their money, power, and influence to create doubt about the problem. The world would be very different today if we had taken prompt action in the 1970s. We lost valuable time and have to live with the consequences. This portion of the chapter was headed "**Some Things Can Be Changed**." But until each of us personally KNOWS the problem is life threatening, we go on as usual.

COLOR ME CLUELESS

I cannot recall when I first heard about global warming. At what point did I even wonder if it could harm my loved ones–or any people for that matter? I remember that by the 1990s my ears perked up when I heard that the water in the Gulf of Mexico was so warm we could expect rougher hurricane seasons.

Living between Houston and Galveston, Texas, I dreaded the season, fearing we could lose everything and have to start over. Our children were young, and the sense of responsibility for their safety and secure future added to our level of anxiety. Alicia was the hurricane that hit us in Texas. Charley and Wilma had their way with us since moving to Florida.

At the start of hurricane season, we plan where to evacuate and consider whether to re-build or re-locate if our home is destroyed. We priced new model homes, but never considered doing something about global warming.

When did the reports of the hottest summers on record, the worst drought since the dust bowl, heat waves killing thousands, or the glaciers melting start fitting into the big picture? I don't remember hearing about the terrible summer of 2003 in Europe that caused 50,000 deaths. How can I not hear, not remember, not understand such a tragedy? Why on Earth did it take until March 2011 for the facts to finally start registering in my brain? If I hadn't read Harmony, not much would have changed. Knowledge has power. People around me go on as usual, just as I had always done.

IF YOU ARE OUR LEADER, WHEN CAN WE EXPECT YOU TO LEAD?

Unfortunately, there's no united, courageous guidance from all, most, or even a notable percentage of our leaders. The power and influence brought down on some elected officials leaves them serving not the people, but the ones who bought them.

> **Thousands of climate scientists agree that global warming is not only the most threatening environmental problem but also one of the greatest challenges facing all of humanity. We must demand a separation between oil and state. We can get off oil and slow global warming.**
> Leonardo DiCaprio

Washington, D.C., state and local governments, where is your leadership and why aren't you trying to save us? Here are two quotes that shed some light on the stalling, resisting, and denying that has our government officials with their backs turned on the deadliest problem man has ever faced.

> **The modern conservative...is engaged in one of man's oldest exercises in moral philosophy.**
> **That is the search for a superior moral justification for selfishness.**
> John Kenneth Galbraith

> **The Earth is not dying—it is being killed.**
> **And the people who are killing it have names and addresses.**
> U. Utah Phillips

You can interpret that as directed to the power elite or to everyone; I support both views. However, I am trying to take my name and address off the list. If I can alert others to the problem, I will rejoice, because that is when we finally go into action. Americans have so much we need to do. The problem is, we are so set in our unsustainable ways of life we can't conceive that we could be happy if we used only our share of what the Earth has to offer.

Some days I try to think of myself as more of an "Earthling" than an American. I do something radical, like carry rainwater to flush the toilet. I don't do it all the time, but I can during our rainy season. Florida's water supply is extremely low, and water restrictions exist year round. Restrictions are ignored until we are in danger of sucking air when we turn on the faucet. On my "Earthling" days, my hope is that I can gain some perspective. Americans are so doped up with consumerism; we're hypnotized. How do we "snap out of it"?

What Can We Do About Global Warming?

Experts point out we need action from our government. That's really what I want, but where would I begin. I have a vote and try to find which candidate will work to address global warming issues. Sadly, it seems to be a non-issue. I feel powerless when it comes to influencing a politician's vote on the floor of Congress. Some elected officials want to take action.

> It's obvious we can't ignore the problem any longer. Locally and nationally, we cannot wait to see how bad it gets. We need to act now.
> Greg Nickels, Mayor of Seattle

This book is the best way I can think of to inform others, and I hope it helps create a voting block that can influence our elected officials. I didn't decide to write a book until I had been studying about global warming for well over a year. As I read, it was discouraging to learn government action was so urgently needed and so not happening.

I could not sit and do nothing. Lilly and my grandchildren will be alive past the middle of this century and perhaps into the 22nd century. Devastating changes to our Earth aren't hundreds of years away, as I had supposed. They've started, and the effects are touching our lives today.

The actions Wally and I took to reduce our electrical use were only because we learned about global warming. That same concern is why we bought our Prius. Learning that being vegan is beneficial for reducing CO_2 emissions was a boost to our spirits. It takes much more than "The Big Three."

The book, *Living Like Ed* (Bagley 2008) offers information gained from forty years of living green and trying many things. We used many of Bagley's ideas to curtail our energy use. He and his wife are a good source of information about toxins in the home. No wonder asthma and allergy problems are on the rise. He also explains why air travel is a last resort. Airplanes burn jet fuel that is similar to kerosene, and emissions are released at high altitudes where little if any of the CO_2 can be filtered out. Ed suggests if flying is your only option, get a direct flight when possible and check with the airlines to see which ones have the newer, more fuel-efficient engines. A direct flight is recommended because the fuel consumption is highest during take-offs and landings.

Reading many books about other's efforts to decrease their carbon footprint gradually opened my mind to try other things. As a result, I live and think differently today and feel good about the changes I've made. Here are some examples of my new and improved lifestyle.

1. I habitually buy much less. Evidence of this shows up on my American Express bill.
2. I ask, "Can I do without this?" Not buying has been a surprisingly happy experience. I'm not racking my brain saying, "I'll never use it; why did I buy it?"
3. We buy used when possible.
4. I try not to buy products that are over- packaged. I have yellow plastic vegetable storage bags for the refrigerator. I take them to the store with me to put my produce in, rather than whipping a line of plastic bags off the dispensers by the tomatoes and the peaches.

That sounds inconsequential, but there is an island "away" out in the Pacific the size of the continental United States that contains billions or trillions of tons of our not-so-inconsequential plastic bags and bottles. It's poisoning fish and entering our food chain.

5. We use MUCH less water. Some of that is just being "mindful" that water is precious.

MARY'S MUSINGS ON WATER

I treat water as if it is very special. The same water has recirculated on Earth since the beginning of time. When I drink it, I think of the people that drank the same drops: Jesus, Mother Teresa, Grandma Meister, Gandhi, Lester Brown, George Washington, Thoreau... When we travel, instead of using paper towels or electric hand dryers, I shake my hands as dry as possible and gently pat the excess water on my face, neck, and arms, knowing where those drops of water might once have been. Wally says he now knows his hands will dry every time without using paper towels or an electric dryer. That is encouraging. We need everyone's help to make a difference. I don't' want this seen as "a girl thing."

6. We like to repurpose things. If there is something we need, our first thought is *can we make it from something we already have*? That thought gets our creative energy flowing.

7. We think before sending things to the landfill. I sometimes wonder when our land will be filled?

8. I clean with vinegar. With all the chemicals that go into everything, I use vinegar rather than do an in-depth investigation of all those products. I mix a spray bottle of equal parts white vinegar, water, and alcohol, then add a few drops of detergent. This was recommended for our laminate floors but works well on everything.

9. Some chemical concoctions are still in use in my home. I'm not willing to give up hair dye, but I only use half as much. It still works.

10. We buy local and organic produce. Thriftiness is one of my virtues, and I have to give myself a pep talk about supporting or creating a larger market for organic items so the demand increases, farmers are more productive, and prices go down. I check the origin of a product and choose the one that needed less transportation to get to me. I don't see myself as someone who would commit to only eating food grown within one-hundred miles or only seasonally. If I had to, I could make that adjustment.

11. I check to see if foods taste as good raw or cold. Some leftover pasta dishes become "salads" and are really good. When I "heat something up," that also heats up my house. In August, many things are tried cold. Leaving the A/C off as long in the day as possible makes me really think about the many ways I heat up the house unnecessarily.

12. We consolidate trips to the store. It dawned on us to shop as we did on Roatan and have a long string of "no-shopping days." See how many days you can "not shop." We mark them on our calendar. If we stop writing them down, our old habits quickly return. We still need that discipline to overcome such an ingrained habit.

13. Our favorite vegan restaurant does everything right, except they use paper napkins. We bring our own cloth napkins. I imagine that in my lifetime I might save a tree. We have travel napkins in the car and ask the people at the drive-through to not give us paper napkins. We bring water with us or use our own glasses. We learned which fast food restaurants allow a person to fill his own glass. Consider how much trash comes from a fast food joint in a day. Everything they use is single use, except the tray.

14. At home we use the same cup all day; that is part of water conservation.

15. We handwash our dishes, heat water in the solar oven, and use minimal water. We are so used to it now, we wouldn't think of doing it the old wasteful way. Once I read about the aquifers and

the "race to the bottom," it was easy to conserve water. I can give lessons when the water is almost gone. Our fair share of water is about twelve to thirteen gallons a day per person. I can get close, but in the United States, we aren't equipped to reach that mark day after day. We would have to convert to the odor-free composting toilet. There are countries that only permit this type of toilet in new buildings. Don't hold your nose they really are odor free. The way we handle our sewage will eventually have to change. Teddy Roosevelt commented that it was insane to take a small amount of human waste, use it to pollute 500 gallons of water, and then have to clean up all that mess.

16. On my list is to lose fifty more pounds; my success is marginal. I've got so much going for me: I'm vegan, I know we will get better gas mileage with that much less weight in the car, and I have my "Matt Lauer suit" to get into.

MARY'S MUSINGS−THE MATT LAUER SUIT AND DREAMING BIG

I want everyone to read *For Lilly*, get curious, start checking out global warming for themselves, and get the fire lit under them. In my musings, I imagine talking to Matt Lauer on *The Today Show* about *For Lilly*. I figured that would be a good way to get the word out.

I have a goal to de-clutter my life, and I am clearing my closet of clothes that are too large, too small, or too something. Years ago, I bought a suit I loved that almost fit. Then the numbers on the scale went in the wrong direction. As I started to put the suit into the box for Goodwill, I decided it was the perfect suit to wear when I meet Matt.

Musing is a fine example of how I can have a wonderful time driving nowhere, buying nothing, and remaining open to the universe conspiring to help me achieve my goals. What sort of thoughts do you let invade your mind? Why not take charge of your thoughts and make them absolutely glorious? Some would call this daydreaming. I believe little Conrad Hilton use to daydream about running a hotel. There is more power in our thoughts than we know. Not knowing does not mean the power is not there. Back up your daydreams with action; give it a test run. I hope Lilly can dream big and step boldly into her future.

17. We use rainwater and gray water for the garden and shrubs, to wash the car, and to clean the patio and driveway.

18. We refuse to buy paper towels, paper napkins, facial tissue, and we are mindful about the quantity of toilet paper we spin off the roll.

19. We never buy plastic bags, storage containers, or plastic wrap and we don't miss it a bit. Once you make a decision not to bring these into the house, answers appear. That's how I discovered I could "can" my leftovers. I store the steaming hot portion of a dish that would be left over if I didn't over eat. I put it in a glass jar, wipe the jar rim with water and screw the top on tight. I let it cool on the counter. When I hear a "pop," I know it will last in the fridge for weeks.

20. I wrote down that I would walk or bike for groceries. I seldom do when the heat and humidity are high in the summer. The "no shopping days" means we sometimes have too much to carry. This also slows buying on a whim or impulse.

Every time I see an adult on a bicycle,
I no longer despair for the future of the human race.
H. G. Wells

21. If we ever move, we will get a much smaller place. We have 1,145 square feet, more than we need, but it's filled. The American way is to buy a house bigger than we really need, pack it full, and look for a bigger place because we need more space. I look forward to being "unencumbered." Notice all the storage spaces people rent. When did that happen? The excess used to take over the attic, basement, and garage, but we only had one of each. Luckily, we can rent more and bigger storage spaces any time we NEED it. Have we gone crazy and lost the ability to know when we have

enough? This is serious; it could take something as devastating as global warming to bring us to our senses.

22. We give a lot of thought to ways we can reduce our amount of laundry. One of St. James' books on simplicity opened our minds to darker prints, one towel a week, and numerous other suggestions. *No Impact Man* is great if you want to really try many things to reduce the infamous carbon footprint. It's strange how reading about someone else's crazy ideas and attempts lures you into actions you never would have considered.

23. Stop junk mail. This is one I haven't completely accomplished. I have a slightly insane reason for stalling. I want my Publisher's Clearing House Sweepstakes entry. You know how big I can dream. Now imagine the party in my brain at the thought of "One Million Dollars a Year for Life." I swear, if I won that, I'd never die. I promptly mail it in and check the calendar to see what day the prize patrol will be at my door. If I have plans, I cancel them so I'm home to accept that first big check. I dream of doing good deeds like sponsoring community gardens, building schools in Africa and Central America, and living green. Jan and I used to joke about this, and every time an entry arrives, I imagine Jan's smile and laughter. I haven't won yet, but the willingness to consider what I want in my life if financial limits were not an issue has paid off. A car with great gas mileage seemed like something we needed to save to buy. The dream of an environmentally-friendly vehicle took root. We have our Prius, no money down, and 0% interest. We're willing to take money from savings to help pay for it, but it hasn't been necessary. Green living has improved our budget. That's the kind of spending we're doing, investing in the environment and Lilly's future. When things come together so perfectly, I have to believe we are on the right path.

24. We haven't bought a rain barrel yet. For now, we use two bins. The rain barrel is a better design. But, I think of all that plastic;

the debate goes on.

25. I get the most out of our very limited garden space. Complying with the homeowners' associations restrictions is a challenge. It's my dream to dine on salads and vegetables from my own garden. That is how local I hope my produce can be.

26. Go to Walmart only one or two times a month. I'm improving.

27. I plan to use drip irrigation for my garden and hope a mentor can show me how.

28. Give away 80% of my clothes as my weight goes down, but not the Matt Lauer suit!

READ YOUR ELECTRIC METER DAILY

Now you are ready to get down to business! Record your daily use of KWHs on your kitchen calendar and see how much you can lower your numbers. You will be able to daily lower your usage for quite some time when you first start. You are in for a shock. A few lights and a few fans left on may not seem relevant, but each little whittle adds to your success. We were surprised at how much phone chargers draw when plugged in but not in use. Stop the loss of phantom energy by using power strips that can be turned off. I think that made a 10% or more difference in our usage.

Maybe you have a friend or group of friends who can read *For Lilly* and start a little friendly competition. Not a bad game, you reclaim your money, and help save the planet. If you really get into the competitive spirit, you will quickly save enough to buy a new high-efficiency washer, when your old one bites the dust.

Did you try any of the things Wally and I did to reduce your consumption of electricity? Many of those changes are not inconvenient at all. They are realistic corrections of bad habits. Readers could lower their electric and gas bills by 10% to 25%, maybe even 50%. You might be pleased with the lower bill, but the REAL benefit is how much it helps the environment.

Can you replace your incandescent light bulbs? The CFLs cost more, but pay for themselves many times over. If cost is the issue, lower the setting on your hot water heater ten degrees, then use the money you save to buy three to six CFLs. Put them in the lights you use most and leave the rest off. We changed all our bulbs so long ago; the switch to CFL didn't appear on the Eureka list.

Make a two-degree adjustment in your thermostat and be as comfortable by dressing cooler or warmer. Try more degrees—now more. Study how to be as comfortable by adjusting your activity and clothing instead of turning on the heat or A/C. Will a fan work instead? It takes half the power for the medium speed on the fan and about one-sixth for the lowest speed. That is part of doing our homework. We were curious about what the difference might be, so we checked it out at Home Depot. Do you leave ceiling fans running for hours when no one is in the room? Why? Is the room happier?

Being retired allows me to be a member of the "leisure majority." It was a pleasure to discover that in order to remain perfectly comfortable I must sometimes do nothing requiring more energy than reading or writing. Picture yourself some hot afternoon, dressed in your coolest outfit, sitting in the shade or in a breeze, sipping ice tea, reading a great book, not needing to turn on the air-conditioning, and doing your part to save the planet. The reason this works is that I get my housework done in the morning when it is cooler rather than procrastinate. This creates more leisure time for me than I ever realized was available.

Can your family take better care of their clothes and only launder them when they are dirty? People in the rest of the world think Americans are totally crazy when it comes to washing so many clothes so often. Dark print shirts, blouses, skirts, and slacks can be worn several times between laundering. The clothes last longer and the colors stay brighter with less laundering.

See if you can cut your laundry by one-fourth or even one-half. If your children wear an outfit forty-five minutes, then leave it on floor for you to collect and launder, teach them to take care of their clothes. Your chores will be lighter. Kids' bad habits are habits that need correcting. Tell them it's for Mother Earth.

Some schools teach about environmentalism, and they may be excited to go over the Eureka list with you and play a game to see how much CO_2 they can prevent from being dumped into the atmosphere. They will know how to use the Internet to find the CO_2 emitted per KWH by your utility company.

Some of our big energy savers were hanging the clothes to dry, using my wonderful solar oven (even to heat dishwater–just because I can), and acclimating to a warmer temperature. All the phantom energy today's appliances, electronics, and endless other gadgets drain from our power lines 24/7 deserve some attention. Using a surge-protecting power strip with an off button for each TV and all its accessories helps.

If your home heats up on a hot summer day, see if you can reduce your need for air-conditioning by using shades, blinds, awnings, or insulated draperies. Some of those items may be on the windows already, but not put to good use. If you decide to buy window coverings, stop by Goodwill to see what they might have. Another possibility is to go to the "free cycle" website to see if someone would like to give them to you.

Sometimes it's good for us to be radical "Earthlings." Might I dare to suggest an afternoon "off the grid?" I'm grateful I can easily do this. The refrigerator and the water softener are the only two items that make it necessary for us to turn it back on after six to eight hours. We use fewer clocks and they run on rechargeable batteries. Turning the power off is educational. I never would have realized how many times I opened the fridge, if I had not gone off the grid. If family members get in the habit of standing in front of the fridge with the door wide open looking and looking for something, they are wasting energy,

Do not buy into the idea of needing a larger refrigerator. Americans buy bigger and bigger everything; we fill or overfill the things, and collect or waste more and more stuff. If you have containers in the back of your refrigerator that have been there so long you wouldn't dare eat the contents, your refrigerator is too big, not too small. In extreme cases of outdated items in the fridge, remember, "If it walks out by itself–let it go."

Instead of hauling home cases of individually bottled beverages, get back into the habit of drinking water from your own faucet. A water-filtering pitcher is an Earth-friendly idea. We enjoy homemade sun tea. No electricity used to heat the water, no transporting and storing bulky cases, no preservatives, and you save a fortune while loading up on antioxidants. Anytime you can mix your drink at home, you have saved oil, oil, oil (for the bottle, for the energy to produce, and for the gas to distribute a lot of water to drive home and store). Moms used to mix up Kool-Aid for the kids on a hot summer afternoon. How many other single use items are in our lives that created multi-million dollar businesses? Which way sounds more convenient and Earth friendly?

Use less and cooler water for your showers. The object of a shower is to get clean, not to remove all the natural oils from your skin. Now, about the towel, hang it up to dry on a pant hanger in an airy space and use it all week. Leaving wet towels on the bathroom floor at our house is a major crime. There will be consequences from Grandma.

What can you do to help slow global warming? It isn't just learning the problems we face and changing the physical and material parts of your life that solves the problem. An emotional recognition and value shift is essential and rewarding. We have been living in a very abnormal way for several generations and believing it is normal. Our culture, advertising, and our family and friends taught us to think that acquiring stuff would make us happier and show we were successful. Our goals to live as movie stars instead of within our own financial limits have ruined relationships and cost lives. We ignore limits and live without setting realistic boundaries. Banks encourage people to over-extend on mortgages and credit cards. Businesses and government rate our economy by how much we produce and how much Americans spend. Prosperity means more—more—more.

At some point, we must take a look for ourselves and ask, "Is this really what makes me feel good about myself and brings me happiness and peace of mind?" We may feel as if we have fallen into a trap that has no way out. There is a way out, and there is no better time than now to redefine what is important and to realize our own value. We do not have to remain forever-consuming victims.

Shed that burden. Forgive our society, your family, and any others who taught you that acquiring possessions, working longer and harder to get them, and having the right image showed you were of value. Let the abnormal fall away and return to a life as nature intended us to live. Take time to relax, appreciate what you have, and let nature be your teacher. Learn to be quiet inside and out, and listen to what your body needs. Enjoy good food, sleep, exercise, and find your ability to connect with the present moment.

Can you list fifty things you are grateful for right now? That is an important exercise to try if you are serious about slowing global warming. We need to get off the path of always looking for what we want next and focus on what we are grateful to have in our life right now. Live in the NOW. Learn to enjoy life now—not when… or if….or after… Let the chronic vague wanting be history. That is not normal; the relentless need for more was instilled in you for others' benefits. You are of value, just as you are. Again, I ask, "What are you grateful for in your life right now?" Do that simple exercise, and recognize that you feel more relaxed and happier than you did fifteen minutes earlier. Real peace, love, and joy comes from within and it feels so much better than anything you can buy. It's not for sale.

CHAPTER 19

ENOUGHNESS

> **As a people we have developed a lifestyle that is draining the Earth of its priceless and irreplaceable resources without regard for the future of our children and people all around the world.**
> Margaret Mead

I FORGIVE ALL WHO TAUGHT ME THIS MADNESS IS NORMAL

Our culture has turned many of our lives into complicated, tiring, and never-ending races to do everything and buy it all. We live on overload thinking our lives are "normal," but they are based on crazy unsustainable ideas. It isn't possible to satisfy the infectious drive Americans have to get all the bigger, better, remodeled, updated, newer, or upgraded items that flood our market. This Dis-Ease has downgraded our lives every day, before we ever get out of bed.

We prize newness; we lost the ability to continue to appreciate what we have, and within days, months, or years, once urgently needed items are replaced or fall into disuse. Our Dis-Ease of overconsumption is triggered by the idea that a newer version has made our recently desired purchase outdated. Never mind that it does enough. Enough is not good enough when more is paraded onto our TV screen. The insanity of thinking we NEED a device that enables us to record four programs at a time from any room in the house seems logical. If the credit card is full or there is enough self-control to not give into the urge to buy the (fill in the blank), we are still left with a desire to have whatever is being hustled. Our awareness of "enoughness" is lacking and marketers are free to roam the airways like pickpockets in a sea of easy-prey.

The tension of living with overwhelming debt puts some people in an escapist-like state of unconsciousness, vulnerable to more spending in an attempt to feel better. Like any addict, the urge to feel better overrides considering the disastrous consequences of repeating the behavior that has them in their sorry state. The trigger for relief from this discontent is not the clink of ice cubes in a glass or the need to unwind with a drink. The hyper-consumer's clink is the news of a newer version, the latest release, a sale, the illusion of having to maintain an image, or fear of not having what everyone else has.

This Dis-Ease is not a normal human condition; it has been cultivated and nurtured by the consumer-oriented culture we call a growing economy. That's how government, industry, and fellow citizens measure success and prosperity. The goal is to produce and consume more. Good news is that profits are up, and the economy is growing. Everyone is happy to hear companies had their highest quarter ever.

There is no mention of the reality that the Earth, its resources, or our wallets are maxed out. We live far beyond what Earth can sustain and still leave anything for our children and grandchildren's survival. We are addicts who deny the problem or cannot stop if we do recognize a crisis. Does anyone or anything tell us this is unsustainable? So many things should, yet, that was a concept absent from my thinking until two years ago. Limits were determined by what I could afford or I was willing to spend. I never heard of peak oil or thought I was robbing Lilly's future.

It seems logical to have a car for every driver in the family, including one vehicle big enough to haul things like boats, travel trailers, or large purchases. We once considered buying a small motor home. The price stopped us, but if our incomes were higher, we would have added that to our list of possessions.

Americans have three cars for every four people. Land the size of a football field is lost to highways, parking areas…for every five cars. The Chinese now buy more cars than Americans, and hundreds of millions more Chinese work for the day they, too, can buy a car. If China were able to have the same number of cars per capita as Americans, an area the size of two-thirds of China's rice lands would need to be paved over. Does that sound sustainable? Can we look at our own spending, polluting, and wasting with the same perspective we have when we see it in others? If we cannot see that the Earth is unable to sustain more than 7 billion people the way we live today, we are in denial.

If you are rich, that doesn't alter the fact that you're living an unsustainable lifestyle. You just do not have financial limitations. An alcoholic millionaire can financially afford the finest liquor, but he is still an alcoholic. His liver is still destroyed, the brain can still suffer from Wernicke-Korsakoff syndrome, drunken behavior still ruins lives, and driving accidents are just as dangerous for the rich. Money does not provide immunity from alcoholism, and neither does it negate an unsustainable lifestyle. Americans are rich compared to most of the world's population.

Being born into the American culture in the 1940s means I was subjected to a distorted perception of the way a normal human being can live on planet Earth. I was taught to work to attain all American industry had to offer. According to the advertisements, success had an image attached. America is the land of opportunity, but somehow opportunity became equated with possessions. We were shown what success could buy and if we were not that successful, maybe we could at least project the image of success. The delusion of being able to afford it all is a trap more and more people fall into. Our buying frenzy encourages businesses to push more on us. Look at some of the junk we buy. It sounds good on TV, but soon clutters our lives. That makes it new and expensive junk.

Our youth have grown up at the peak of this runaway consumerism. Believing they need it all seems totally normal to them, and in some ways they've been taught not to care about others. Often their primary concern is to have the latest electronic device, shoes, or jeans and they beg, demand, insist, connive, and act as if they are deprived until they get it. They learned this behavior from the society in which they live. This response to consumer pressure is a tragedy. The real world may have some great disappointments. Things seem like absolute necessities to them and often to their parents. Many young adults return to their parents' homes because they cannot make it on what they earn. They can't stop buying the cute shoes, the nice car, the manicure, the high-maintenance hairstyle, the lattes, the lunches, the nights out, the clothes... We are crippling our children, leaving them ill prepared to live independently as adults. Over-indulgence is a form of child neglect. Were you one of those children who learned that what you wanted you must have? It is good for business, but our planet can no longer afford such extravagances—and neither can our children.

Admitting we have limits both financially and what nature can provide might be easy to voice, but living within those limits is a challenge. Not many people can teach us healthy boundaries, but the Earth and we desperately need to live sustainably.

Rethinking what I wanted and really needed in my life was made easier by the idea of forgiving my culture, my family, my friends, and myself for teaching me that a hyper-consuming lifestyle was normal. We are all caught in the same trap. Companies want to prosper, parents want to give their children more than what they had as children, and we want to have an image others admire. Everyone is doing what seems like the right thing to do.

I forgive, let go, and move into a lifestyle that feels freeing. I wish I hadn't learned a false normal and participated in teaching it to my children. I am improving with my spending, but I find it daunting to let go of all the accumulated possessions that now feel like burdens. I want to live simply, but agonize over such things as clearing a bookshelf. We wait to "sort through" the VCR and cassette tapes. Part of me is still hooked on useless things.

> **I believe we need to live simply so that others may simply live.**
> Ed Bagley, Jr.

Do We Have the Ability to Live Sustainably?

It is a quandary: how can Americans desire and be happy with the correct amounts of things we actually need? Right now we are so pumped up with the false belief that more, multiples, newest, the entire series...is what we must have. There's nothing normal about living far beyond our own and the Earth's means.

We line up in the early morning hours to buy things we don't need that replace some things we lined up in the early hours to get just a year or two ago. This thinking is not an inborn trait, but cultivated by advertisers. This abnormality has been perpetuated and increased within the last few generations, and seems natural to many young and not-so-young people. We believe one of life's goals is to accumulate endless amounts of the latest and greatest.

What do teens or preteens expect or wish to have for their own? The list of gadgets might include the latest iPhone with endless apps, an iPod, a computer, a Kindle Fire, a tablet, an Xbox with Kinect, a Wii with added games, a DS, a PSP, a PlayStation, a digital camera, their own TV with a Blu-Ray player, and an Internet bundle fast enough and with enough band width and satellite service to do all the things the gadgets promise. The Walmart price for midrange of the products listed is about $3,500, not including accessories, movies, games, monthly service fees, and apps. More than half the list will be considered outdated within two years. Teens are primed for activation when the already planned new version is released. Is this normal? Kids think it is. We grumble about not being made of money, but in the end, many kids have most of the things on the list. And they're used as toys. These are the sort of things Americans don't want to feel deprived of. We were sold a bill of goods without realizing how frivolous we are about our spending.

If this is considered normal, our young people are hypnotized. Teens expect to get a car when they are old enough to drive. Parents say the kids need to get jobs and buy their own cars, but the parents end up helping buy the cars or paying the insurance. They have bought into the idea that this is what kids need in today's world. Our children are saddled with debt they will carry for the rest of their lives. Families are buried in debt. I'm talking about large credit card balances that cause constant worry about how to pay all the bills.

The list above is only one example. Other areas where Americans have lost touch with reality are clothing, vehicles, eating out, the latte factor, entertainment, oversized homes... All have a tremendous negative effect on the environment. I had no idea what was involved environmentally with something as simple a T-shirt that I reached for just because it was on sale. Now I see a much bigger picture.

I was surprised at the donation I was able to make to a women's recovery program after I learned their patients needed clothing. That prompted me to again weed out my closet. I donated ten pairs of slacks and thirty-six shirts, sweaters, blouses, and jackets. What is enlightening is that I don't even miss them.

Wally and I have learned not to charge more than we can pay off each month. That has only been in the last fifteen years and has to do with being older and wiser. Many lives have become living nightmares because of spending far beyond their means. People have declared bankruptcy and lost their homes. We are a country of shopping and spending addicts. We unconsciously keep charging with little thought of the consequences of living or wanting a celebrity life style on an average income. We live paycheck to paycheck and have very little in savings. Every time there is an emergency, life turns into a panic attack.

THIS is what I would like to deprive you of.

How quickly could you right your finances if you only bought necessities? How freeing would that feel? Start immediately saving 10% of your earnings and be able to take a relaxing breath and have money for true emergencies. An emergency is not that something is going off sale. There is money to be found by changing your current spending habits to pay off bills. Rather than thinking what you might cut back on, do as I suggested for becoming vegan. Make a radical change and cash in on amazing immediate benefits. Write down everything you spend your money on and only buy the absolute necessities. That means no more jeans, T-shirts, books, dining out, lattes, gas station snacks, movies, individual over-processed meals, magazines, vacations, manicures-pedicures, having your hair done.... This is aimed at the people who are prisoners of their loans and credit cards. Like an addict who stops binging, the mall is not a safe place to frequent, any more than a bar is the place for a recovering alcoholic to meet friends. If you decide to try this exercise, you will be amazed at how freeing it feels to discover you really can get out from under piles of debt. It involves setting boundaries, considering consequences, and being accountable for your choices.

Years ago, Oprah had a series of programs called *The Debt Diet*. The show featured three families buried in debt, their lives and relationships were in shambles. Each had the help of a financial expert, and by the end of the series all three families had a clear path out of debt, had made outstanding progress, and the projections of around a million dollars saved during the next thirty years for a comfortable retirement. Each family felt as if a terrible burden had been lifted, their relationships saved or improved, and they had a new life of freedom from debt. Americans go through their paychecks with far more discretionary spending than they realize.

Over-consumption is an epidemic in America that is more pervasive than obesity. We don't see it because everyone is trying to keep up an image so others don't realize they can't afford to live like everyone else. Many don't realize this is happening. Big business and banking have had their way with us far too long.

As you look at your household, can you see the benefits for your family and the good role model you could be for your children? Raising children who expect to have everything that is popular and advertised is not showing them love; it is parental neglect. How prepared are they to face the real world?

Imagine the peace of mind a family would feel if they had not spent all that money on the earlier list of toys for the kids. If there is a large credit card balance, that $3,500 could actually end up being $5,000 to $10,000 or more by the time it is paid off. How can we reverse this trend? It is only getting worse, and many Americans have stress-filled lives because they have lost sight of "enoughness."

The goal of advertising is to create a chronic emotional state that is like a vague anxious depression leaving us constantly looking to buy a "fix." We're manipulated to the point that we keep buying things and forfeit the peaceful life we could enjoy.

There are many divorces and breakups over financial problems. People work long hours trying to make ends meet. Often it takes a second job to do this. It would be great if we all had a budget guru step into our lives and help. Can Americans free themselves of this consumer hamster wheel we find ourselves spinning, constantly needing and desiring more? We call it needing when most of it is a programmed-in anxiousness to think of the next thing we must work to obtain or pay off. How do we shed this horrible burden that has been placed upon us? Can we even recognize what has happened to us?

It's a comforting and calming feeling when the wanting ends and appreciation for all we have settles on us. "Enoughness" is a luxury we can relax into. The pile of debt may last quite a while, but with recognizing we already have enough, the debts will dwindle instead of climb. One day you will be free of debt. Enjoy each credit card you pay off. The current thinking is that it is better to tackle the card with the lowest balance and eliminate the annual fee and the chance of late fees. Then roll that amount spent each month for paying off the next lowest. Chew through those cards as you start moving toward building wealth instead of accumulating stuff. You will never open an over-stuffed bank account and think, *why did I spend my money on that?*

I asked the question, "Can Americans live sustainably?" Eventually we or our children will be forced by dire circumstances to do just that. The good news is we can make changes now, rather than allow the waste and misery to continue until the situation is most dire. We can get off the treadmill, the hamster wheel, the mounting suffocating debt, and the chronic anxious wanting to which we keep responding as if we were hard-wired to live this way. This madness makes Americans the most environmentally destructive people on Earth.

I hope *For Lilly* motivates you to "choose to," "want to," or even "love to" live a new way. Taking positive steps opens doors to a new feeling of freedom and hope. It may be only a tiny flicker of hope, but that feeling is richer than any spending can provide. Instead of a guilt hangover, you like the new you. Some people find the difference so satisfying and different that they refer to themselves as the new me and refer to the time of their previous ways as "before." They literally step into a new way a living and happiness.

Oh, Frivolous Me

My husband phoned a woman, I'll call her Jodie, with some business questions. She was very helpful and we learned she was born and educated in India and moved to the United States nine years ago at the age of twenty-five. The opportunity to interview and get the perspective of someone raised and educated in India and who has now been influenced by the American culture for nine years seemed like a gift. Webster defines "perspective" as the power to see or think of things in their true relationship to each other. My first thought was, *have*

Americans ever had a true perspective of how our destructive ways relate to the planet and the seven billion people who call Earth home?

Jodie is of the Hindu faith, is single, lives and works in Los Angeles, and shares an apartment with her American boyfriend. Her Indian home had been in a small city of a few million in southern India. She explained, "It is a small city because it is very packed in."

Jodie agreed to an interview after we discussed the book I'm writing. She shares my interests and attends meetings about some of the problems she sees as most pressing in the Los Angeles area. I asked how she would describe Americans when it comes to environmental issues. She thought for a while and then said, "Americans are very frivolous." Webster defines frivolous as, "Of little importance, TRIVIAL, not serious or practical (a frivolous attitude)."

In India she lived in a combined family home with her father, her uncle, and their families sharing a six-room home. Male cousins and their wives lived there at times while she was growing up. There were usually about ten people living in the home. This is typical, and she never felt crowded. Her childhood was happy. She particularly liked always having one of the wives around, and she described her home life as fun. She had two drawers and almost three-feet of personal closet space.

She compared how things are for her in the United States. Instead of two drawers, she has fifteen, and her closet has fifteen feet of rod space, all full. She commented she's lived here so long she is becoming more frivolous. That didn't please her and she hopes to make some changes. She asked, "Who needs that many things? I need to give some to people who really need them."

Being Hindu, she remains vegetarian and cooks most of her food at home. Her electrical use is conservative, and she stays within the minimal-use range the light company charges as a base rate. In India her family had all the modern conveniences, like a TV, a phone, a computer, heat, and air-conditioning. When not in use, they turned things off, and they never left the air-conditioning on if no one was home.

Public transportation by bus in India was excellent and it was easy to get anywhere. The buses were on time and had good connections. She finds it frustrating how poor the public transportation is in Los Angeles. She wanted to use the bus, just as she did in India. However, in Los Angeles the buses are never on time and they sit in traffic so long that connections are missed. She was forced to buy a car to get to work on time.

She said in the last nine years India has added three times as many cars, has traffic jams, and the air is polluted, just like Los Angeles. As the people of India earn higher incomes, they want the luxuries Americans enjoy. She explained, "That has a lot to do with American influences on TV and especially the Internet. Even with the added cars, India's 1.2 billion people will not cause as much pollution as America. Homes are smaller and more people share the homes. There just is not enough space to own endless possessions."

In India, water is not wasted the way it is in America. To bathe, each person gets a bucket of water and a tumbler and it works very well. Rising sea level is a concern and the islands off the coast are noticing rising water now. She thinks those islands will be under water in less than forty years.

"Scary" is the word she used when she was talking about how the people of India want to have the luxuries like Americans. When she considered how her own habits changed after being in America for nine years, she said, "It just happens with so much available and all the advertising." Even with her increased spending, which she points out is much less than Americans spends, she doesn't believe she could become as frivolous as Americans. She said, "Americans just go so overboard about everything."

> **Earth provides enough to satisfy every man's need,**
> **but not every man's greed.**
> Mahatma Gandhi

I hope readers can recognize what I call enoughness. Taking positive steps to live sustainably starts opening doors. Can you think of someone in your life, probably in your past, who could serve as a role model? I am fortunate to have had my Grandma Meister as a good example.

> **Deviation from Nature is deviation from happiness.**
> Samuel Johnson

What Can I Learn from Grandma Meister?

I felt an unexpected contentment and a new awareness of what I can learn as I recalled the way she lived her daily life. Grandma's memory adds to my desire to lift the burden I, as an American, have lived with for many years. One of her favorite sayings was, "We have a great plenty." She didn't have to wait for some future time "when she could buy," "if she could be, do, or have," or "after it's paid off." She focused on the now and did not fall victim to advertising. She knew her worth and did not need possessions to show her importance or value.

My grandparents moved to a small house after their five children were adults, but it felt large, airy, and uncluttered. She had beautiful flowers. Her vegetable garden produced enough for the entire year and she had plenty to give to others. From spring to fall, her day started with a prayer and a sunrise "tidying up her gardens." Then she made breakfast, and after Grandpa was off to the farm to help uncle Elwood for the day, she did her chores. She didn't know how to procrastinate and her chores didn't mean boring or tiring work. She was grateful to do things for her home and family. I have a letter holder that reminds me of her. It says, "Let's Do It Now!" She approached everything with joy and eagerness. Whether she was walking through her garden or her home, she always left it "tidy." She did not have an abundance of useless possessions scattered about; she appreciated what she had and everything was always in its place. The frustration of having to search for something misplaced was never a problem. That is possible when life is simple, focused, and uncluttered. Shopping meant driving four miles to Carthage for groceries every other Thursday. If there was some other item she needed, she bought it on that trip to town. She didn't have that vague, constant wondering if there was something she needed or wanted to get or do that seems to always linger in the back of our minds today. Where did that uneasiness come from and when did it start? I felt a little of that wanting lift when we were living on Roatan. It felt peaceful—like being at Grandma's.

I can live like that. Thinking about Grandma prompted me to do things differently today. Everything was eagerly "done up" and "tidied up" in an attitude of appreciation before moving on to the next. It sounds like a minor thing, but it creates a peacefulness. I have more free time and I don't have to remember to go back and finish anything. When writing, I'm not distracted with the "mind-chatter" of lists of things to do.

This has an impact on global warming. Americans live with a chronic vague discontent, and they look for things to make them feel better. If changing the way we go through our day, staying focused, can ease our minds, there may be something of value we let go of over the years that is important to our quality of life. There is calmness and gratitude rather than pressure from trying to do too many things at once. This means setting boundaries with others and for ourselves. Grandma always had time to appreciate everything in her day. Gratitude was woven into her thoughts and her speech.

She acknowledged Nature's blessings: buds on plants, songs from birds, rainbows, shade, breezes, dawn, fresh food, sweetness and crispness of vegetables fresh from the garden to the table, kittens, giggling children, hens laying plenty of eggs, earthworms, ladybugs, the sweet smell of newly-mown grass, the river to swim in, and the warm sun. She let us dance in the warm rain, roll in the autumn leaves, and eat fresh snow with maple syrup on it. Nature was simply enjoyed, and she always felt blessed by it. Every meal started with thanking God for all He had provided.

Are you beginning to see the reasons Grandma didn't have a sense of lack? Her happiness was not found in stores or catalogs and her happiness was never dependent on waiting until she could have some material thing.

Twenty years ago I read two books by Elaine St. James called *Simplify Your Life* and *Inner Simplicity*. Elaine and her husband had been eaten up by the "yuppie" lifestyle of the 1980s. They looked at what being hyper-consumers and over committed was doing to them and decided to get off the treadmill to success. They "way down-sized" their life and shared their new, happier way of life with their readers. Three things stand out as a base for a life with the freedom of knowing enoughness. First, have few enough and small enough things that you can easily afford and take care of your own stuff. Second, cut out obligations and commitments you do not enjoy, so you have time to do the things you really want to do. Third, learn to live in harmony with nature and the environment. Grandma could have written those books, except she never fell into the consumer trap to begin with.

Let Nature Nurture You

Grandma looked on nature as providing her with "a great plenty" of food, beauty, relaxation, inspiration, comfort, and happiness. She was in her garden as the sun rose in the morning. She never woke anyone to help her. I suspect it was her time for meditation and welcoming her new day. Today, I got up and applauded the sunrise. Somehow, I knew my day was already on the right track. Tonight, I plan to applaud the sunset, as well. We have great views of both from our home. Is that being rich? I know how blessed I feel when I take the time to notice all that nature offers me so freely.

Studies show one week of gardening reduced the symptom for people with mild to moderate depression. That could cut down on compulsive shopping and compulsive eating for some of us. I used to conduct an outpatient group for elderly people with chronic depression. One of the mood elevators we used was to go outside for a relaxing walk on a wooded path. After being in nature the patients were more willing to take positive steps toward recovery. It was amazing.

A Japanese study found that women who walked in the woods for two to four hours on two consecutive days elevated the cancer-fighting ability of their white blood cells by nearly 50%. Perhaps humans have a physical need to spend time in nature for maximum health. Will you try an experiment? Next time you think of heading to the mall, go to the park and take an extended walk. It may seem very unnatural to you at first, but see how your physical body and your emotions feel. If you are deconditioned, it's a good thing to discover that information. It's the emotional change I'm wondering about. Nature has healing powers; can you feel them?

The negative ions released into the air by a rain shower, waterfalls, rushing rivers, or a rolling surf can increase a person's energy level after being in that environment for one hour. Our bodies physically respond, and a chemical in our blood drops, leaving us energized.

Search for chances to be in nature and reap the physical and emotional benefit there for the taking. You may find a new attitude, where happiness is no longer found in getting more, but in wanting less. Look at all you have with gratitude and treat the good things in your life with honor and respect. I think I am going to clean, polish, and honor our Prius. She is a treasure. We have a "great plenty." I have a contentment that comes from embracing the concept of enoughness–I feel rich and blessed.

> **'Tis a gift to be simple.**
> **'Tis a gift to be free.**
> **'Tis a gift to come down**
> **Where we ought to be.**
> **And when we find ourselves**
> **In a place that is right,**
> **'Twill be in the valley**
> **Of love and delight.**
> Shaker Hymn

I believe we can correct our course and be grateful for the gifts these changes bring to our lives. We can live sustainably and leave our children and grandchildren a world that provides for their needs. We can help our children and grandchildren learn to live happily within nature's limits and their own financial limits. That is a part of raising our children that must not be neglected.

> **Every action or inaction has an impact—good or bad—upon our surroundings, and anything we do today will have an impact on the lives of our grandchildren.**
> Ted Turner

CHAPTER 20

LEAVING SOMETHING TO THE KIDS THAT REALLY MATTERS

The inheritance I most want to leave Lilly is a planet with food, clean air, safe water for everyone, and an atmosphere that is just right. Weather would be more stable, energy would come from pollution-free renewable sources, and the rat race to be a hyper-consumer would be a thing of the past.

World peace would be attained by valuing all people, appreciating the good we have, and being willing to share. Man has been slowly progressing in that direction in recent centuries. When people work together to solve global warming and all it entails, we may progress faster. I saw a beautiful statue of a mother holding her child. The inscription read, *"A MOTHER'S PEACE—KNOWING HER CHILD WILL NEVER DIE IN WAR."* That world would be a wonderful gift for Lilly.

UNITED WE STAND—DIVIDED WE FALL

Can man find peaceful ways to settle issues so that not one of our brothers or sisters dies in war? The current destruction on television is the civil war in Syria. Whether the headlines read, "The Evil Dictator is Ousted" or "The Murderous Rebel Movement is Squashed," the warring is like a madness that has infected brother against brother. Men, women, and children lie dead in the streets. Homes and businesses are piles of rubble. Schools, hospitals, places of worship, water purification and power plants are demolished. Everyone is the victim, and the madness that ruled their minds is the enemy. Poor Syria and its people, poor Mother Earth, suffering yet another assault. How is either to recover? Syria was ranked 48th on the Failing States Index from 2009 through 2011. In 2012 the index ranked Syria twenty-third, and in 2013 the rank slipped to twenty-first. The violence grows deadlier each day. How can humanity do this to our brothers and sisters?

> **Peace with all the world is my sincerest wish.**
> George Washington   August 15, 1789

Let Us Have Peace Instead of This

The first time I read pages 72 and 73 of *"A NEW EARTH: Awakening to Your Life's Purpose"* (Tolle 2005), my heart ached. I thought, *That is why we kill each other and how we can go to war.* We really do have to buy into madness before we are able to kill thousands of men, women, and children, and destroy all they hold dear.

I want Lilly's world free of the infectious madness Tolle describes so well.

> **Both sides believe 'we are right' and 'they are wrong.'**
> **Both sides are deeply identified with their own perspective.**
> **Both sides are equally incapable of seeing the other's perspective.**
> **Both sides believe themselves to be in possession of the truth.**
> **Both sides regard themselves as victims and the 'other' as evil.**
> **They 'dehumanize' the evil other as their enemy.**
> **Once the enemy has been dehumanized, they can kill and inflict all kinds of violence on the other, even on children without feeling their humanity and suffering. They become trapped in an insane spiral of perpetration and retribution, action and reaction.**

The infectious and insane "us" against "them" thinking can infect families, religions, politics, races, ethnic groups, gangs, and nations.

I pray for lasting PEACE for Lilly's world, the kind of PEACE that only comes when ALL people ALWAYS remember the humanity in EVERY person and remember we are all brothers, and are connected!

I know we share that connection and feel others' pain. We're glued to the TV and wait for the updates about the terrible earthquake, crash, or epidemic. We shed tears, reach into our wallets, and volunteer to go to their aid. When our brothers in our neighborhood or around the world face tragedy, the best in us bursts forth and we become heroes. Please awaken America's heroes; let's save all our brothers and the world from a global warming disaster.

We each have a marvelous brain, especially when we realize how to select the thoughts that guide our day. Instead of being programmed by advertisers or allowing people to divide us against our fellow man by casting others as the enemy, we can choose better thoughts. I want Lilly to accomplish what is important to her by focusing on the positive things in her life. I didn't always know how to focus my mind on the present, how to decide what was truly important to my life, how to set personal goals, or how to make them happen. I have discovered tools to help me achieve my goals. My desire is to be an author who is helping to slow global warming, and my tools are helping me achieve that goal. The same tools are available to everyone and fit any task—including reducing global warming. Grab these tools, decide what you want, adjust your attitude, and follow your dreams.

AFFIRMATIONS

Affirmations are positive statements about ourselves, in the present tense, as if to acknowledge they are true. These three are current favorites while writing *For Lilly*.

I know that the first 65 years were only a warm up.

***

When I really want something,

the whole universe conspires to help me achieve it.

***

My impossible dreams that have come true

inspire me to even greater heights.

Affirmations are backed up by relaxing for a moment and taking on the feelings we would have if our goal were already accomplished. Isn't that what we do when we dread something? In that case, we are getting results we fear. Our minds are always telling us something, and I plan to have what mine is saying be useful. How else would I write a book?

This tool can help us leave a sustainable world to our children. Try this affirmation: "I reduced my electric bill by 50%." Write it down and repeat it many times a day. Then imagine your bill arrives, you open it, and you feel the joy and sense of accomplishment when charges are cut in half! Your mind is now fertile ground for the ideas and actions you need to attain your goal. Remember the tool of affirmations is always in the present tense and charged with the feeling of accomplishment. Now you are in the driver's seat, rather than letting others control your thoughts and decide your actions.

GRATITUDES

There must be more to life than having everything.

Maurice Sendak

Another tool to take control of my thoughts is to maintain "An Attitude of Gratitude." An ongoing practice of mine, one I have asked patients and families to try, is to list one hundred things for which you are grateful. I have a standing list of four hundred. If I'm irritable, I grumble for ten minutes and then say, "Times up!" To remove myself from the grumpy state I either read my list or write a new one. The first few dozen entries are easy, but you then have to start digging deeper. List things that bring contentment, like a beautiful song, or notice things in your home with an attitude of love. Gratitude fills that hole the advertisers are always trying to create or take aim at. A favorite saying of mine is, "We are so rich and someday we may have money." There is so much to be thankful for in all our lives. It's a way you can lift your spirits in fifteen minutes or less. Learning to appreciate what we have moves us in the direction of being happy living a sustainable life.

I CHOOSE HAPPINESS

Choosing to be happy is a decision. You can start your day in a happy mood and maintain it. Consider your current train of thought as you greet your day. I hope you have incorporated some positive practices. I have a comfy chair in our "east wing" with windows over-looking our patio, my potted veggie garden, and our sailboat. This is my "sanctuary." It's understood that when I come to my sanctuary, I first take a few deep relaxing breaths drawing my attention to the present moment. This doesn't mean I am there to meditate, although I can if I choose. I'm there to take time to use my mind, rather than my mind pulling me into the "boardroom meeting" to start my day.

The ways I focus on NOW are quick, simple, and varied. Sometimes I feel my breath with air going in my nose, my lungs filling, and then I feel the air leave. Other times I study and appreciate an orchid that has a beautiful new bloom. Once I am in the NOW moment, I can ask, "What is mine to do today?" My sanctuary is never frantic. In this focused attitude I can plan my day, make my list, and remain relaxed, knowing my MGIG (Mary Guay Intuitively Guided) is up and running. With this guidance comes the energy, creativity, and enthusiasm it takes to do what is mine to do today.

> **I fairly sizzle with zeal, energy, and enthusiasm;**
> **eager to do that which ought to be done by me today.**
> Charles Fillmore,
> Co-founder of Unity Church of Practical Christianity

At the age of 92, Fillmore shared that statement, saying it was how he always greeted his day. I would like Lilly to have tools to start her day in a positive, productive, and peaceful way.

Verbal gratitudes are an uplifting way to greet a new day. Before we get out of bed, my husband and I go back and forth telling each other what we are grateful for in our lives. When grandchildren visit, they join us. It's nice to hear what's important to them. It opens the lines of communication and makes it a natural step to later asking each to share the best thing and the worst thing that happened in their day. This creates a time when the focus is on each other, rather than the TV, computer, or electronic devices that intrude into the time spent on relationships with those most important in our lives. I have to wonder about the quality of relationships when teens are on devices hour after hour with their two hundred "best friends."

A big part of living with peace, love, and joy is to be happy and grateful when we have enough. That includes food. I'm a compulsive overeater, and I know that sugars, refined carbohydrates, fat, and my own specific weaknesses for certain foods have diminished the quality of my life in many ways. I hope our children are spared that problem. Right now, fast food is adding to the problem and it is becoming standard practice to tote addictive nutrient-deficient "healthy snacks" wherever we go.

These are thoughts I'd like to pass on to Lilly. Enjoy enough healthy natural food to have the energy to do all you want.in life. Be satisfied and happy when you've had enough. To some people, that might not sound like a big deal, but for others it's a freedom they long for, for themselves, and for their loved ones. Being vegan is helping me.

Eating foods that are close to their natural state has done miracles for my health and the planet.

UNENCUMBERED

Oprah had a guest who describing how "unencumbered" her life has become since she moved into a tiny house, taking only the items she actually needed. She has a new freedom and happiness she had never known. "Unencumbered" became a mantra for me. I have visions of my entire house as a peaceful sanctuary.

Oprah interviewed a mother in Denmark. The lifestyle in Denmark, which is ranked number one as the country with the happiest people, sounded so nice. A saying the people in Denmark often speak is, "More stuff–less life, more life–less stuff." I remember thinking how much simpler, happier, and more peaceful her life seemed. People spent time outdoors and met neighbors in the parks, which were where we would have streets. Everyone rode bikes, and children were safe playing anywhere outside. A baby could be left outside in a carriage while the mother went to the market, and the other women in the area cared for the baby.

The home was small. The two young children had spaces like alcoves in the wall. Each had a mattress and space at one end for a few clothes and at the other end for some toys. Imagine the task of cleaning your room, putting away your clothes, or finding a favorite toy. The child could almost stand before his space and reach everything at arm's length.

I'd like to live in Denmark for two months and see how much of that ability to live life in an uncluttered and natural manner I could absorb. How can I pass to Lilly the appreciation of having a few treasures that don't burden her life and having extra time to play outside with friends and family? I want to live "unencumbered," but how do I get there from here?

I am gravitating in that direction. This morning I was doing the laundry. As I took the sheets off the bed, I considered that we seldom use the top sheet during the summer, and I decided to put only one sheet on the bed. It no longer makes sense to cover up and turn on the air-conditioner. My thinking has changed, not covering up sounds comfortable, peaceful, and natural. When I first read about Americans consuming so much more, using up the natural resources, and polluting the earth to the point of unbalancing nature, I thought, *how can I give up that much? Am I willing to deprive my family and myself of all the things we have worked for and are so used to?* Now I think how freeing it feels to sleep on the bed with no top sheet. That is less than an iota of change, but it is less cotton, less laundry, less work, more time, less electricity, less water, very comfortable, and I feel good about it.

Time–Any Way You Choose It

We turned the TV off to reduce energy consumption. At first it felt as if we gave up something by not turning on *The Today Show* to see what was going on, switching to *The Weather Channel* for the day's forecast, and then maybe watch *Ellen DeGeneres*. The energy savings is a small part of the benefits we gained. How many times have you said you would like some time for yourself? We found it! Now it's easy to skip most of the evening programs, especially reruns. Time for myself often means I can experience more creativity and intuitive guidance can surface. Inspiration pops up, answers come, and the day is just plain great! What a freedom it is to have "just plain" be "great!"

Sitting quietly, doing nothing, Spring comes and the grass grows by itself.
Zen saying

Lilly, please take time for yourself. Don't squander it in the name of entertainment. I don't miss the endless commercials, either. I do a better job of programming my mind than the commercials ever did. They are never for our benefit; they are designed to reach into our pockets and sell us yet another gismo. Let Lilly be free from being convinced that she wants or needs something that actually clutters her life. While we were singing "The Lord's Prayer," at church, the words, "Lead us not into temptation" had added meaning.

MEDITATION

For fast-acting relief, try slowing down.
Lily Tomlin

Meditation is a practice I hope to use more. Everyone who tries it has his or her own unique way and with varying results. Oprah interviewed Deepak Chopra who said he has meditated every day for the last forty years. That is amazing, but even more impressive was that he has not had an argument with his family in over thirty years. He said there is nothing that can get him upset, no matter what.

I have learned, but can forget at times, to stay in the present moment, "The Now." I can always handle "Now." Thoughts slipping in from the past can bring feelings of guilt and anger, while being pulled into the future leaves the mind open to worry and doubt. Meditation keeps Deepak centered, and he reports that he tries to live in a meditative state. When he was asked who he considered his greatest teacher, he said, "These days my greatest teacher is my own inner silence." I wonder if my children or grandchildren ever get a glimpse of inner peace. It is not easy to experience in today's busy world.

I LIKE TO PUT MY TOES IN THE WATER

Meditation with visualization can produce a peaceful calm. Living in Naples is wonderful. I jokingly say, "They took paradise and filled it with things for millionaires and billionaires to enjoy, and every so often we get to stick our toes in the water." We have a philharmonic orchestra, incredible entertainment, art, endless white sand beaches free to all, and hundreds of miles of beautifully landscaped roadways. There is one "toe in the water" that means the most to me. I invite you to join me.

Find a quiet and comfortable spot to sit, close your eyes, take a few deep breaths, and with each exhale let yourself melt into the chair. See yourself walking on our beautiful sandy beach. The day is perfect; the sun and gentle breezes caress your skin. In this quiet, you have a sense that you can breathe in peace. Let that peace flow through you, relax, then exhale any and every stress. You linger along the shore, aware of a calmness you treasure. Your toe touches the warm water. Slowly step into the water a little more and a little more. A feeling of joy engulfs you as you stroll into the water to chest level. You know you are special and in a special place. You are here to be healed. You fold into a drop, relax, and sink into a Holy place where you are supported, suspended, and you are at peace. You are a drop in the sea of God. As the gentle current sooths you, your edges that had kept you separate from the sea of God wash away. You lazily drift and willingly let any barrier between you and God drift away. Then slowly but overwhelmingly you remember; you are a drop in the sea of God and you have the qualities of God. You remember; "YES" you are a part of the sea of God. In this silence there is peace that passes all understanding. Gently let any and all concerns dissolve away and know you have a God-given inner guidance you can call on in any present moment.

Relax into this peacefulness as long as you wish.

When you are ready, gently touch your toe to the sandy bottom. Leisurely emerge from the sea refreshed, cleansed, and remembering who you really are. That is how I put my toe in the water. You can come to this silence for guidance, comfort, and to nourish your soul any time.

Eckhart Tolle teaches us to live in the present–the NOW. That is the time to put your toe in the water. For a brief time, let go of the past with its guilt and anger. Let go of the future with its worry and fear. Come to NOW. Find a comfortable spot and I'll see you at the beach.

Don't search for joy–go into the silence and remember it all.

If being deprived of some possessions can make room in our lives to remember who we are, we win the grand prize!

When Deepak says his greatest teacher these days is his own inner silence, I understand, admire, and desire what he has. That is a treasure I wish for Lilly. If I could leave Lilly the ability to go into a meditative state, feel at peace, and be able to trust her intuitive guidance, I believe that is a gift that really matters.

I Can Hardly Wait to See the Good That Will Come of This

This saying means so much to me and it works in all situations. Wally made a little shelf that sits in the mirrored corner above my bathroom sink. On the edge facing me as I start and end each day, I painted, "I can hardly wait to see the good that will come of this." That reminds me there is good in all situations when I am open to accepting life as it is. I am not alone; there is an intuitive guidance within me. I do not need to know what to say or do; I am at peace, and all is well.

Mother Earth cannot keep giving and giving so much to so many. It may be that having to re-evaluate the way we live today forces us to discard the frantic pace that has Americans trying to buy happiness. Could it be that it took something as life threatening as global warming to free us to live in a manner that allows PEACE, JOY, and LOVE to enter our lives?

Sleep tight little one, Great-Granny will keep you from harm.

THE RUG

WHAT HAPPENED IN JULY AND AUGUST OF **2003?**

Question: Was there anything newsworthy?

Answer: The people of Europe thought so; 50,000 people died in the heat wave that hung over Europe during July and August.

Question: How newsworthy was this in the United States?

Answer: Not very. I found on the Internet the top ten news stories for 2003 listed in order of importance in America:

1. U.S. space shuttle Columbia crashes
2. U.S. launches war on Iraq, Saddam captured 12-13-03
3. U.S. releases "Roadmap for Peace Plan in Middle East"
4. SARS (Acute Respiratory Syndrome-bird flu) in 32 countries; 812 die
5. U.S.-Canadian Rolling Blackout
6. China, U.S., S. Korea, Russia, and Japan hold talks to solve nuclear crisis in Korean Peninsula
7. India and Pakistan reach ceasefire
8. Iran signs additional protocol to nuclear non-proliferation treaty
9. There were many car bombs in Middle East
10. Powerful earthquake rocks Iran, killing over 20,000 people

I agree these were newsworthy, but wouldn't 50,000 killed by a heat wave rank right up there with 812 deaths from SARS, many car bombs in the Middle East, U.S. releases "Road Map for Peace in the

Middle East", and Iran signs an additional protocol to nuclear non-proliferation treaty? One key difference might be that none of these have a connection to global warming, except when one considers that war is the ultimate in pollution and the destruction of natural resources.

No wonder I have only a faint memory of some little old lady that died in a Paris apartment. That was probably the extent of the news coverage. President Bush didn't believe there was global warming, and anything that caused us to question the idea was swept under the rug.

During the 2000 presidential campaign, oilman and Texas governor George W. Bush needed votes from moderates and people concerned about the environment. During one debate Bush stated, "Global warming needs to be taken very seriously." He made it clear that he supported regulating CO_2 and agreed that limits should be set on emissions. Those statements were again repeated in an energy policy paper his campaign released two months before the election. He boldly stated he supported mandatory limits on CO_2, while Gore was only asking for voluntary limits. What was swept under the rug was that the Bush campaign planned to make whatever claims it took to make sure that an environmentally-friendly president was not elected. He tried to look like more of an environmentalist than Gore.

Big Coal author Goodell explained, "Nobody in the coal industry took Bush's campaign rhetoric seriously. Whatever he said or did not say during the campaign, they knew he was a fossil fuels man to the core." A cynic might read that to mean the fossil fuel industry knew he was only lying to get the votes to be elected. The cynics would have been right this time.

A COAL-BLACK DUST-BUNNY WITH VAMPIRE TEETH—THE MYSTERY
Produced and Directed by Coal, Railroads, and Utilities

Here is a mystery with some hidden plots. The scope and depth of how big contributions might be or how much influence these alliances bought is far beyond anything I can delve into. I limit my review of this mystery to the information available at the local library. An especially enlightening book is *Big Coal* by Jeff Goodell, who spent three years investigating. He interviewed politicians, miners, and coal mining families. He went into coal mines and was there for a small 55,000 pound blast of ANFO to "fluff up" the dirt to reach the coal.

He tracked down the cast of characters that pulled the strings at the very top of our government. When George W. Bush accepted the contributions, this cast got their money's worth. This coal mystery tells what money and influence the coal, railroad, and utility companies were able to collect when George repaid his debt. Another separate mystery might be, "Did the Oil Companies Buy a War Paid for By the American Taxpayer That Cost Trillions of Dollars and Thousands of American Lives?"

Coal, the energy supply that, according to then President George W. Bush, "has crept back into our economic destiny," was supplying the fuel for half of our electricity (2006). Coal is a huge part of the railroad profits and a cheap fuel for utility companies. This trio makes a formidable alliance that can buy power in Washington. The buying and trading is not done in plain view. It is best done under the rug and names aren't always what they seem. Meet the cast of characters that could be found.

CAST CHOSEN BY THE PRESIDENT
WHO CAMPAIGNED THAT HE WAS MORE
ENVIRONMENTALLY FRIENDLY THAN GORE

BNSF (Burlington Northern Santa Fe) Railroad hauls the coal from Wyoming to power plants across the country, especially the Northeast and Southeast. The coal transport provides about 20% of the railroad's profits.

Matt Rose, CEO of BNSF and $100,000 (known) Bush campaign contributor. Rose opposed Kyoto Protocol because it would place limits on CO_2 emissions. Recognizing how much profit BNSF makes transporting coal, Rose, in a speech to BNSF employees in 2003 said, "I think the future looks bright, with one exception…if an environmental bill is passed that caps CO_2 emissions, employment would be cut by half or more, because coal would be seriously hurt or even eliminated." What's so sad is that Wyoming coal's business, hauled by BNSF, expanded when the 1970 Clean Air Act limiting sulfur was passed. Wyoming coal has less sulfur than eastern coal. BNSF wants limits on sulfur dioxide but not on carbon dioxide. Another environmental contradiction is BNSF's publicity material, which boasts how railroads are a more environmentally friendly means of transportation than trucking because of the lower level of CO_2 emissions. If indeed Rose's contribution to Bush's campaign was only $100,000, he certainly got a big bang for his bucks. Bush was the man to buy; consider the Gore option. For some reason Bush, once elected, "didn't believe in global warming" and thought the "Kyoto Protocol was a lousy idea for America." What a "lousy" price our Earth and my Lilly paid for that change in opinion.

The 2012 Republican National Convention is on the week I am writing this. I may be becoming cynical, but I have to wonder what sort of "lousy" price our Earth and my Lilly will be paying for the millions or billions of dollars in contributions going into the buying of our government in 2012. Too many contributors expect great returns at the expense of our environment. These are not the people I want writing the laws, forming the policies, deciding subsidies, or running the regulatory agencies to "protect" our environment.

Marc Racicot, BNSF board member, chair of the Republican National Committee and head of Bush's reelection campaign.

John Snow, Bush treasury secretary, was the former head of a Florida-based railroad that hauls millions of tons of Appalachian coal.

Steven Griles, coal lobbyist, became Bush's deputy secretary for the United States Department of Interior. One of his crowning achievements was the changing of **ONE** word, "WASTE" became

"FILL." That one word change has a "lousy" price. With that change, mountaintop removal debris containing hazardous acids and heavy metals can now be dumped anywhere. This is a terrible threat to water supplies. For years, environmentalists and local citizens have waged legal battles to slow mountaintop removal. That one-word change derailed the pending lawsuits dealing with toxic pollution of the water and land in the affected mining communities. In many cases, the water is lethal and the land unlivable. This is not a small area. By cutting legal challenges, an area larger than the state of Rhode Island is now a "go" for continued devastation.

Big coal would have to give a thumbs up to that maneuver and say, "George Bush and Steven Griles, what a team, job well done." To use George Bush's own words, THIS is something Great-granny thinks is truly "a lousy idea for America."

Irl Engelhardt, Peabody Coal, America's largest coal company contributed a known $846,000 to the 2000 federal campaigns. The Republican Party got 98% of that money. What might one expect in return if that money was meant to buy control of policies. Bush appointed Peabody's chairman and CEO, Irl Engelhardt, to the Environmental Protection Agency transition team.

John Wotten, Peabody Coal Vice President, was appointed to the Energy Department Team.

Steven Chancellor, Chief Executive of Peabody subsidiary, Black Beauty Coal, was also appointed to the energy department.

Thomas Sansonetti, former lobbyist representing Peabody Coal, headed the group choosing the top personnel for the Interior Department.

All this and did it make the news? I do not recall much about mountaintop removal mining, except thinking it would ruin the scenery. Being clueless is not good for America.

I wish George Bush hung around with a better crowd. For eight years they did all they could to kill legislation that would limit America's burning of coal. They derailed legislation that taxed or regulated coal's emission of CO_2. Their power was great enough that the United States remains the ONLY country that did not sign the Kyoto Protocol. We are the black sheep of the world when it comes to global warming.

When I see a political advertisement showing the owner of a small business walking through his company saying he needs to get big government and all those regulations off his back, I see a very big black shadow looming in the background. I wonder if those deregulations would really benefit that business owner at all. He is such small potatoes compared to the main cast of characters in all these mysteries. They pay thousands for the ad and collect billions if the message works. Great bang for the buck!

The owner is presented like a friendly guy who just wants what's good for us all. It reminds me of the friendly names like GLOBAL CLIMATE COALITION or GREENING EARTH SOCIETY. What would those names imply if they were honest? They're not honest; they are clever, deceptive, and dangerous. They are also part of the cast in this mystery.

Global Climate Coalition was formed as an alliance of corporations in the early 1990s, with Exxon Mobile, coal, electric power, and BNSF as supporting members. The Global Climate Coalition's mission is "to undercut, obfuscate, and confuse the science of global warming."

The Greening Earth Society is a group largely funded by the coal industry and until recently by BNSF to promote the idea that global warming is "good for the planet because it allows crops and trees to grow faster." What an environmental group that turned out to be!

Bush is history, and it was not the person of George W. Bush that was the real problem. The problem is that people and corporations will use their power, money, and influence to put people in office by election or appointment whose only concern is controlling the government to further their cause. This would include:

1. Not paying taxes on most of their earnings

2. Not being regulated to prevent pollution of our air, water, land, and food supply

3. Not having to compensate victims for death, damage, or injury

4. Getting the government to subsidize their companies with billions of dollars

5. Not subsiding a competitive industry

6. Ignoring global warming

Their ethics are not ethical at all. Regard for the environment or individuals are not factored into their plans, and there is an absolute determination to dominate. The entitled elite pull the strings on whatever puppet they buy.

America now has laws that allow anyone or any group to make massive contributions to a candidate without divulging who they are. Airwaves are flooded with unlimited political advertisements, saying anything they want by way of the unknown supporter. The candidates never have to respond to questions about the truth of claims made by the cleverly named backer. It's not the candidate who made the claims and the candidate does not have to acknowledge endorsement. Once the candidate is in office, he pays his debts to his supporters, and the supporters step into position of influence and control in our government. All this is done under that darn rug.

I hope it becomes illegal to accept unlimited contributions from deceptively named groups. If this doesn't change the time may soon come when the power elite has bought and paid for a Senate and House of Representatives that votes as the nameless supporters tell them to vote. Over time that would mean control of the Supreme Court and heads of many government agencies.

We've been clueless long enough. Now let's get out there and save the world for our Lillys!

BIBLIOGRAPHY

Aebi, Tania with Brennan, Bernadette. 1989. *Maiden Voyage.* New York: Ballantine Books.

Bagley, Ed Jr. 2008. *Living Like Ed: A Guide to the Eco-Friendly Life.* New York: Clarkson Publishing.

Barlow, Maude and Clarke, Tony. 2002. *Blue Gold: The Fight to Stop the Corporate Theft of the World's Water.* New York: The New Press.

Beavan, Colin. 2009. *No Impact Man: The Adventures of a Guilty Liberal Who Attempts to Save The Planet and the Discoveries He Makes About Himself and Our Way Of Life In The Process.* New York: Farrar, Straus and Giroux.

Brower, Kenneth. 1990. *One Earth: Photographed By More Than 80 of the World's Best Photojournalists.* San Francisco: Collins Publishers.

Brown, Lester R. 2003. *Plan B: Rescuing a Planet Under Stress and a Civilization in Trouble.* New York: W.W. Norton & Company.

Brown, Lester R. 2006. *Plan B 2.0: Rescuing A Planet Under Stress and a Civilization in Trouble.* New York: W.W. Norton & Company.

Brown, Lester R. 2009. *Plan B 4.0 Mobilizing to Save Civilization.* New York: W.W. Norton & Company.

Brown, Lester R. 2011. *World on The Edge: How to Prevent Environmental and Economic Collapse.* New York: W.W. Norton &

Company.

Brown, Paul. 2007. *Global Warning: The Last Chance for Change.* Pleasantville, NY: Dakini Books.

Brune, Michael. 2008. *Coming Clean: Breaking America's Addiction to Oil and Coal.* San Francisco: Sierra Club Books.

Campbell, T. Colin Ph.D. and Campbell, Thomas II. 2006. *The China Study: Startling Implications for Diet, Weight Loss and Long-term Health.* Dallas: Benbella Books.

Casten, Thomas R. 1998. *Turning Off The Heat: Why America Must Double Efficiency To Save Money and Reduce Global Warming.* Amherst: Prometheus Books.

Crosby, Alfred W. 2006. *Children of the Sun: A History of Humanity's Unappeasable Appetite for Energy.* New York: W. W. Norton & Company.

Deffeyes, Kenneth S. 2009. *Beyond Oil: The View from Hubbert's Peak.* New York: Hill and Wang.

Charles, HRH The Prince of Wales. 2010. *Harmony: A New Way of Looking at Our World.* New York: Harper Collins Publishers.

Cravens, Gwyneth. 2007. *Power to Save The World: The Truth About Nuclear Energy.* New York: Random House, Inc.

DeVilliers, Marq. 2000. *Water: The Fate or Our Most precious Resource.* Toronto: Stoddart Publishing LTD.

Dobson, Clive, and Beck, Gregory Gilpin. 1999. *Watersheds: A practical Handbook for Healthy Water.* Altona, Manitoba: Firefly Books.

Fox, Josh. 2002. *Gasland.* New York.

Fuhrman, Joel, MD. 2011. *Eat to Live: The Amazing Nutrient-Rich Program For Fast And Sustained Weight Loss.* Revised Edition, New York, NY: Little Brown and Co., Division of Hachette Book Group.

Goleman, Daniel. 2009. *Ecological Intelligence: How Knowing the Hidden Impacts of What We Buy Can Change Everything.* New York, NY: Broadway Books.

Goodell, Jeff. 2006. *Big Coal: The Dirty Secret Behind America's Energy Future*. New York, NY: Houghton Mifflin Company.

Gore, Al. 2006. *An Inconvenient Truth*. Emmaus: Rodale Publishing.

Henson, Robert. 2011. *The Rough Guide to Climate Change: The Symptoms, The Science, The Solutions*. New York: Penguin Putnam Inc.

Klare, Michael T. 2008. *Rising Powers Shrinking Planet: The New Geopolitics of Energy*. New York: Metropolitan Books.

McGraw, Dr. Phil. 2008. *The Ultimate Weight Solution: The 7 Keys to Weight Loss Freedom*. New York: Simon and Schuster, Inc.

McKibben, Bill. 2006. *The Bill McKibben Reader: Pieces From An Active Life*. New York: Henry Holt and Company.

Melville, Greg. 2008. *Greasy Rider*. Chapel Hill: Algonquin Books of Chapel Hill.

Ornish, Dean, MD. 1993. *Eat More. Weigh Less: Dr. Dean Ornish's Life Choice Program for Losing Weight Safely While Eating Abundantly*. New York: Harper Collins.

Pearce, Fred. 2008. *Confessions of an Eco-Sinner: Tracking Down the Sources of My Stuff*. Boston: Beacon Press.

Pollan, Michael. 2009. *Food Rules: An Eater's Manual*. New York: Penguin Books.

Pope, Carl and Rauber, Paul. 2004. *Strategic Ignorance: Why the Bush Administration is Recklessly Destroying a Century of Environmental Progress*. San Francisco: Sierra Club Books.

Powers, William. 2010. *Twelve By Twelve: A One Room Cabin Off The Grid & Beyond The American Dream*. Navota: New World Library.

Rothfeder, Jeffrey. 2001. *Every Drop for Sale: Our Desperate Battle Over Water in a World About to Run Out*. New York: Penguin Putnam.

Schucman, Helen and Thetford, William. 1975. *A Course in*

Miracles. Tiburon: Foundation for Inner Peace.

St. James, Elaine. 1994. *Simplify Your Life: 100 Ways to Slow Down and Enjoy the Things That Really Matter.* New York: Hyperion.

Tolle, Eckhart. 1997. *The Power of Now*. Vancover, BC, CA: Namaste Publishing.

Tolle, Eckhart. 2005. *A New Earth: Awakening to Your Life's Purpose*, Vancover, BC, CA: Namaste Publishing.

Walsch, Neale Donald. 2011. *The Storm Before the Calm: A New Human Manifesto*. Ashland: Emnin Books.

Willcox, Bradley J. MD, Wilcox, D. Craig, and Suzuki, Makoto MD. 2001. *The Okinawa Program: How the World's Longest- Lived People Achieve Everlasting Health - And How You Can Too.* New York: Clarkson Potter Publishers.

Winfrey, Oprah. 2012, *Oprah Talks To Deepak Chopra, O: The Oprah Magazine,* New York: Hearst Publications, Inc.

ACKNOWLEDGMENTS

Wally, my husband, has been a devoted assistant, worked tirelessly, and encouraged me every step of the way. Our daughter, Michelle Sheldon, spent many hours with revisions and proof reading. Our daughter, Monica Estrada, shot the cover and author photos.

> **When I really want something,**
> **the whole universe conspires to help me achieve it.**

That affirmation explains how this book was published. I was advised to join The Gulf Coast Writers' Association, Marco Island Writers, Naples Authors, and The Critique Critters. The guidance and assistance from fellow members made the difference between a dream and reality. Martha Jeffers, "The Grammar Granny," did the line-by-line editing. She was like a lifeboat for this novice. Jennifer Fitzgerald, "Mother Spider," did the layout and design. Joining a group of like-minded writers gave me people to go to with hundreds of question. They pointed out the land-mines to avoid and helped clear my path.

People at our church, Master Mind members, fellow vegans, and friends in Green Scene groups inspired me.

The greatest motivation came from Lilly. The promise to keep her from harm goes all the way to my soul. Thank you universe and all who appeared to help me fulfill my divine purpose.

A Personal Request

From Mary

For my readers who really "get it," please join me in my mission. Let the next gift you give to a friend or loved one be a copy of this book. It will:

- Save them money
- Improve their physical and emotional health
- Help slow global warming

Please contact me if there is any way I can assist you in educating and involving others. I provide motivational/environmental workshops. This really is my mission/purpose and I welcome ways to further the awakening of my caring but clueless brothers and sisters.

https://www.createspace.com/4373226

ABOUT THE AUTHOR

Mary Guay has a Master's in Social Work and was a hospice social worker. Retirement took on new meaning when she discovered the devastating issues our children face in a world plagued by global warming. She has done extensive research to answer her own questions and learn what she could do, and then put them into play in her own life.

This book is a compilation of what she learned. Mary is available for motivational workshops to help others understand global warming, its causes, and to share the actions we can take to protect our children's futures.

Get updated information by visiting http://www.MaryGuay.org.

www.ingramcontent.com/pod-product-compliance
Lightning Source LLC
Chambersburg PA
CBHW060448290526
45791CB00001B/23